Cross-Purposes

Cross-Purposes: Lesbians, Feminists, and the Limits of Alliance

EDITED BY
Dana Heller

Indiana University Press

BLOOMINGTON AND INDIANAPOLIS

© 1997 by Indiana University Press

The paper used in this publication meets the minimum requirements of
American National Standard for Information Sciences—Permanence of
Paper for Printed Library Materials, ANSI Z39.48-1984.

MANUFACTURED IN THE UNITED STATES OF AMERICA

Library of Congress Cataloging-in-Publication Data

Cross-purposes : lesbians, feminists, and the limits of alliance / edited by
    Dana Heller.
        p.   cm.
    Includes bibliographical references and index.
    ISBN 0-253-33246-X (alk. paper). — ISBN 0-253-21084-4 (pbk. : alk.
paper)
    1. Lesbianism. 2. Lesbians—Identity. 3. Lesbian feminism. 4. Feminist
theory.   I. Heller, Dana A. (Dana Alice), date.
HQ75.5.C76   1997
306.76'63—dc20   96-32929

1 2 3 4 5   02 01 00 99 98 97

CONTENTS

ACKNOWLEDGMENTS

My sincere thanks goes to the friends and colleagues who helped make this book. Above all, I am grateful to the authors whose work appears in this volume and whose commitment to the larger concept of "the project" often helped sustain my own. Thanks to Teresa de Lauretis, SDiane Bogus, and Emma Perez for their participation at a special session of the 1994 Modern Language Association Convention in San Diego, where many of the issues and debates that define this volume were rehearsed. Joan Catapano at Indiana University Press provided indispensable editorial guidance and expertise. Joan Nestle and the staff/friends of the Lesbian Herstory Archives in Brooklyn arranged for generous access to the collection, helped me track down sources, and engaged me in lively conversation during my visits. The College of Arts and Letters at Old Dominion University helped materially support this project with a grant to cover research and production-related expenses. Jill Dolan and Andrea Slane offered feedback and suggestions on various parts of the manuscript. Lastly, I am indebted to Janice Conard for her encouragement and companionship throughout the entire process of assembling this volume.

Norfolk, 1996

Katie Hogan's "Where Experience and Representation Collide: Lesbians, Feminists, and the AIDS Crisis" appears in modified form in *Found Object* 6 (Fall 1995). Passages from this essay appear also in "'Victim Feminism' and the Complexities of AIDS," in *Bad Girls/Good Girls: Women, Sex, and Power in the Nineties*, ed. Donna Perry and Nan Bauer Maglin (New Brunswick, N.J.: Rutgers University Press, 1996). Reprinted with permission of the author.

Cross-Purposes

Purposes: An Introduction

DANA HELLER

The fourteen essays collected in this volume stage a long-overdue critical intervention into the history, current condition, and evolving shape of lesbian alliances with feminisms in the United States. Of course, it could also be said that these essays—constructed through the diverse idioms of academic theory and personal experience, alert to the precariously intertwined cultural discourses of gender, sex, and sexuality—tell stories, stories that push the analytic relationship of lesbian and feminist studies to its limits. In this spirit, I begin with a story of my own—an origin story, you could call it. My goal here is necessarily contradictory: to affirm the continuing vitality of lesbian feminism and to account for the development of a project that would interrogate the sacred ground of this union.

For the better part of my formation as a feminist subject, lesbianism and feminism remained deadlocked in a kind of defensible conflation of purpose. In New York City in the mid-1980s, as I worked toward a doctorate in American literature and began to act, with equal tenacity, on a long-repressed sexual desire for women, this conflation remained for the most part axiomatic, even though recent events such as the 1982 Barnard Conference on sexuality had revealed a certain lack of theoretical commensurability. Nevertheless, at the institutional level the presumption of overlap between lesbian and feminist studies posed no practical impediments to my dissertation on female homosociality in quest-romance, or, for that matter, to my social relations with straight women and gay men. In graduate seminars, I was a feminist whose lesbianism was engulfed by theories of gender; at the pride marches and in the bars, I was a lesbian whose feminism was engulfed by a nexus of objects—erotic and judicial—which drew me to queer activism.

This all changed when I awoke one morning in 1990 to find myself overwhelmed by a virtual avalanche of new books on gay and lesbian literature, film, popular culture, history, sociology, philosophy, psychology, etc. Leading up to this point, I had become increasingly frustrated with the unquestioned assumption of a normative female heterosexuality that informed much of the women's studies research and teaching at the southern university where I had recently taken a job. As a new assistant professor of women's literature and feminist literary theory, and as the only "out" lesbian faculty member in the college, I frequently found myself at odds with feminist colleagues who were either reluctant to address sexual differences, let alone lesbian differences, or who would address lesbianism as a "separate but equal" category, a distant relation of feminism whose significance remained tied to a subjective process of "coming out," a process seemingly isolated from conditions of nationality or from the social dynamics of class, race, region, generation, etc. I became a regular feature of the sole lesbian roundtable at our annual Women's Studies conference, and I began to notice a correlation between the token panel—which nevertheless did serve to promote my lesbian visibility—and the token essay on lesbianism that had been for some time a standard inclusion of many popular feminist anthologies. Sensing that it would be my unique task to represent lesbian studies and force the arguments for its curricular vitality among those who were supposedly my allies, I grew somewhat detached from the feminist community and doubtful of the disciplinary tradition that I had been hired to pass on. Gradually, I stopped referring to my position as "feminist" and began describing it in terms of "gender" and "queer" engagements.

Still I retained a primary, albeit ambivalent, identification with feminist theory and politics. It was, after all, feminism that had given me the tools necessary to read against "tradition," feminist or otherwise. It was feminism that had shown me the value of resisting monolithic abstractions of the sort that have been strategically deployed throughout Western history to misrepresent women, queers, minorities. It was feminism that had taught me to appreciate contradictions, the necessity of living with and within them. I knew this, and yet it wasn't something I could easily convey to my undergraduates—many of them first-generation college women, some with families and full-time jobs—students for whom I must have seemed something of an anomaly: a feminist who openly rejects the unifying category "women"; a queer-rights advocate who believes that the movement owes a huge unacknowledged debt to feminism.

One day a very bright student came to my office and asked me, in earnest, if being a lesbian meant she *had* to be a feminist. She sincerely hoped not. Of course, the fact that she even discerned a connection between the two might be read as a triumph, especially since so many of her peers, regardless of gender and sexual orientation, remain smugly certain that whatever the feminist movement was—way back before they were born—it didn't change anything and doesn't really exist anymore save for a few cranky extremists who show up on *Larry King Live* every so often. In my courses, students watch episodes of *Roseanne* and films such as *Paris Is Burning*. They read novels such as *Sula* and "zines" like *Hothead Paisan: Homicidal Lesbian Terrorist*, and I ask them to think about how these texts signify confluences and inconsistencies of sex, gender, race, and class. They are often surprised and sometimes a little embarrassed to learn that they are thinking and talking in ways that could be described as "feminist." "What is feminism anyway?" they ask. To be honest, I don't always know what to tell them. Is it anything anyone says it is? Is it NOW? Is it *Oprah*? Is it the sum total of required textbooks that they enthusiastically purchase and even more enthusiastically sell back at the end of the semester, books that provoke the small-group discussions of the moment? I think about these students and I wonder, can feminism be all these things and still give them the sense that they are aligned with a history and a live movement of lesbian activism? I think about that student who came to my office and I wonder, is feminism a live movement for lesbians?

In 1993, I entered into a correspondence with Bonnie Zimmerman, a scholar whose work seemed to reflect a concern with similar questions. I set about articulating my dilemma, hoping to find the words that would elicit her participation in a proposed collection of essays on the complex ways in which lesbianism and feminism inform and resist one another. In a letter from her, I was struck by a remark that she had "never separated out lesbian and feminist in [her] work." This prompted me to go back and reread some of her writings. In the process, I noticed that in Zimmerman's famous 1981 essay, "What Has Never Been: An Overview of Lesbian Feminist Criticism," she proposes, among other things, "to investigate some of the problems, strengths, and future needs of a developing lesbian feminist literary criticism" (201), while in her 1992 essay, "Lesbians Like This and That: Some Notes on Lesbian Criticism for the Nineties," the "feminist" is . . . well, where did she go?[1] How did "lesbian feminist criticism" become "lesbian criticism," and what are the implied gains and losses in this progression, not only for lesbian and feminist writers, but for all writers whose work is concerned with gender, sex, and sexuality? I asked Zimmerman if she would consider writing about what had happened over the course of that ten-year period. The result is "'Confessions' of a Lesbian Feminist," the essay which opens the third section of essays in this volume.

The writers who have contributed to *Cross-Purposes: Lesbians, Feminists, and the Limits of Alliance* situate themselves in multiple and sometimes contradictory ways within the interrelated fields of lesbian and gay studies, women's studies, and queer theory. As editor my goal is to create a forum for discussion on the strengths, risks, and limits of the lesbian alliance with feminism at a time when the former is defining its own disciplinary space within gay studies, while the latter continues to question the presumed coherence of its foundational category, "women." Indeed, now that gay studies and "queer" theory have established habitable disciplinary spaces for lesbian inquiry, have feminists and lesbians reached a parting of the ways, or is it time to redefine the value and purpose of their alliance? This collection will explore a complicated albeit increasingly apparent dilemma within the overlapping discourses of feminist studies and lesbian studies: if the social and aesthetic significances of the terms *lesbian* and *feminist* can be said to derive from the same historical moments, or if the development of lesbian studies has been defined in some sense as coextensive with the development of feminist studies, then how are contemporary scholars and critics participating in the emergent articulation of a lesbian studies paradigm that is exploring (in necessarily diverse contexts) a distinctly lesbian approach to cultural production, political participation, and identity management?

This collection proceeds from the recognition that histories of lesbianism and feminism, and the subjects represented by these histories, remain distinct and at the same time intersect at flashpoints of mutual appropriation, idealization, and repudiation. "I have met many, many feminists who were not Lesbians—but I have never met a Lesbian who was not a feminist" (308), wrote Martha Shelley in 1969.[2] Six years later, the radical feminist group Redstockings rejected lesbian feminism on the grounds that the relationship between the terms consisted of no more than "hyphenating the word" (191).[3] Throughout the twentieth century, lesbianism has been viewed as both everywhere and nowhere within feminism, a cause as well as an effect. Lesbians have been idealized as both the "vanguard of the women's movement" and the movement's greatest liability, a contradiction that renders the very idea of lesbian feminism at once a redundancy and a contradiction in terms.

From the Lavender Menace to the Leather Menace, from NOW's Second Congress to Unite Women to the 1982 Barnard Conference, eruptions of conflict between lesbian feminists and straight feminists have significantly shaped and reshaped histories of the women's movement. Debates have centered on lesbians' appropriation of feminism for the promotion of sexual radicalism, as well as on a dominant liberal feminism's totalizing claims, its resistance to sustaining a critique of heterosexuality, its reluctance to address the confluence of sexuality, race, and class, and its failure to register the lack of continuity between the various theoretical, cultural, and activist positions of feminism and the subjects who produce and are produced by these positions. In this way, critics claim, feminism maintains the coherence of its foundation rather than trying to understand how multiple differences in concert with sexual orientation destabilize the very logic of that foundation. Consequently, Katie King has argued that narrative accounts of the "gay/straight split" represent a "kind of mistake" (83).[4] But are constructions of a political identity free of internal contradictions the only mistake effected by the gay/straight split? If origin stories of the women's movement are all interested stories, as King has rightly observed, then what are they interested in besides disproving one another?

My interest in examining and specifying the tensions between lesbianism and feminism has to do, among other things, with my ongoing exploration of the ways in which social histories are narrated and revised in relation to mass culture forms and investments. To put it another way, I suspect that the gay/straight split in feminism has less to do with sexual orientation per se than with the ways sexual orientations are produced and made consumable through various modes of popular storytelling. For example, in Margaret Cruikshank's informative history of the Lesbian and Gay Liberation Movement (1992), we are told that lesbians who joined women's liberation found "that they could be heterosexual, homosexual, bisexual, or asexual and that these choices were equally valid."[5] And while the movement did provide many women with an environment in which to address and explore sexual options and desires, this representation of a supportive feminist sisterhood relies on and at the same time feminizes a popular sentimental trope of familialization, a trope that is contested by Alice Echols's historical account of Rita Mae Brown's accusation, issued after her resignation from the National Organization for Women, that NOW "consciously oppresses other women on the question of sexual preference," and that "lesbian is the one word that can cause the Executive Committee a collective heart attack."[6]

The tendency of this "one word" to elicit such contradictory expressions of the heart is further revealed when we read feminist history in connection with storytelling conventions and mass culture narratives of origin that have similarly undergone widespread discursive remapping. How, for example, might we read the gay/straight split in terms of the de-Oedipalization of American culture, and its intensification in the decades following World War II? In this sense, I'd like to think of the gay/straight split as a romance that both complies with and critiques cultural histories in an age when Oedipus, like the lesbian, is everywhere and nowhere. My purpose in doing this is to locate the fault lines of feminism by way of the fault lines of family romance, one of the most massively produced unifying cultural myths. In U.S. feminist and lesbian feminist writings of the years between 1968 and 1981, these fault lines cross one another to produce revealing sites of competition and ambiguity developing out of newly articulated configurations of sexual desire, gender identification, Oedipal politics, and narrative form.

Of course, the family romance has significant links to histories of American and European mass culture in addition to feminism and other liberatory discourses of bourgeois modernity.[7] In this sense, the familial master narrative may be understood as one of the many discursive threads that entangle U.S. feminist politics with popular culture, unevenly cross-stitching sentimental tropes of kinship to shifting notions of legible sexual citizenry and productive public-sphere participation. In the process, it is no surprise that feminists have tended to regard family romance with ambivalence and outright angst. While some contemporary feminist writers have retained and revised the romance, often to counter right-wing depictions of feminism as a homogeneous movement set on the complete eradication of traditional "family values," others have regarded family romance disdainfully as an ideological extension of cultural patriarchy, a policing instrument of social boundaries and gender hegemony that feminism would do well to avoid.[8]

Part of the problem, undoubtedly, is due to the family romance's lingering association with Sigmund Freud, who coined the phrase in a famous 1908 essay. Within feminism the romance has retained much of the same value that Freud originally ascribed to it as a fantasy that structurally unifies normative subjectivity and social consensus, or the personal and the political. Origin stories of the women's movement are similarly organized by means of spatial tropes and tensions that are by no means unique to histories of feminism or lesbianism, but circulate through all forms of cultural discourse. The gay/straight split is a romance that paradoxically retains a narrative apparatus of sexual oppression in order to consolidate feminist goals and rewrite the master narratives of Western bourgeois culture. Ultimately, however, this is a romance that demonstrates the discontinuity of the identity category purportedly represented by it: the category "women."

The fault lines of feminist narratives of origin are foregrounded in movement writings that queer the romance, thus subverting the family's ideological centrality while at the same time asserting its formal pervasiveness. These subversions become actively self-consuming, ultimately destabilizing feminism itself. In such instances, political myths, whether they stress coalition or contradiction, are aimed at articulating history for cultural consumption; in which case, the gay/straight split may be the kind of mistake that sees political narratives and popular narratives as discrete.

For many lesbian feminists and straight feminists in the period between 1968 and 1972, a political commitment to feminist politics involved a rhetorical commitment to a feminization of the family trope. This move, not unlike the nineteenth-century women's suffrage movement, was aimed at relocating relations of affect in the private sphere to relations of power in the public sphere. A feminized family romance—organized largely around metaphors of sisterhood and maternity—held particular significance for lesbians entering the movement, especially for those who were questioning the rhetoric of brotherhood that described relations between lesbians and gay men in the homophile movement.

In a 1970 issue of the *Ladder,* Del Martin, one of the "founding daughters" of the Daughters of Bilitis (DOB), bids farewell to Gay Liberation and the "alienated brothers" of the homophile organizations who for fifteen years had dismissed and excluded their lesbian "sisters" in the struggle for homosexual civil rights.[9] Martin cites Assemblyman Willie Brown of California, who, in his speech to the North American Conference on Homophile Organizations, encouraged unity among homophile groups and racial, ethnic, student, and women's liberation movements by cautioning them that differences "should be kept within our own families." Martin finds Brown's analogy "unfortunate." "Families usually include women," she writes, "and they usually include youth—both of whom are integral parts of the homophile community, both of whom were ignored . . ." (4). Martin describes herself as "pregnant with rage" as she bitterly decries a "brotherhood" whose preoccupation with bars, camp, pornography, drag, and role playing has resulted in homosexuals becoming the "laughing stock" of the public.

Martin concludes, "It is a revelation to find acceptance, equality, love and friendship—everything we sought in the homophile community—not there, but in the women's movement. I will not be your 'nigger' any longer. Nor was I ever your mother. Those were stultifying roles you laid on me, and I shall no longer concern myself with your toilet training. You're in the big leagues now, and we're both playing for big stakes. They didn't turn out to be the same" (6). While Martin's metaphorization of incest, racism, and momism constructs a complex vector of oppression within the Gay Liberation Movement, the feminist trope of egalitarian sisterhood emerges from the ashes of a failed family romance to sentimentalize relations between lesbian feminists and straight feminists. Martin's familial rhetoric of "moral mission" has been noted by Sue-Ellen Case, who argues that DOB's goal at that time was to convert lesbians into lesbian feminists (296).[10] These multiple rhetorical displacements that recuperate classism and racism equate the rejection of male supremacy with the rejection of sexual practices considered nonegalitarian—the sexuality of bar culture, butch-femme, and s/m—practices presumably based on heterosexual patterns of male domination and female submission. However, in her demonization of these sexualities Martin recuperates forms of racism and classism within an emergent lesbian feminist alliance by separating out women of color, working-class lesbians, bar dykes, and older lesbians from the movement. In this instance, the feminist family romance closets difference and offers a romance of consensus based in the primacy of white middle-class heterosexual women.

The Lavender Menace uprising registered, among other things, lesbian frustration with the liberal reformist wing of the women's movement. Subsequently, in 1972, Charlotte Bunch metaphorically cast the lesbian feminist as a forsaken sister and dissident daughter, although this time at the hands of movement women themselves. Martin's contradictory image of a lesbian "pregnant with rage," an image that suggests at once movement incest, life-producing anger, and mythical female powers capable of transforming political action, is restored to its classical context in the rhetoric of the Furies collective, a name derived from a Greek family romance that rivals Freud's Oedipus.[11] In Volume 1 of their publication, the Furies define themselves as "the avengers of matricide, the protectors of women" and "the primacy of mother right." In retrospect, Charlotte Bunch explains her disillusionment with the homophobia of the women's movement, a disillusionment that would lead her, along with several other movement women, to declare themselves *"lesbian-feminist separatists."* "The movement had been our family—our mother and child. When we began to proclaim our love for one another in ways that went beyond the boundaries of 'familial love,' most of us did not realize how savagely we would be disinherited by our 'sisters.'"[12] Bunch's statement is rhetorically marked by a failed maternal romance that points to the dangers, and the inevitability, of mixing political identifications with desires. The affirmative symbiosis of the mother-daughter romance—an alliance that resonates with feminist psychoanalytic theory's recuperation of lesbianism as an idealization and metaphorization of the maternal sublime—is bitterly reinterpreted here. Feminism's rhetoric of sisterhood is questioned along with its commitment to decentering Oedipus. The feminist family romance is critically diagnosed as centrally ambivalent, a de-Oedipal narrative not entirely unlike Julia Creet's reading of the contemporary lesbian s/m fantasy, "Daughter of the Movement." Publishing thirteen years later, Lacanian psychoanalytic theory substituting for Greek mythology, Creet positions feminism "as a kind of symbolic mother, a locus of law" against which lesbian s/m fantasies play out lesbian ambivalence toward the power of feminism (138).

While recognition of multiple differences and fractured alliances threatened the foundation of early feminism, it is has become clear that there is no articulation of a gay/straight split in the history of the United States Women's Movement that is not conversant with contradictions of race and class, although these contradictions take different forms in histories of women's movements and histories of gay and lesbian movements. An epistemology of cross-purposes within the parameters of a disunified subject was developed and amplified in writings by African American, Latina, and Third World lesbian feminists in the late 1970s and early eighties. A transformative theme throughout much of these writings is familial and maternal displacement and reclamation. These themes occasion family romances far more contradictory and ambiguous than white feminism's dream of a common language, and they demonstrate the extent to which racial and ethnic differences within the movement were disavowed by the focus on a gay/straight split.

"My dear *hermanas*," Gloria Anzaldúa writes in *This Bridge Called My Back*, "the dangers we face as women writers of color are not the same as those of white women though we have many in common."[13] In the same anthology, Cherríe Moraga questions familialized movement rhetoric that culturally unifies the meanings of the mother-daughter relationship by basing it exclusively in affirmative gender identifications. "When I finally lifted the lid to my lesbianism, a profound connection with my mother reawakened in me," she writes. "It wasn't until I acknowledged and confronted my own lesbianism in the flesh, that my heartfelt identification with and empathy for my mother's oppression—due to being poor, uneducated, and Chicana—was realized" (29). For Moraga, lesbianism does not initiate a romance with white feminism, but rather awakens her to the cross-purposes that define her unique cultural position. Moraga demonstrates the elusive and culturally contingent nature of the mother-daughter romance, a romance freed from social paradigms tied to notions of linguistic and class consensus. "Words are a war to me / They threaten my family."[14] Many of the writings published in groundbreaking feminist anthologies such as *This Bridge Called My Back* avoid the construction of a singularized or bifurcated identity. Rather, as Moraga demonstrates, Chicana lesbians persistently move across and occupy multiple subject positions interstitially, so that the multiple nuances of a hybrid romance redefine feminism and its feminized family plot as a movement of voices engaged in external and internal contradictions.

Similarly, in a conversation entitled, "Across the Kitchen Table: A Sister-to-Sister Dialogue," Beverly Smith expresses her concern that "there is so much about Black identity that doesn't get called into practice" (119) through her involvement with the women's movement.[15] What's missing, she suspects, is not something that movement women can give "to each other as peers because there is a kind of family bonding across generations that is very Black that doesn't happen" (120). She asks, "Do black lesbians, who do not identify as feminists and base their lives in the black community, feel this struggle?" Barbara Smith responds, "I think the isolation is probably a result much more of being a feminist" (120). Her response reveals the extent to which lesbian feminist separatism, as a strategy aimed at fostering cultural coherence and bonds of feminist sisterhood, constrains modes of community exchange and engagement with kin that are perhaps more central to African American cultural identities. Feminism's family romance thus fosters a deep sense of alienation for Beverly and Barbara Smith, sisters for whom political organization remains interdependent with familial and community structures inclusive of men and nonlesbians. As several contributors to this volume point out, identity as well as disciplinary constraints could be said to produce parallel forms of professional alienation and critical misrepresentation.

These textual occasions all figure as points of contention and slippage that may be read as participatory in the construction of a lesbian feminist genealogy. They demonstrate the expansion of methods of political self-formation in the wake of cultural redescription. They illustrate lingering formal constraints in combination with new ethical and aesthetic imperatives to write across private/public divisions as well as identity categories. By examining the ways in which the family romance is grafted onto the narratives and accounts of both gay/straight splits and gay/straight alliances, we see how popular and political myths reinforce and support one another while at the same time dissolving one another. These crossings present political desires and familial identifications as mobile and transgressive, as sites where popular and political narratives circulate inseparably, affirming and contesting one another, to construct feminist romance as history and feminist history as romance.

But what does this mean for the future of political coalition? Do the limits of lesbian and feminist alliances become more inhabitable when they are studied as the contiguous effects of mass-cultural paradigms and with the expectation that they render some histories and subjects more coherent than others? I believe they do, and I also suspect that feminism was queer studies before queer studies was queer studies, although feminism still remains to be productively expanded by lesbian, gay, and queer studies. Indeed, we may feminize queer studies and queer feminist studies, and rigorously critique the history of heterosexuality without abandoning belief in the romance of effective social alliances that make it expedient, in certain strategic instances, to claim kin. However, the de-Oedipalization of feminism necessarily disrupts appearances of consensus within feminist culture, thus troubling the boundaries between history and romance, the personal and the political, the lesbian and the feminist. To be at cross-purposes, in this respect, is to persistently dislocate and resituate alliance, by means of acknowledging the contradictions of a romance that sustains it.

Cross-Purposes is organized in three groups of essays, although admittedly almost any single essay could be appreciated for its contribution to more than one group. Each section establishes, and continues, a loose conversation about the conditions, inconsistencies, limits, and hopes of lesbian feminist alliances. Essays in the first section, "Crossings," stress the multiple entanglements and interactions of feminist and lesbian studies, exploring the ways in which feminism and lesbianism are inevitably, even if problematically, linked. Essays in the second section, "Collisions," underscore moments and points of critical impasse where lesbian and feminist subjects, politics, and representational strategies delineate strategic, albeit imprecise, boundaries and oppositions. Essays in the third section, "Coalitions," locate and reconstruct sites of possible coaction—generational, disciplinary, cultural—where lesbian studies and feminist studies might redefine their alliance and work toward common goals in the context of their acknowledged differences.

Cross-Purposes will rely on and advance the current scholarly investigation of the specificity of lesbian histories, self-concepts, and cultural representations. However, this collection is unique in its emphasis on locating lesbian studies in relation to feminism, which as Annamarie Jagose argues in this volume, often tends to negate the lesbian presence within its own histories, studies, and self-concepts. How has feminism, as an academic and political discourse, retained the authority to speak for the lesbian even at the expense of the lesbian herself? In order to address this question we need to explore the margins of feminist discourse where, to reiterate Carolyn Dever's assertion in the essay that opens this collection, lesbians have often been situated literally as "dykes," obstructionary figures that redirect and redefine the flow of feminism's mainstream. At the same time, we need to consider the lesbian's own sense of feminist discourse as central, yet somehow indifferent to her evolving analytical focus on lesbian-specific theories and practices, a historical process mobilized through her political insistence on space, visibility, and difference.

As several contributors to this volume note, generational shifts have impacted on lesbianism's uncertain alliance with feminism, particularly as a generation of lesbians came to political awareness not through the women's movement but through groups such as Queer Nation and ACT UP, organizations that placed them in a viable post-Stonewall alliance with gay men. According to numerous observers, the shift away from lesbian feminism to queer was decisively marked by sex radicalism.[16] In "Toward a Butch-Feminist Retro-Future," Sue-Ellen Case targets 1981–82 as "the great divide," the years that saw the outbreak of the "sex wars," fervid debates motivated not only by s/m lesbians' frustration with antipornography feminists but by an increasingly urgent political crisis stemming from government inattention to HIV and AIDS. By the end of the 1980s, queer "performativity" would effectively re-present lesbian feminism as essentialist and binary-happy, thus overturning the movement's socialist roots in consonance with the new global capitalism and changing political terminologies that worked to obscure worldwide material conditions.

From lesbian feminist collectives to queer constituencies, stagings of cross-purposes based on gender-specific versus sex-specific analyses, assimilationist versus antiassimilationist strategies, and essentialist versus constructivist approaches have significantly shaped and reshaped feminism's generational imaginary. In their cross-readings of gender, sexuality, and sex-directed critique, Michèle Aina Barale and Colleen Lamos argue that feminism and gay studies may share more intellectual and political kinship than they are as yet prepared to acknowledge. One reason for this lack of acknowledgment, as Bonnie Zimmerman points out, may be that while the New Left and dialectical materialism produced the theoretical and activist consciousness of a lesbian feminist generation that came of age in the 1960s and 1970s, a subsequent generation's political consciousness was shaped by the sex wars, poststructuralism, performativism, agitprop, and Queer Nation. According to Case, these latter generational engagements produced a new "queer dyke" who identified more with gay men than lesbians, and whose exit from feminism contributed to the widespread closing down of women-centered bars, bookstores, and cultural centers, many of them collectively owned and operated. This shift from movement to market sector generated a politics of celebratory commodification fixated on cultural production and organized around individual market intervention. Nevertheless, as Karin Quimby's essay on the cultural and historical development of the women's music industry demonstrates, forms of lesbian subjectivity were empowered through the concurrent emergence of feminist and lesbian political energies, energies that were—and continue to be—staged at women's music festivals.

In various arenas of queer cultural production, global capitalism's capacity to repackage historical structures of lesbian feminist subjectivity is being thoughtfully explored, as Tania Modleski demonstrates in her essay on the parodic confluences of race, gender, and sex that mark the work of actress and performance artist Sandra Bernhard. Such repackagings are currently the focus of academic cultural production as well. For example, Teresa de Lauretis observes the tendency of self-styled "postmodern lesbians" to speak in the "very lexicon of the feminist theory that I have been practicing for some twenty years . . . long-familiar terms like *unsettle, destabilize, test limits, undermine, heterosexual hegemony,* and so forth." Same vocabulary, different generational imaginary. This leads de Lauretis to ask, "what is Pomo about the lesbian without quotation marks, besides her rightly postmodern lack of historical memory?" The answer, it seems, is to be found in this rising generation's wholesale repudiation of femininity and the female body. In its place we now find a semiotic fascination with cyborgs, female-to-male-transsexuals, and Barbie. The current fixation is on creatures "beyond gender . . . efficient, clean, indestructible, and sexless."

De Lauretis's critique of the lesbian postmodern echoes, in many respects, recent critiques of "queer theory," a term that she herself coined and has since distanced herself from because of its deployment in contexts that neutralize rather than specify differences. On these grounds, lesbian studies has taken issue with queer theory in the interest of retaining the specificity and diversity of lesbian existence. For some, however, the neutralization of bipolarities implicit in the category "lesbian" is precisely what made queer politics and its academic consort, queer theory, viable. Queer's inclusion of multiple subjectivities that produce discontinuities of sex and gender in socially and racially diverse historical contexts promises stronger coalitions among gay, lesbian, transgender, transsexual, and bisexual communities in their efforts to reform institutionalized heterosexism. While such coalitions are urgently needed they remain seriously hindered by the strategic reinsertion of a bipolar gender system, a tendency which Kathleen Chapman and Michael du Plessis trace in their critique of the elisions of transgenders and transsexuals in lesbian, feminist, and queer discursive contexts.

A rising generation of lesbian scholars identify neither with lesbian feminism nor queer, believing that the latter retains gay men as its implicit referent while the former has become increasingly elitist, centrist, and removed from the material and political realities of women's lives. While this is not a new concern, it is one that feminism can scarcely afford to put off as congressional threats to women's welfare, housing, and health become enacted in punitive funding cutbacks, and as the violent rhetoric that fuels the radical Right's defense of traditional "family values" continues to demonize women, latinas/os, blacks, queers, the elderly, the poor, and the sick. Katie Hogan, for example, argues in her essay on lesbian studies, feminist studies, and representations of AIDS for the need of academic feminism to recognize that HIV/ AIDS is an urgent health and representational issue for all women. Hogan's essay, like several others in this volume, raises the important question of what can count as feminist theory, a question as central to Ruth Salvaggio's exploration of the lesbian and feminist energies that mobilize "interventions in language" as to Karman Kregloe and Jane Caputi's analysis of feminism's misrepresentation by the popular pundits of lesbian chic.

At the risk of stating the obvious, I believe that feminists, lesbians, and queers need one another's energies, theories, histories, communities, and politics as we continue to rethink and remake the coalitions that remain necessary for our survival. For this reason, it is important that the essays in this collection not be taken as representative of all feminists or lesbians. I hope *Cross-Purposes* will be received in the spirit with which it is intended, as a part of the story. This book is an invitation to begin questioning alliances in the interests of reforming and strengthening them; for when we examine the points of division between feminism and lesbianism we acknowledge the limits of identity politics and we discover the differences that inhere within discourses and within self-concepts. This collection stands on the borders between the multiple articulations of a lesbian or queer critical perspective and the multiple articulations of a feminist perspective. Its objective is to take these articulations to the limit, to see how and why we situate lesbianism in relation to feminism, and against it.

NOTES

1. Bonnie Zimmerman, "What Has Never Been" and "Lesbians Like This and That." See Works Cited for full publication data.

2. Martha Shelley, "Notes of a Radical Lesbian."

3. Redstockings of the Women's Liberation Movement, "The Pseudo-Left/Lesbian Alliance against Feminism."

4. Katie King, "Producing Sex, Theory, and Culture: Gay/Straight Remappings in Contemporary Feminism."

5. Margaret Cruikshank, *The Gay and Lesbian Liberation Movement* 149.

6. Quoted in Alice Echols, *Daring to Be Bad* 213.

7. For a more elaborate account of these ties, I would direct readers to my book, *Family Plots*.

8. Jane Gallop, for example, seems particularly invested in this latter position when she cautions "that feminists need to stop reading everything through the family romance." See her *Around 1981* 239.

9. Del Martin, "If That's All There Is."

10. Sue-Ellen Case, "Toward a Butch-Femme Aesthetic."

11. *The Furies: Lesbian/Feminist Monthly* 1 (January 1972).

12. Charlotte Bunch, "Learning from Separatism" 433.

13. Gloria Anzaldúa, "Speaking in Tongues" 165.

14. Cherríe Moraga, from *Loving in the War Years*, quoted in Anzaldúa, "Speaking in Tongues" 166.

15. Barbara Smith and Beverly Smith, "Across the Kitchen Table" 113–27.

16. See, for example, the essays collected in Carole S. Vance, *Pleasure and Danger: Exploring Female Sexuality* (Boston: Routledge & Kegan Paul, 1984); Ann Snitow, Christine Stansell, and Sharon Thompson, eds., *Powers of Desire: The Politics of Sexuality* (New York: Monthly Review Press, 1983); Samois, *Coming to Power: Writings and Graphics on Lesbian S/M* (Boston: Alyson, 1982).

WORKS CITED

Anzaldúa, Gloria. "Speaking in Tongues: A Letter to Third World Women Writers." In *This Bridge Called My Back: Writings by Radical Women of Color.* Ed. Cherríe Moraga and Gloria Anzaldúa. New York: Kitchen Table, Women of Color Press, 1981, 1983.

Bunch, Charlotte. "Learning from Separatism." In *Lavender Culture.* Ed. Karla Jay and Allen Young. New York: Harcourt, 1978.

Case, Sue-Ellen. "Toward a Butch-Femme Aesthetic." In *The Lesbian and Gay Studies Reader.* Ed. Henry Abelove, Michèle Barale, and David M. Halperin. New York: Routledge, 1993, 294–306.

Creet, Julia. "Daughter of the Movement: The Psychodynamics of Lesbian S/M Fantasy." *differences* 3.2 (Summer 1991): 135–59.

Cruikshank, Margaret. *The Gay and Lesbian Liberation Movement.* New York: Routledge, 1992.

Echols, Alice. *Daring to Be Bad: Radical Feminism in America, 1967–1975.* Minneapolis: University of Minnesota Press, 1989.

The Furies: Lesbian/Feminist Monthly 1 (January 1972).

Gallop, Jane. *Around 1981: Academic Feminist Literary Theory.* New York: Routledge, 1992.

Heller, Dana. *Family Plots: The De-Oedipalization of Popular Culture.* Philadelphia: University of Pennsylvania Press, 1995.

King, Katie. "Producing Sex, Theory, and Culture: Gay/Straight Remappings in Contemporary Feminism." In *Conflicts in Feminism.* Ed. Marianne Hirsch and Evelyn Fox Keller. New York: Routledge, 1990, 82–104.

Martin, Del. "If That's All There Is." *The Ladder.* 15. 3 and 4 (December–January 1970–71): 4–6.

Moraga, Cherríe. "La Guerra." In *This Bridge Called My Back* 27–34.

Redstockings of the Women's Liberation Movement. "The Pseudo-Left/Lesbian Alliance against Feminism." *Feminist Revolution.* New York: Random House, 1975, 190–96.

Shelley, Martha. "Notes of a Radical Lesbian." In *Sisterhood Is Powerful: An Anthology of Writings from the Women's Liberation Movement.* Ed. Robin Morgan. New York: Vintage, 1970, 306–10.

Smith, Barbara, and Beverly Smith. "Across the Kitchen Table: A Sister-to-Sister Dialogue." In *This Bridge Called My Back* 113–27.

Zimmerman, Bonnie. "Lesbians Like This and That: Some Notes on Lesbian Criticism for the Nineties." In *New Lesbian Criticism: Literary and Cultural Readings.* Ed. Sally Munt. New York: Columbia University Press, 1992, 1–16.

———. "What Has Never Been: An Overview of Lesbian Feminist Criticism." In *The New Feminist Criticism: Essays on Women, Literature, and Theory.* Ed. Elaine Showalter. New York: Pantheon, 1985, 200–24.

Part One

CROSSINGS

Obstructive Behavior

Dykes in the Mainstream of Feminist Theory

CAROLYN DEVER

The "obstructive behavior" I hope to analyze in this chapter involves the consideration of "dykes," by which I mean obstructions that impede or redirect a current or flow. I want to argue that feminist theory has come into being in relation to a set of "dykes," through contact with critical obstructions that shape, divert, and otherwise help to define the mainstream. The function of these dykes is an ambiguous one; they are at once necessary and problematic, central yet diversionary. Dykes are not *of* the mainstream, but the mainstream necessarily shapes itself in response to the presence of dykes.

At its most literal level, my title should signify a concern with the tendentious shape-shifting that has characterized feminist theory, producing new and innovative theoretical concerns and applications. At another level, however, it should signify its concern with the discourse of "obstruction," with impudent behaviors and political impediments that have confronted, ideally to challenge and to change, academic feminism. At still another level, I am concerned with the discourses of sexuality in feminism, and the sense in which the issue of sexuality itself operates as a "dyke," as a shaping impediment. For colloquially, *dyke* itself signifies, sometimes rudely, sometimes not, a way of being named or self-identifying as lesbian.[2] And the question of lesbians in the mainstream of feminist criticism has been the single most powerful "dyke" in the evolution of this critical discourse.

The *Oxford English Dictionary* definition of *dyke* or *dike* (the latter is the "more conventional" spelling), depends on an interestingly redoubled sense of ambiguity. The *OED* traces the etymology of *dyke* through a series of exchanges of masculine and feminine cases, evolving, perhaps ironically, from versions of the word *dick* in the masculine to versions of the word *dyke* in the feminine, pausing only in Icelandic at the neuter. Its history of etymological indeterminacy notwithstanding, *dyke* consistently signifies a form of diversionary obstruction, whether ditch, trench, mound, embankment, or dam, though the obstruction is conceived alternately as *either* a trench or a wall: "The application thus varies between 'ditch, dug out place,' and 'mound formed by throwing up the earth,' and may include both." Under its first definition, a dyke is "an excavation narrow in proportion to its length, a long and narrow hollow dug out of the ground; a DITCH, trench, or fosse," "such a hollow dug out to hold or conduct water." Under its second, it is "an embankment, wall, causeway," and still more specifically, "'a bank formed by throwing the earth out of the ditch' (Bosworth)," or "a wall or fence. . . . The wall of a city, a fortification."

Dyke is a word that presupposes the complication, conflation, even the collapse of binary categories. Confounding notions of masculinity and femininity in the case of etymology, of structure in the architectural significance of a barrier, conflicting definitions of *dyke* exploit an ambiguity at the heart of the concept itself. In its first definition, a "narrow hollow dug out of the ground," the function of the dyke is to enable another activity, such as the holding or the conducting of water, but is essentially passive: it exists primarily not as a presence but as an absence, as negative space sculpted from the positive surface of the earth. Yet in its alternate definition, the dyke exceeds that positive surface, existing as the highly visible *surplus* of earth in fortifying relation to the populace whose existence it protects and enables; whether as a canal permitting transport from one place to another or as a protective wall impeding that transport, the well-being of its architects depends on the dyke's structural integrity. In either incarnation, the transformative capacity of the dyke remains its most powerful capital: articulating a space that is, by definition, both marginal and central, the dyke demarcates difference, transition, liminality, and vulnerability. That vulnerability inheres in the status of the dyke as a protective structure: without the need to guard against difference, against the threat of difference to destroy, the dyke would be completely unnecessary.

A slang definition, listed below and separated from the nearly three columns of dykes in the *OED*, reads as follows: "dike, dyke . . . [Of obscure origin.] A lesbian; a masculine woman."[3] Citing as its earliest usage a 1942 entry in the *American Thesaurus of Slang*, this dyke, of obscure origin, remains distinct from the *OED*'s other dykes, yet shares with them certain implications of liminality. Not only a lesbian but also a "masculine woman," the dyke, in this definition, blurs the borderline between masculinity and femininity. In her appearance, presumably in her affective alliances, she, like her fellow dykes, marks, embodies, and deconstructs that borderline by disrupting conventional practices of self-presentation and desire. Like the other dykes, this dyke offers a limit case and a liminal space, enabling definitions of inside and out-side, enabling, through her location of and as a border, binary systems of logic which exploit fixed notions of identity and identifiability.

Mainstream feminism, I want to argue, has been defined by and against its relationship to dykes, depending precisely on the dyke's function as a borderline to mark the parameters of feminist theory and practice. For twenty-five years, feminists have displayed dramatic, symptomatic forms of ambivalence to lesbians in the mainstream. At once needing and abhorring the dykes that exist at and as the shaping margins of its discourse, feminist theory has struggled to accommodate competing desires for mainstream acceptance and individual sexual diversity. Catalyzing questions about sex, sexuality, eroticism, pleasure, identity, politics, and power, the dyke in the mainstream has always been the site of contention, the source of troubling questions, both for and within feminism.

FEMINIST THEORY IN THE 1970s

A RIDGE, EMBANKMENT, LONG MOUND, OR DAM, THROWN UP TO RESIST THE
ENCROACHMENTS OF THE SEA, OR TO PREVENT LOW-LYING LANDS FROM
BEING FLOODED BY SEAS, RIVERS, OR STREAMS.

—OXFORD ENGLISH DICTIONARY

From the vocabulary of lesbian separatism in the 1970s through queer theory today, feminists have always engaged questions of sexual-ity. But although the vantage point of history often associates the early women's movement with the political enthusiasms of the Sexual Revolution, in fact, the very personal politics of sexual difference have historically marked the most dramatic fault lines among feminists. As early as 1970, at the Second Congress to Unite Women, twenty women stormed the meeting's plenary session with the words "Lavender Men-ace" emblazoned on their chests. Prompted to act by Betty Friedan's notorious, and perhaps apocryphal, remark that lesbians in the women's movement were a "lavender menace" who would ultimately impede cultural acceptance of feminist sympathies, the women calling themselves the "Lavender Menace" challenged conference members to confront discrimination against lesbians in the women's movement.

Later renaming themselves "Radicalesbians," this group soon produced an essay titled "The Woman-Identified Woman," which argued that all sexualities exist in the service of patriarchy and that a challenge to rigid notions of sexuality must accompany feminist critiques of patriarchy. Women who fail to consider the erotic potential of other women are trapped in a patriarchal web, living their lives, setting their expectations, only in terms of their relationships to men; thus feminists fail to confront their full investment in patriarchal power until they confront the personal politics of their bedrooms. "Real" women, "feminine" women, the Radicalesbians suggest,

> are authentic, legitimate, real to the extent that we are the property of some man whose name we bear. To be a woman who belongs to no man is to be invisible, pathetic, inauthentic, unreal. He confirms his image of us—of what we have to be in order to be acceptable by him— but not our real selves; he confirms our womanhood—as he defines it, in relation to him—but cannot confirm our personhood, our own selves as absolutes. As long as we are dependent on the male culture for this definition, for this approval, we cannot be free.[4]

The Radicalesbians identify female homosexuality as a political choice. Lesbianism, within their rubric, is a political mandate more than an erotic one; the utopic vision of a lesbian-separatist community, often figured as the return of the Amazons, is frequently represented as the only plausible alternative within a radical and thoroughgoing critique of patriarchy. And indeed, this is a notion that looms large over the culture of feminist discourse to this day, for, as lesbian separatists throughout the early days of the Women's Movement insist, separatism remains a logical extreme of feminist critiques of patriarchy, a logical solution to often painfully paradoxical attempts to live a "feminist life." As Catharine MacKinnon writes, "Feminism is the epistemology of which lesbianism is an ontology."[5]

Lesbian separatism was one of the greatest challenges to and the greatest anxieties of early feminists. Ti-Grace Atkinson presents a summary of the theory informing political lesbianism in the collection *Amazon Odyssey:* "It is the commitment of individuals to common goals, and to the death if necessary, that determines the strength of the army. . . . Lesbianism is to feminism what the Communist Party was to the trade-union movement. Tactically, any feminist should fight to the death for lesbianism because of its strategic importance."[6] Invoking metaphors ranging from the martial to the economic, Atkinson emphasizes the importance of linking feminist theory and feminist practice: "I'm enormously less interested in whom you sleep with than I am in with whom you're prepared to die."[7] Atkinson interrogates the inherently "political" nature of lesbianism, suggesting that affectional and erotic object choices themselves do not necessarily make a politics, but that lesbianism has occupied a politically significant structural position within feminism.

> Because of their particularly unique attempt at revolt, the lesbian role within the male/female class system becomes critical. Lesbianism is the "criminal" zone, what I call the "buffer" zone, between the two major classes comprising the sex class system. The "buffer" has both a unique nature and function within the system. And it is crucial that both lesbians and feminists understand the strategical significance of lesbianism to feminism. (136–37)

In Atkinson's analysis, the liminal lesbian position, the "buffer," becomes strategic turf: it is the battlefield of actual feminist practice, the space intervening between "oppressor" and "oppressed," men and women. Semantically, however, within the discursive structure of Atkinson's vision, lesbians are not women, nor are they men, feminists, oppressors, or oppressed; they exist, as dykes so often have, as the means of defining the difference between feminists and their oppressors; significantly, though, lesbians themselves manage to elude definition, categorization, political importance, even inclusion in this framework. That both "lesbians" and "feminists" must understand the crucial significance of lesbianism to feminism sacrifices lesbian interests to a larger feminist cause; nowhere are lesbians supposed to consider the significance of feminists, they are simply assumed to *be* feminists. Despite Atkinson's comment that "feminists should fight to the death for lesbians," she more frequently assumes the opposite logic: she sees lesbians as the front lines of the feminist army. Mainstream feminism for Atkinson, regardless of its radical politics, is a heterosexual movement; dykes exist merely to facilitate, protect, and maintain that mainstream. Unlike the Radicalesbians, for whom lesbianism is feminist theory in its purest form, for Atkinson, lesbianism is a means to an end, a strategic position on a much larger battleground.

Atkinson's interest in the concept of lesbianism originates in the persistence of homophobic invective against feminists: "from the outset of the Movement, most men automatically called all feminists 'lesbians.' This connection was so widespread and consistent that I began to wonder myself if maybe men didn't perceive some connection the Movement was overlooking" (135–36). Atkinson, like the Radicalesbians, wonders why feminism engenders this response: "Generally speaking, the Movement has reacted defensively to the charge of lesbianism: 'No, I'm not!' 'Yes, you are!' 'No, I'm not!' 'Prove it.' For myself I was so puzzled about the connection that I became curious. . . . Whenever the enemy keeps lobbing bombs into some area you consider unrelated to your defense, it's always worth investigating."[8] As Miriam Schneir points out in a recent discussion of the Radicalesbians, "The lesbian issue continued to generate personal and ideological splits among feminists—including among radical feminists—that sisterhood could not always surmount. Lesbians and straights both played a part in this unfortunate turn of events: Some straight feminists were afraid of being labeled dykes and wished to dissociate both the movement and themselves from lesbianism, while some lesbians claimed that lesbianism was an example of feminism in action and preached that the only true feminists were those who renounced relations with the opposite sex entirely."[9] Rather than disavow the label "dyke," Atkinson attempts to appropriate it as "buffer": within her theoretical paradigm, lesbians exist on the front line of the gender wars. The logic here is that of a speech act: the men lobbing the explosive word *dyke* succeed in labeling all practicing feminists as dykes. Atkinson assumes that those who are called dykes necessarily become dykes, whether in theory or in practice. And within her vision of feminist activism, these dykes will be sacrificed, in theory or in practice, for a mainstream feminist utopic vision.

FEMINIST THEORY IN THE EARLY 1980s

> THE APPLICATION THUS VARIES BETWEEN 'DITCH, DUG OUT PLACE,' AND 'MOUND FORMED BY THROWING UP THE EARTH,' AND MAY INCLUDE BOTH.
>
> —OXFORD ENGLISH DICTIONARY

Split between defensive responses to internalized homophobia and the political logic of separatism, feminist definitions of *lesbian* during the early 1980s are marked by a noteworthy ambivalence toward questions of sexual practice and erotic pleasure: lesbianism, when it enters into definitions of *feminism* at all, enters almost exclusively as a political ideal, undistinguished by any real erotic significance. Adrienne Rich's landmark essay "Compulsory Heterosexuality and Lesbian Existence" appeared in *Signs* in 1980. Rich's articulation of a "lesbian continuum" indicates a significant development in popular feminist attempts at self-definition. Interrogating heterosexuality as a vestigal structure of patriarchal power, Rich argues in the tradition of early political lesbians that "the denial of reality and visibility to women's passion for women, women's choice of women as allies, life companions, and community, the forcing of such relationships into dissimulation and their disintegration under intense pressure have meant an incalculable loss to the power of all women *to change the social relations of the sexes, to liberate ourselves and each other.*"[10] In the terms of Rich's argument, feminists historically have been their own worst enemies, thwarting their own political agendas through their failure to truly challenge "the social relations of the sexes." Rich suggests that homophobia informs feminists' unwillingness to ally themselves fully—politically, personally, or intellectually—with lesbians, duplicating the oppression of women more generally under patriarchal power structures and undermining the viability of all feminist theory. Recalling the Radicalesbians' argument about the need to theorize heterosexuality rigorously, not as a "natural" category but as a complex and problematic construct, Rich modifies their concluding exhortation of lesbianism as the feminist political ideal through the development of two strategic arguments.

The first, which encompasses the mission statement of Rich's essay, calls for a more comprehensive and rigorous feminist theory that takes into consideration all forms of erotic, political, and intellectual individuality; extending a critique of Dorothy Dinnerstein to feminist theory as a whole, Rich writes: "[Dinnerstein] ignores, specifically, the history of women who—as witches, *femmes seules,* marriage resisters, spinsters, autonomous widows, and/or lesbians—have managed on various levels *not* to collaborate. It is this history, precisely, from which feminists have so much to learn and on which there is overall such blanketing silence" (230). Rich's form of feminist theory would have at its center the interrogation of "compulsory heterosexuality":

> The assumption that "most women are innately heterosexual" stands as a theoretical and political stumbling block for feminism. It remains a tenable assumption partly because lesbian existence has been written out of history or catalogued under disease, partly because it has been treated as exceptional rather than intrinsic, partly because to acknowledge that for women heterosexuality may not be a "preference" at all but something that has had to be imposed, managed, organized, propagandized, and maintained by force is an immense step to take if you consider yourself freely and "innately" heterosexual. Yet the failure to examine heterosexuality as an institution is like failing to admit that the economic system called capitalism or the caste system of racism is maintained by a variety of forces, including both physical violence and false consciousness. (238–39)

Calling for a rigorous analysis of the power dynamics at stake in "compulsory heterosexuality," Rich is sharply critical of feminist unwillingness to consider the full range of sexual diversity. Her suggestion

that this analysis would be anxiety-producing because feminists themselves have something at stake in the institution of heterosexuality
recalls the Radicalesbians' arguments about the political inconsistencies in most attempts to combine feminist theory with a bourgeois,
heterosexual life. But Rich stops short of calling for political lesbianism,
insisting instead on a feminist theoretical analysis of issues previously
hidden by assumptions of normative heterosexuality.

In fact, Rich's second argument represents a neat appropriation of
the anxieties that inevitably seem to accompany discussions of political
lesbianism. She argues, through the radical expansion of the term
lesbian, that all feminists, in fact, all women, are already lesbians;
feminist thus becomes a subset of lesbian, rather than the other way
around. She explains:

> I mean the term *lesbian continuum* to include a range—through each
> woman's life and throughout history—of woman-identified experi-
> ence, not simply the fact that a woman has had or consciously desired
> genital sexual experience with another woman. If we expand it to
> embrace many more forms of primary intensity between and among
> women, including the sharing of a rich inner life, the bonding against
> male tyranny, the giving and receiving of practical and political
> support, if we can also hear it in such associations as *marriage resistance*
> and the "haggard" behavior identified by Mary Daly (obsolete mean-
> ings: "intractable," "willful," "wanton," and "unchaste," "a woman
> reluctant to yield to wooing"), we begin to grasp breadths of female
> history and psychology which have lain out of reach as a consequence
> of limited, mostly clinical, definitions of *lesbianism*.[11]

Rich's identification of the "lesbian continuum" is the logical yield of
her interrogation of compulsory heterosexuality. She emphasizes that
the deconstruction of the assumptions and dynamics informing compulsory heterosexuality will bring into view many forms of profound
interconnections among women, connections that have always existed
but have been obscured from view by assumptions of normative heterosexuality. In naming these relationships "lesbian," Rich accommodates
and thus begins to value women's relationships with one another across
a wide range of behaviors that presumably includes, but is not limited
to, the erotic: "As the term lesbian has been held to limiting, clinical
associations in its patriarchal definition, female friendship and com-
radeship have been set apart from the erotic, thus limiting the erotic
itself" (240).

In addition to the notion of the "lesbian continuum" and the critique
of compulsory heterosexuality, the other significant innovation of Rich's

argument is its shift in the locus of activism. Identifying her task as a primarily critical one, Rich targets an audience composed principally of feminist academics. She identifies literary criticism, as well as related modes of historical and social scientific research, as central to feminist praxis and instrumental in the process of locating the lesbian continuum; literary critics and other academics possess the ability to produce a more accurate version of women's history. Significantly, however, even as Rich empowers academics within feminist activism, academics also occupy the center of her target of critique: she condemns "the virtual or total neglect of lesbian existence in a wide range of writings, including feminist scholarship" (229). By the early 1980s, literary criticism is at ground zero in what was previously a grassroots political movement, as academic work is increasingly valorized as a primary form of feminist activist intervention. Rich's focus on literary criticism constructs feminist politics as a battleground of metacriticism; the issues at stake concern not only the practicalities of feminist critique in the world at large, but also the novels of Colette, Charlotte Brontë, and Toni Morrison, and the theoretical paradigms of Mary Daly, Catharine MacKinnon, and Nancy Chodorow. Focusing on the historical period from which Rich's essay emerged, Jane Gallop, in *Around 1981: Academic Feminist Literary Theory*, argues that in the early 1980s, feminism "entered the heart of a contradiction": "It became secure and prospered in the academy while feminism as a social movement was encountering major setbacks in a climate of new conservatism. The Reagan-Bush years began; the ERA was defeated. In the American academy feminism gets more and more respect while in the larger society women cannot call themselves feminist."[12]

Underscoring Gallop's argument regarding the yawning divide between academic feminism and the lives of women "in the larger society," bell hooks, writing in 1984, sees academic discourse as part of the problem, alienating mainstream women from feminist activism. "The ability to 'translate' ideas to an audience that varies in age, sex, ethnicity, degree of literacy is a skill feminist educators need to develop. Concentration of feminist educators in universities encourages habitual use of an academic style that may make it impossible for teachers to communicate effectively with individuals who are not familiar with either academic style or jargon."[13] hooks's critique of self-conscious academic language extends from the same metacritical impulse as Rich's critical rereading of feminist texts for their prescriptions of compulsory heterosexuality. But hooks's target audience is somewhat different from Rich's; hooks sees the exclusionary language of academic feminism as part of a problematic system of oppressive power relation-

ships relating to race, class, and gender. Far from escaping the pernicious implications of these power relations, hooks argues that feminists
consistently *duplicate* them in their blindness to and exclusion of women
of color and poor women. While Rich's critique focuses on assumptions
of normative heterosexuality, hooks's focuses on assumptions of normative white middle-class status:

> White women who dominate feminist discourse today rarely question
> whether or not their perspective on women's reality is true to the lived
> experiences of women as a collective group. Nor are they aware of the
> extent to which their perspectives reflect race and class biases, al-
> though there has been a greater awareness of biases in recent years.
> Racism abounds in the writings of white feminists, reinforcing white
> supremacy and negating the possibility that women will bond politi-
> cally across ethnic and racial boundaries. Past feminist refusal to draw
> attention to and attack racial hierarchies suppressed the link between
> race and class. (3)

Given hooks's useful insistence on sex, race, and class discrimination as
symptoms of larger systemic problems, it is noteworthy that discrimination based on sexuality drops out of her larger structure of critique.
hooks is deeply concerned that feminist theory address issues across
lines of race and class, but to do so, she argues, feminism must begin to
disassociate itself from its image as a movement consisting primarily of
lesbians; she sees feminism as a movement dominated by dykes at the
expense of diversity. hooks is sharply critical of what she perceives as
the facile equation in mainstream feminism of lesbian sexuality with
political correctness: "women who are not lesbians, who may or may
not be in relationships with men feel that they are not 'real' feminists.
This is especially true of women who may support feminism but who
do not publiclly [*sic*] support lesbian rights" (151).

Unwilling to apply the same critique to homophobia that she does to
racism, hooks exhorts feminists to "diversify" the public face of feminism by making clear that feminists are not necessarily lesbians or man-
haters. In hooks's view, the failure of feminism to become a truly
massive social movement inheres in its anxiety-producing association
with nonhetero sexualities:

> My point is that feminism will never appeal to a mass-based group of
> women in our society who are heterosexual if they think that they will
> be looked down upon or seen as doing something wrong. . . . Just as
> feminist movement to end sexual oppression should create a social
> climate in which lesbians and gay men are no longer oppressed, a
> climate in which their sexual choices are affirmed, it should also create

a climate in which heterosexual practice is freed from the constraints
of heterosexism and can also be affirmed. One of the practical reasons
for doing this is the recognition that the advancement of feminism as
a political movement depends on the involvement of masses of
women, a vast majority of whom are heterosexual. As long as feminist
women (be they celibate, lesbian, heterosexual, etc.) condemn male
sexuality, and by extension women who are involved sexually with
men, feminist movement is undermined. (153)

The rhetoric of comprehensive, systemic analysis of power relations has
shifted by this point to a more coercive rhetoric of marketing: "feminism
will never appeal to a mass-based group of women in our society who
are heterosexual *if* . . ." While hooks claims concern here for the
discriminatory assumptions of heterosexism, nowhere else does she
suggest that feminist theory pander to the comfort of the "vast majority" in exchange for a rigorous consideration of the rights and the
existence of an endangered minority.

My critique of hooks's position is not a new one; in fact, the quote
above is part of hooks's response to "lesbian feminist" Cheryl Clarke,
who wrote an essay titled "The Failure to Transform: Homophobia in
the Black Community," in which she remarks: "'Hooks delivers a
backhanded slap at lesbian feminists, a considerable number of whom
are black. Hooks would have done well to attack the institution of
heterosexuality as it is a prime cause of black women's oppression in
America.'"[14] hooks replies, "Clearly Clarke misunderstands and misin-
terprets my point. I made no reference to heterosexism and it is the
equation of heterosexual practice with heterosexism that makes it appear that Clarke is attacking the practice itself and not only
heterosexism." Clarke's point, reminiscent of Rich, that hooks should
examine "the institution of heterosexuality," is revealingly translated
by hooks directly into "heterosexism": it is not Clarke but hooks who
makes the equation of heterosexual practice and heterosexism.[15] The
question of the problematic institutional dynamics of heterosexuality is
neatly subsumed under this equation; hooks's discussion continues on
into a critique of feminist heterophobic impulses, in defense of "the
choice women make to be heterosexual" (154). Heterosexuality, not
normally seen as an endangered category, makes a strange bedfellow
with the other forms of oppression and exclusion hooks treats in this
text, including racial and class prejudice. hooks's heterosexuality is
vulnerable, defensive, embattled, but ironically, her need to defend
heterosexual practice duplicates a function of the dyke: she is eager to
set up protective walls around heterosexuality, thus liberating women
everywhere into the radical freedom of heterosexual object choice. In

another twist of irony, hooks begins to set up dykes to defend against dykes.

hooks's logic at this point is complicated, for several reasons. In her larger argument, her desire to ensure that feminists are consistent in their critique of *any* form of compulsory sexuality, whether gay or straight, is a direct extension of powerful early feminist critiques of limiting patriarchal roles for women. However, in a book critiquing feminist marginalizations of women of color, it is strange that hooks's analysis of phobic exclusionary practices should fail to extend to her discussion of sexuality. The apparent suggestion that feminists should disassociate themselves—at least publicly—from the issue of lesbian sexuality seems linked to another paradigm of the 1970s, the antifeminist rhetoric which labeled feminists, often arbitrarily, as dykes, intimidating through the invocation of internalized homophobia. Instead of reading "mass-based" anxiety about lesbianism as a need for "mass-based" education about forms of prejudice as pernicious in the case of sexuality as in the case of race, hooks seems to suggest that feminists need only change the window dressing in order to appeal to a wider range of women; her feminist paradigm seems to sacrifice sexual diversity in the cause of racial diversity, while she bars altogether the possibility that lesbians of color might exist. This platform clearly—and perhaps ironically—returns to the scene of the "lavender menace," and backlash against the suggestion that the marketing of the feminist movement must occur under the aegis of "normative" sexuality.

While Barbara Smith echoes hooks's sharp criticism of white, middle-class feminist narcissism, she does not see the interests of black women and lesbians as mutually exclusive or even in competition, insisting on the importance of a feminist discourse that considers race and sexuality together: "Long before I tried to write this I realized that I was attempting something unprecedented, something dangerous, merely by writing about Black women writers from a feminist perspective and about Black lesbian writers from any perspective at all. . . . All segments of the literary world—whether establishment, progressive, Black, female, or lesbian—do not know, or at least act as if they do not know, that Black women writers and Black lesbian writers exist."[16] Jane Gallop claims, in a discussion of *The New Feminist Criticism* (the anthology in which Smith's essay is reprinted), that feminist criticism of the early and mid-1980s struggled explicitly with problems of self-definition and with issues of inclusion and exclusion.[17] Judith Roof argues that "the myriad differences among women are often reduced to the formula 'black and lesbian.' . . . I suspect that this . . . critical reliance upon black and lesbian is symptomatic of some underlying critical difficulty with multiplicity."[18] I would concur that within the discourses of feminist theory and criticism of the mid-1980s, the categories "black" and "lesbian" demarcate similar modes of "difference," both existing, in most cases, as "other than" a norm. The white, middle-class, hetero-sexual assumptions of that norm are made visible only through the tension produced by the defining presence of the other.

FEMINIST THEORY IN THE LATE 1980s

A MASS OF MINERAL MATTER, USUALLY IGNEOUS ROCK, FILLING UP A FISSURE IN THE ORIGINAL STRATA, AND SOMETIMES RISING FROM THESE LIKE A MOUND OR WALL, WHEN THEY HAVE BEEN WORN DOWN BY DENUDATION.

— OXFORD ENGLISH DICTIONARY

Feminist theorists became increasingly preoccupied with the discursive politics of "difference" in the years that followed these publications, to the extent that race and sexuality are equated less often. But the contentious and persistent question of dykes in the mainstream continued throughout this period to serve a uniquely definitional func-tion for feminist theory. In the early 1980s, feminism was faced with a central division: some critics argued that feminism was all about, too much about, lesbianism and lesbian sexuality; others argued that the heterosexist bias in feminist discourse betrayed itself constantly in the marginalization and the silencing of lesbians and lesbian writers. This particular "dyke" shaped the peculiar path of feminist discourse in the second half of the 1980s.

Literary theory more generally was reinfused with the politics of activism in the mid-1980s; as the AIDS epidemic ravaged the gay male community, many critics turned to the complexities of male homoeroticism, discourses, and representation with a sense of political urgency unseen since the early days of the women's movement. Using the tools of feminist theory, literary theorists began to focus on homo-sexuality through the newly repoliticized disc   ses of masculinity. Interestingly and ironically, this development created yet another "dyke" in the world of literary criticism: while lesbians belonged to the gay rights movement and the feminist movement, suddenly they were *centrally* implicated in neither. Although questions of homosexuality were central to both feminist and gay male discourses, they were primarily about male homosexuality. Lesbians themselves existed at the discursive margins, in and as the space between these two newly prominent theoretical positions.

Through the middle years of the 1980s, the central terms of feminist literary theory underwent a significant paradigm shift, refocusing from a concern with the politics of female sex and sexuality to a theoretically broader concern with the notion of gender. As Elaine Showalter points out in the introduction to the anthology *Speaking of Gender,* which first appeared in 1989, "talking about gender means talking about both women and men." "The introduction of gender into the field of literary studies marks a new phase in feminist criticism, an investigation of the ways that all reading and writing, by men as well as by women, is marked by gender. Talking about gender, moreover, is a constant re-minder of the other categories of difference, such as race and class, that structure our lives and texts, just as theorizing gender emphasizes the parallels between feminist criticism and other forms of minority dis-course."[19] The rise of gender studies over the course of the 1980s served practical as well as theoretical functions. Among other things, it opened the doors of feminist theory unambiguously to male practitioners, and as Showalter points out, presented a much more sophisticated notion of the ways in which language and power converge to shape a speaking subject, whether "male" or "female." The focus on gender served to further dismantle monolithic notions of "maleness" and "femaleness" per se, in exchange for a theory of gender as cultural construct, symp-tomatically reflecting larger cultural investments.

Gender theory has proved both invigorating and problematic for more conventional feminist political concerns. As Showalter notes,

> some readers . . . worry that "gender studies" could be a pallid assimi-lation of feminist criticism into the mainstream (or male stream) of English studies, a return to the old priorities and binary oppositions that will reinstate familiar male canons while crowding hard-won courses on women writers out of the curriculum. Others fear that talking about gender is a way for both male and female critics to avoid the political commitment of feminism. Still others raise the troubling possibility that gender will be isolated from issues of class and race. (10)

Showalter suggests that many feminists were and remain concerned that to forsake the focus on "women" in favor of a broader focus on "gender" is to retrench on feminist inroads in the academy; if there is no longer any basis for a practical concern for and with women specifically, then what is the difference, they ask, between the academy now and the academy before early feminist pioneers appeared on the horizon? The generalization outward of feminist political and theoretical interests reflects more complex notions about the ways in which structures of gender and sexuality are supported; in a poststructuralist theoretical universe which privileges indeterminacy, to talk about "women" alone is, in some sense, a return to an artificial and potentially simplistic means of categorization. Yet this artifice is belied by the materialist concerns of patriarchal class politics: the opening out of feminist theory into gender theory certainly risks the reinstitutionalization of male-centered concerns, a loss of ground in some sense, even as it represents an enriched understanding of prevailing cultural constructs.

Feminist ventures in gender theory constantly engage this ambivalence. The important linkage of feminist and gay male theories of discourse and narrative was facilitated by several prominent feminist critics, who are necessarily prompted at every turn to theorize, even to justify, the gender politics of their methodologies. For example, Eve Kosofsky Sedgwick, in the groundbreaking study *Between Men: English Literature and Male Homosocial Desire,* both avows a feminist methodology and defends her exclusive focus on male subjectivity and male homosociality. In her introduction, Sedgwick discusses "the isolation, not to mention the absolute subordination, of women, in the structural paradigm on which this study is based." She writes: "The absence of lesbianism from the book was an early and, I think, necessary decision, since my argument is structured around the distinctive relation of the male homosocial spectrum to the transmission of unequally distributed power. Nevertheless, the exclusively heterosexual perspective of the book's attention to women is seriously impoverishing in itself."[20] Profoundly feminist in its methodology, Sedgwick's rereading of Freud, Girard, and the structure of triangulated desire does not offer a deeper understanding of the place of the woman in that structure but instead demonstrates as central the vector connecting its two male subjects in a rich analysis of the male homosocial relations previously concealed by assumptions of normative heterosexuality. However, the single theoretical distinction Sedgwick makes between male and female homoeroticism is a significant one; she justifies her focus on the distinction between homosociality and homosexuality in men based on the fact that this is *more* of a distinction for men than for women:

> The diacritical opposition between the "homosocial" and the "homosexual" seems to be much less thorough and dichotomous for women, in our society, than for men. At this particular historical moment, an intelligible continuum of aims, emotions, and valuations links lesbianism with the other forms of women's attention to women: the bond of mother and daughter, for instance, the bond of sister and sister, women's friendship, "networking," and the active struggles of feminism. The continuum is crisscrossed with deep discontinuities—with much homophobia, with conflicts of race and class—but its intelligibility seems now a matter of simple common sense. (2)

Writing off the theoretical complexity, even the specific discernibility, of lesbian erotic desire as "simple common sense," Sedgwick inaugurates an era in which feminist practitioners fixate on male homoeroticism as an interesting problematic while dismissively relegating the "dyke" to the outer reaches of feminist discourse. Implicitly accepting Rich's notion of the "lesbian continuum" as theoretically exhaustive, Sedgwick ironically reinscribes the very problem Rich herself was hoping to dismantle. For Rich was concerned with precisely "how and why women's choice of women as passionate comrades, life partners, co-workers, lovers, community has been crushed, invalidated, forced into hiding and disguise; and . . . the virtual or total neglect of lesbian existence in a wide range of writings, including feminist scholarship." Rich concludes, in a startling prediction of a predicament redescribed a decade later: "I believe that much feminist theory and criticism is stranded on this shoal."[21]

In *The Apparitional Lesbian: Female Homosexuality and Modern Culture,* Terry Castle explores Sedgwick's resistance to or "blockage" against any form of rigorous consideration of female homosexuality:

> Lesbians, defined . . . with telling vagueness only as "women who love women," are really no different, Sedgwick seems to imply, from "women promoting the interests of other women." Their way of bonding is so "congruent" with that of other women, it turns out, that one need no longer call it homosexual. "The adjective 'homosocial' as applied to women's bonds," [Sedgwick] concludes, *"need not be pointedly dichotomized as against 'homosexual'; it can intelligibly denominate the entire continuum."* By a disarming sleight of phrase, an entire category of women—lesbians—is lost to view.[22]

Castle's objection to Sedgwick's "uncharacteristically sentimental" (71) reliance on the "continuum" metaphor begins to indicate a major problem in conventional feminist analyses of homoeroticism. Castle's critique implicitly returns to and begins to trouble Adrienne Rich's notion of the "lesbian continuum," which pointedly desexualizes lesbianism in favor of a more pan-feminist vision of meaningful engagement among women. Castle's discomfort with the "lesbian continuum" betokens a new negotiation for feminist theory: a theoretical practice that interrogates the specificity of male homoerotic desire cannot rely complacently on a notion of lesbianism that is vague, deliberately broad, and explicitly detached from any form of eroticism or desire whatsoever. Rich's argument for the "lesbian continuum" was the product of a specific historical moment and served several important functions within the discourse of feminist theory, particularly in its defusing of the term *lesbian* and its situation of feminist methodology firmly in the center of literary critical practice. However, as Castle implies, Rich's project is not the lesbian equivalent to the carefully theorized analysis of male homosociality that Sedgwick conducts in *Between Men*. Indeed, Rich's essay announces as its goal the more rigorous *inclusion* of lesbians throughout the range of academic discourses; thus Sedgwick's appropriation of Rich, in order to justify the *exclusion* of lesbians, represents a perfect, if ironic, example of the phenomenon Rich had hoped to counteract.

Pursuing the implications of Castle's argument, I would agree that feminists, working from the heritage of such broad definitions as Rich's "lesbian continuum," are quick to assume that they already fully understand "lesbianism," most conventionally as something inherently "feminist" or as something having to do with (not necessarily sexual) "female bonding." Accompanying this model are assumptions suggesting that lesbianism is only occasionally or tangentially related to sex and sexual pleasure. These assumptions are engendered in part by the history, within feminism, of a political lesbianism which constructs lesbianism as a separatist opting out of patriarchy rather than as an erotic object choice. They are also facilitated by historical conventions of female friendship and Boston marriage, which again are perceived as related more to women's mutual empathy than to mutual erotic pleasure. These assumptions suggest a dramatic historical difference in cultural perceptions of female and male homosexuality. From Gay Liberation to queer theory, analyses of male homosexuality have rarely assumed that eroticism, sexual attraction, and sex acts, covert or explicit, are marginal or irrelevant issues. Following Sedgwick's lead, feminist and queer analyses of polymorphous sexualities ironically continue to fixate on problems of *male* homoeroticism because of the perception that these relations are somehow underexplored or more complex than female homoeroticism. In turn, lesbianism is too often dismissed as either coextensive with any sort of feminist practice or completely accessible within any conventional understanding of female friendship. "What may appear 'intelligible' or 'simple common sense' to a nonlesbian critic," writes Castle, "will hardly seem quite so simple to any female reader who has ever attempted to walk down a city street holding hands with, let alone kissing or embracing another woman." She continues:

> The homosexual panic elicited by women publicly signaling their sexual interest in one another continues, alas, even "at this particular historical moment," to be just as virulent as that inspired by male homosexuality, if not more so. To obscure the fact that lesbians are

women who have sex with each other—and that this is not exactly the same, in the eyes of society, as voting for women or giving them jobs— is, in essence, not to acknowledge the separate peril and pleasure of lesbian existence. (71–72)

Explicitly detaching lesbianism from the broader concerns of feminism in general, Castle returns to Rich again, this time replacing the term that Sedgwick appropriates, "lesbian continuum," with the term that Rich uses in her title, the far more insistent and aggressive "lesbian existence." With this gesture, Castle begins to call for an analysis of female homosexuality, not homosociality, that accounts for the sexual pleasure and personal danger that accompany living as a lesbian. In response to Sedgwick's contention that male homosociality is the figure of patriarchal power, Castle suggests the insurgent potential of a theory of lesbian desire: "To theorize about female-female desire . . . is precisely to envision the taking apart of this supposedly intractable patriarchal structure. Female bonding, at least hypothetically, destabilizes the 'canonical' triangular arrangement of male desire, is an affront to it, and ultimately—in the radical form of lesbian bonding—displaces it entirely."[23]

Castle's discomfort with the feminist absorption of lesbian concerns is also reflected, somewhat differently, however, in the initial theoretical formulation of "queer theory," which occurred in a 1991 special issue of the journal *differences* dedicated to "Lesbian and Gay Sexualities." Again, the voice behind this formulation is that of a prominent feminist, Teresa de Lauretis. In her introduction to this issue, de Lauretis notes that while gay male and lesbian discourses have evolved along basically separate paths in the past, recent critical tendencies to see them as versions of one phenomenon, "lesbian and gay" (ladies first, of course), threaten to erase the specificity of that history. She writes, "our 'differences,' such as they may be, are less represented by the discursive coupling of those two terms in the politically correct phrase 'lesbian and gay,' than they are elided by most of the contexts in which the phrase is used; that is to say, differences are implied in it but then simply taken for granted or even covered over by the word 'and.'"[24] Thus occurs the birth of "queer theory," a metacritical praxis which is "intended to mark a certain critical distance" from the formulaic and reductive phrase "lesbian and gay." "Queer theory," writes de Lauretis, "conveys a double emphasis—on the conceptual and speculative work involved in discourse production, and on the necessary critical work of deconstructing our own discourses and their constructed silences" (iv). By definition a self-interrogating methodology, conditioned by a tradition of oppression, erasure, and silence to constantly examine its own "constructed silences," queer theory is, in theory, a school of thought that is always going back to school.

De Lauretis's logic is both provocative and problematic. To replace a phrase like "lesbian and gay" with a phrase like "queer theory" is quite literally to cover over any notion of lesbian and gay difference, to subsume male and female homosexuality within the single, potentially monolithic category "queer," to depend on the self-policing integrity of queer theorists themselves to "deconstruct . . . our own discourses and their constructed silences." In its ideal form, queer theory would be a constantly self-interrogating practice, and through that self-interroga-tion would succeed in retaining the specificity of lesbian and gay histories while also exploring the theoretical complexity of lesbian and gay difference. However, the replacement of a tripartite term—"lesbian and gay"—with a bipartite term—"queer theory"—appears to counter-act de Lauretis's desire for increased specificity. And as queer theory begins to articulate itself as a practice distinct from feminist theory, the question of women, and particularly the question of lesbians, is persis-tently sidelined.

In the introduction to *Epistemology of the Closet*, Sedgwick addresses the question of a specifically lesbian-centered theoretical practice: "It seems inevitable to me that the work of defining the circumferential boundaries, vis-à-vis lesbian experience and identity, of any gay male-centered theoretical articulation can be done only from the point of view of an alternative, feminocentric theoretical space, not from the heart of the male-centered project itself."[25] Within the context of a book that is quite explicitly at "the heart of the male-centered project itself," Sedgwick's discussion of a lesbian implication to gay male theory demonstrates great ambivalence. While this introduction, like the intro-duction to *Between Men*, gives a nod to the urgent necessity for "feminocentric theoretical space," the place of lesbians in *Epistemology* is at best marginal. Acknowledging lesbian activists' work in the AIDS epidemic, Sedgwick writes, "The newly virulent homophobia of the 1980s, directed alike against women and men even though its medical pretext ought, if anything, logically to give a relative exemptive privi-lege to lesbians, reminds urgently that it is more to friends than to enemies that gay women and gay men are perceptible as distinct groups." Noting that lesbians, too, are vulnerable to AIDS, Sedgwick sees gay and AIDS activism as deeply indebted to lesbian practitioners and feminist theories:

> The contributions of lesbians to current gay and AIDS activism are
> weighty, not despite, but because of the intervening lessons of femi-
> nism. Feminist perspectives on medicine and health-care issues, on

civil disobedience, and on the politics of class and race as well as of sexuality have been centrally enabling for the recent waves of AIDS activism. What this activism returns to the lesbians involved in it may include a more richly pluralized range of imaginings of lines of gender and sexual identification. (38-39)

Sedgwick is significantly vague about the yield of lesbian investment; that activism "*may* include a more richly pluralized range of imaginings" seems tepid consolation within a context of "virulent homophobia." Sedgwick is cautionary about the tendency of gay male discourse to "subsume" lesbian "experience and definition":

> The 'gay theory' I have been comparing with feminist theory doesn't mean exclusively gay male theory, but for the purpose of this comparison it includes lesbian theory insofar as that (a) isn't simply coextensive with feminist theory (i.e., doesn't subsume sexuality fully under gender) and (b) doesn't a priori deny all theoretical continuity between male homosexuality and lesbianism. But, again, the extent, construction, and meaning, and especially the history of any such theoretical continuity—not to mention its consequences for practical politics—must be open to every interrogation. (39)

Sedgwick, like de Lauretis, is always careful to argue that male and female homosexuality are very different phenomena, a useful and critical point. In fact, in this passage, as she tries to articulate a sufficiently specific and differentiated theoretical agenda for her text, Sedgwick recurs to an implicit structure of triangulation: gay male theoretical concerns, lesbian theoretical concerns, and feminist theoretical concerns are all related yet distinct entities. Once again, the "dyke" operates as the border, the literal site of connection and distinction between feminist and "gay" concerns in general. But as with all triangulated structures, as Sedgwick has demonstrated, one term is inevitably subordinated in favor of a dynamic connection between the other two. In Sedgwick's *Epistemology*, as in *Between Men*, the coincidence of feminist methodology and gay male subject matter consistently produces lesbian concerns as that third term, emerging occasionally, marginally, and principally in introductory matter. This is one example of a larger critical phenomenon in which, once again, the dyke demarcates the border of internal and external, offering a frame of reference but not a *mise en abîme*.

At the risk of the inevitable pun, I would argue that while feminist theory engendered queer theory, the two remain distinct. By now the dualism that so profoundly shaped feminist discourse at the end of the

1970s and into the early 1980s is literalized in the separate entities of feminist and queer scholarship. But what has been factored out here, oddly enough, is the specificity of lesbian discourse: caught between the feminist and the queer, the lesbian, again, occupies the problematic third position in the triangle of contemporary critical discourse. And as with the triangular structure posited in Sedgwick's early analysis, the third term is not the one that counts; the animate connection here is the one between feminists and queers, while the third, the site of literal connection and disjunction, marks the space between without signifying itself. Lesbians occupy the subordinated place of the woman in the structure of triangular desire, in which the desiring relationship is constituted between feminists and queers.

Back in 1980, in "Compulsory Heterosexuality and Lesbian Existence," Rich produced what seems today a startlingly prescient commentary. She writes, "Lesbians have historically been deprived of a political existence through 'inclusion' as female versions of male homosexuality. To equate lesbian existence with male homosexuality because each is stigmatized is to erase female reality once again."[26] Equated not only with male homosexuals but with feminism in its most generalized form, lesbians remain consistently—and paradoxically—marginalized. And as a marginalized population, dykes serve a useful function within the context of feminist and queer theories alike, acting as the border against which the mainstream can define itself. The specific location of that margin, of that "dyke," is revealing of particular, often-shifting engagements within theoretical discourses as they struggle to define themselves, their constituencies, their politics, and their activism. The dyke in the mainstream marks the space of margin and connection, offering at once a point of view that is and is not of the central flow.

Within the metaphorical structure I have explored throughout this essay, I have argued that feminist theory has consistently seen the "dyke" as marginal, protective, and contingent, as facilitating the existence of a larger whole rather than independently significant. Yet the specificity of lesbian discourses and desires has independently significant value, not only as a metacritical instrument for the analysis of a broader feminist theory, but also as an historically complex cultural phenomenon it its own right. Behind the metaphorical, architectural dyke is another dyke, a figure too often marginalized, too frequently and too vaguely appropriated within larger theoretical paradigms of sexuality and politics. For let us recall that listed below and separated from the nearly three columns of *dykes* in the *OED* is the slang definition: "dike, dyke . . . *slang*. [Of obscure origin.] A lesbian; a masculine woman."

NOTES

With thanks to Kathryn Schwarz, Sarah Blake, David A. Hedrich Hirsch, and Marvin J. Taylor.

1. "Dike, dyke," *Oxford English Dictionary*, 2d ed., vol. 4, 659–60. All epigraphs that follow are excerpted from *OED* definitions of *dyke*, as cited here.

2. For a discussion of theoretical appropriations of such disparaging terms as *queer*, see Judith Butler, "Critically Queer," *Bodies That Matter*, esp. 226–30.

3. *OED*, vol. 4, 660.

4. Radicalesbians, "The Woman-Identified Woman" 166. Authorship of this essay has been attributed to Rita Mae Brown.

5. Catharine A. MacKinnon, "Feminism, Marxism, Method, and the State" 247n46.

6. Ti-Grace Atkinson, "Lesbianism and Feminism: Justice for Women as 'Unnatural,'" *Amazon Odyssey* 134, 132.

7. Ti-Grace Atkinson, "Strategy and Tactics: A Presentation of Political Lesbianism," *Amazon Odyssey* 138.

8. Atkinson, "Lesbianism and Feminism" 131.

9. Miriam Schneir, Introduction to Radicalesbians, "The Woman-Identified Woman" 161.

10. Adrienne Rich, "Compulsory Heterosexuality and Lesbian Existence" 244. Italics in original.

11. Ibid. 239. Italics in original.

12. Jane Gallop, *Around 1981* 10.

13. bell hooks, *Feminist Theory from Margin to Center* 111.

14. Quoted in hooks, *Feminist Theory* 153. hooks responds again to the emotional, if not the intellectual, implications of this issue in the essay "Censorship from Left and Right," *Outlaw Culture* 71.

15. Interestingly, hooks herself later criticizes Madonna's book *Sex* for *its* conflation of the heterosexual and the heterosexist: "Even in the realm of male homoeroticism/homosexuality, Madonna's image usurps, takes over, subordinates. Coded always in *Sex* as heterosexual, her image is the dominant expression of heterosexism. . . . In the context of *Sex*, gay culture remains irrevocably linked to a system of patriarchal control framed by a heterosexist pornographic gaze" ("Power to the Pussy," *Outlaw Culture* 16–17).

16. Barbara Smith, "Toward a Black Feminist Criticism" 168.

17. See esp. Gallop's chap. 2, "The Problem of Definition," *Around 1981*.

18. Judith Roof, *A Lure of Knowledge* 217.

19. Elaine Showalter, "Introduction: The Rise of Gender," in *Speaking of Gender* 2-3.

20. Eve Kosofsky Sedgwick, *Between Men* 18.

21. Rich, "Compulsory Heterosexuality" 229.

22. Terry Castle, *The Apparitional Lesbian* 71. Italics in original.

23. Ibid. 72. For an interesting revisionary reading of Sedgwick's paradigm of triangulated desire, see Castle's chap. 4, "Sylvia Townsend Warner and the Counterplot of Lesbian Fiction," ibid. 66–91.

24. Teresa de Lauretis, "Queer Theory: Lesbian and Gay Sexualities, an Introduction" v–vi.

25. Eve Kosofsky Sedgwick, *Epistemology of the Closet* 39.

26. Rich, "Compulsory Heterosexuality" 239.

WORKS CITED

Atkinson, Ti-Grace. *Amazon Odyssey: The First Collection of Writings by the Political Pioneer of the Women's Movement.* New York: Links Books, 1974, 131–89.

Butler, Judith. *Bodies That Matter: On the Discursive Limits of "Sex."* New York: Routledge, 1993.

Castle, Terry. *The Apparitional Lesbian: Female Homosexuality and Modern Culture.* New York: Columbia University Press, 1993.

de Lauretis, Teresa. "Queer Theory: Lesbian and Gay Sexualities, an Introduction." *differences* 3.2 (Summer 1991).

Gallop, Jane. *Around 1981: Academic Feminist Literary Theory.* New York: Routledge, 1992.

hooks, bell. *Feminist Theory from Margin to Center.* Boston: South End Press, 1984.

———. *Outlaw Culture: Resisting Representations.* New York: Routledge, 1994.

MacKinnon, Catharine A. "Feminism, Marxism, Method, and the State: An Agenda for Theory." In *The Signs Reader: Women, Gender, and Scholarship*, ed. Elizabeth Abel and Emily K. Abel. Chicago: University of Chicago Press, 1983, 227–56.

Oxford English Dictionary, 2d ed. Oxford: Clarendon Press, 1989.

Radicalesbians. "The Woman-Identified Woman." In *Feminism in Our Time: The Essential Writings, World War II to the Present*, ed. Miriam Schneir. New York: Vintage, 1994, 162–67.

Rich, Adrienne. "Compulsory Heterosexuality and Lesbian Existence." In *The Lesbian and Gay Studies Reader*, ed. Henry Abelove, Michèle Aina Barale, and David M. Halperin. New York: Routledge, 1993, 227–54.

Roof, Judith. *A Lure of Knowledge: Lesbian Sexuality and Theory.* New York: Columbia University Press, 1991.

Schneir, Miriam. Introduction to Radicalesbians, "The Woman-Identified Woman." In *Feminism in Our Time* 160–62.

Sedgwick, Eve Kosofsky. *Between Men: English Literature and Male Homosocial Desire.* New York: Columbia University Press, 1985.

———. *Epistemology of the Closet.* Berkeley: University of California Press, 1990.

Showalter, Elaine. "Introduction: The Rise of Gender." In *Speaking of Gender*, ed. Elaine Showalter. New York: Routledge, 1989.

Smith, Barbara. "Toward a Black Feminist Criticism." In *The New Feminist Criticism: Essays on Women, Literature, and Theory*, ed. Elaine Showalter. New York: Pantheon, 1985, 168–86.

Fem/Les Scramble

TERESA DE LAURETIS

The question of the relations between lesbian studies and feminist studies—their shifting configuration over the past twenty-five years, the limits, limitations, boundaries, and constraints of their alliance, the notion of alliance itself—is a tangled knot of issues. In this short chapter, an intervention solicited by Dana Heller for a Modern Language Association special session on the Cross-Purposes project, I will consider only two points of contestation, or rather two areas of theoretical slippage concerning one common stake, one segment of the border, so to speak, and that is sexuality. Obviously, sexuality too is a complex question, imbricated with issues of identity, representation, epistemology, politics, and practices, to name a few besides race, class, and gender. For a discussion of several of these, I must refer the reader to my recent book on lesbian sexuality, which I emphatically titled *The Practice of Love*.

One area of contestation in lesbian and feminist studies is the discourse on *female* sexuality. Here the common frames are psychoanalytic theory and feminist psychology, and to these I will refer; for "talking sex" is not a discourse, or a practice, that lesbians and nonlesbian feminists have shared. The second area of contestation is the discourse on *lesbian* sexuality in the (lesbian) studies now performed under the aegis of "queer theory." In both instances, the contestation has to do with the divided or eccentric position of lesbians vis-à-vis both feminist theory and what is now designated by the term *queer theory*. This brief intervention proceeds from such an eccentric position; that is to say, I will not align myself with either feminist or queer theory but will try instead to scramble or disturb the terms of this latest polarity.[1]

THE FEMINIST DISCOURSE ON SEXUALITY

In a chapter of *The Practice of Love*, I advance the argument that in feminist psychoanalytic theory and in feminist psychology, lesbianism, though hardly mentioned, figures prominently as a subtext and a fantasy of seduction; lesbianism figures, for all women, the site of a specifically female desire and the possibility of a desiring subjectivity, of being the active subject of a desire of one's own. To reclaim for women the position of subject of desire, feminist theory has constructed and relied on a sex-specific notion of homosexuality, deriving from the pre-Oedipal relation to the mother, which obviously obtains for all women. But I said that lesbianism *figures*—not *represents*—the possibility of a female subject of desire because, in fact, lesbianism is not represented in this feminist theory, which has more often elided the actual sexual difference, the psychosocial and sociosexual difference, that lesbianism signifies and, while avoiding that signifier, it has instead spoken it as a trope, a figure of discourse, what I call "the homosexual-maternal metaphor."

Let me backtrack a moment. Since the late 1970s feminist psychology and psychoanalytic theory have reclaimed the mother as the primary, if not the only, formative influence in female psychosexual development, and have postulated that a "homosexual factor" or a latent homosexuality is constitutive of female sexual subjectivity from birth on, owing to the girl-child's pre-Oedipal attachment to the mother. This early attachment or first love is subsequently renounced under the social or instinctual pressures of heterosexuality, this feminist theory maintains; but it remains active, whether conscious or not, throughout the course of a woman's life, causing a strong tendency toward bisexuality and a labile, fluid, or oscillating pattern of identifications and object-choices that make a feminine sexual identity inherently unstable, fundamentally compromised, even unachievable.

(This argument evolved out of the feminist readings of Freud's case history of "Dora," the name he gave to his hysterical patient. For many feminists in the 1970s and early 1980s, Dora's hysteria became paradigmatic of female sexuality as sexual "undecidability," and has been at times explicitly conflated with lesbianism. The contemporary analogue of Dora's hysteria is gender dysphoria as represented in queer theory. I'm thinking of a volume entitled *Dagger: On Butch Women* or Leslie Feinberg's novel *Stone Butch Blues*.)

But in postulating a latent or potential homosexuality of all women (which closely resembles Freud's fudgy notion of a latent or potential bisexuality of all humans), feminist theory has been careful not to qualify it as lesbian: indeed, the phrase *homosexual-maternal* equivocates on the "same-sex relation" of mother and daughter, because, on the one hand, it intimates homo*sexuality,* with emphasis on the sexual, even genital, connotations of the word; but, on the other hand, it may be taken on a purely descriptive or constative level—that is to say, the "fact" that a daughter has the same sex or the same body as her mother (which, incidentally, is not at all a "fact," since the body of desire is a fantasmatic body and not an anatomical one). Then there are those cases in which this "same-sex relation" between women *is* qualified as lesbian, as in the phrase "the lesbian continuum"; but here the lesbian qualifier is most often de-sexualized, if not de-eroticized, and metaphorized to mean a continuity of woman-identified women—who *may* sleep with each other *or not,* but that, in this feminist theory, *makes no difference.* So we have a problem, an area of slippage and contestation, because for some of us the difference is there.

In other words, conceptually, the homosexual-maternal metaphor projects onto female *sexuality* certain features of an idealized female *sociality*—sisterly or woman-identified mutual support, antihierarchical and egalitarian relationships, an ethic of compassion and connection, an ease with intragender affectionate behavior and emotional sharing, a propensity for mutual identification, and so forth. And, up to a time, these ideal values appealed to lesbian feminists as much as to hetero-sexual feminists.

But the seductiveness of this metaphor—the seduction it both implies and performs—derives from the erotic charge of a desire for women which is specifically lesbian; which, unlike masculine hetero-sexual desire, affirms and enhances the female-sexed subject and represents her possibility of access to a sexuality autonomous from the male. By charting the road of access through the maternal, and thus displacing the perhaps difficult question of women's heterosexual desire, the homosexual metaphor erases the particular relation between women that is lesbianism, a relation that is both sexual and sociosymbolic, and that entails not only a different configuration of desire but also a different production of reference and meaning, though not always and not necessarily in the terms of feminism.

In sum, the homosexual-maternal metaphor elides the sexual specificity of lesbian desire and its effects in the body, in subjectivity, and in political subjecthood. This is one of the reasons, I believe, why some lesbians have abandoned or outright refused the feminist "homosexual" imaginary (even as others have literalized the maternal metaphor with the help of sperm banks and international adoption). To some, queer activism and queer theory have offered an alternative set of tropes, a nonmaternal but equally voluntaristic and redemptive imaginary where sexualities and genders are indefinitely recombinable and re- fashioned through technology or performance.

SEXUALITY AND LESBIAN POMO

And so I come to the second area of contestation, the discourse on sexuality in lesbian studies in the age of queer theory or, as the title of a recent book proposes, "the lesbian postmodern." I take this book as symptomatic of the current predicament of lesbian studies, caught between an older generation of lesbian scholars whose lives and works and political formation intersected with 1970s and 1980s feminisms, and the pressing consumer demand for new and sexier academic per- formances. In her introduction to the volume, Robyn Wiegman suggests that the book's project is adventurous, a leap into the unknown, and the juxtaposition in its title daring: *The Lesbian Postmodern* would not only replace a worn lesbian-feminist imaginary but also displace "the les- bian" (in quotation marks), that is, the lesbian as commodity—a com- modity circulating not only in the mass media but in the academy as well. And here Wiegman wisely remarks that her own writing is inevi- tably complicit with that commodification of "the lesbian." The title phrase, therefore, embodies a contradiction: it names a category, "the lesbian," which remains "in excess" of the system that names it. For the lesbian (now without quotation marks: the real lesbian, I presume? or perhaps the real postmodern lesbian, a more fitting oxymoron) has abandoned "the dream of symmetry and equivalence, moving away from the epistemology of identities, rights, and reason that would guarantee [a bourgeois] cultural legitimacy" ("Introduction: Mapping the Lesbian Postmodern" 16).

The language of this introduction is familiar: words like *excess, displace, contradiction,* and *complicity* are the very lexicon of the feminist theory I have been practicing for some twenty years. The editor's preface, too, promises that the book will tread on "a new and unpredict- able terrain," but speaks in long-familiar feminist terms like unsettle, destabilize, test limits, undermine, heterosexual hegemony, and so forth (ix–x). So what is PoMo about the lesbian without quotation marks, besides her rightly postmodern lack of historical memory?

Flipping through the book, one encounters images or figures of speech whose kinship is to both feminist theory and queer theory: the images of "dynamic and fluid gender pluralities and sexual positionings" (Laura Doan, "Jeannette Winterson's Sexing the Postmodern" 153) or of "borderlands of racial, sexual, and national identities" (Judith Raiskin, "Inverts and Hybrids" 168) are clearly the discursive progeny of feminism. Another trope, that of "the feminine cyborg assemblage" standing for a lesbian "politics of transformation and hybridity" (Cathy Griggers, "The Age of (Post)Mechanical Reproduction" 126–27), is still feminist, if updated by the cultural-studies word *hybridity*. And if you don't believe me, if you think that feminism is old-fashioned, take a look at Mary Russo's *Female Grotesque:* the hybridity in this book, in its grotesque, prosthetic, oozing, or aging bodies, by far surpasses that of the cyborg, which is not only beyond gender, or ungendered, but also efficient, clean, indestructible, and sexless.

However, as I will point out in a moment, other technological or cosmetic articulations of identity in lesbian PoMo, notably transsexuality and gender dysphoria, are definitely creatures of queer theory.

Interestingly, Wiegman takes issue with the term *Queer Theory,* whose coinage she correctly traces to me and the special issue of *differences* I edited from a conference I organized in 1990. She notes that the ways in which queer theory has since been deployed "actually neutralizes differences" (17); and this is indeed the opposite of the effect I had hoped for in coining the phrase *queer theory,* by which I wanted to displace the undifferentiated, single adjective *gay-and-lesbian* toward an understanding of sexual*ties* in their historical, material, and discursive specificities. Obviously, therefore, I agree with Wiegman. And so does Simon Watney, in an essay entitled "Queer Epistemology" (no need to speculate on the provenance of this title). He writes: "The great convenience of the term 'queer' today lies most immediately in its gender and race neutrality." For him, however, this is a plus: "'queer' asserts an identity that celebrates differences within a wider picture of sexual and social diversity" (15).

Watney, in a British context, and similarly Michael Warner in a U.S. context, define queer in opposition to "the sanctimonious moralism" of lesbian and gay identity politics. The latter, Watney writes, in challenging stereotypes and invisibility, have tended "to suppress the actual diversity of 'queer' sex in the name of 'gay community' values" and thus have produced "a set of highly normative pictures of 'gay life'" (23–24).[2] On the contrary, queer culture—whose figures of sexual diversity range, for Watney, from Oscar Wilde and Rimbaud to Tom of Finland and are all men with the single exception of Madonna—queer culture, he claims, challenges "the authority of the dominant epistemology of sexuality" (23).

The corresponding pantheon in lesbian PoMo lines up such figures as Annie Sprinkle, Susie Bright, and Barbie. Here the exception is Les, formerly Linda, the F2M sex partner of Annie Sprinkle in a docu-video called *Linda/Les and Annie*. And it is an important exception because, amid the preoccupation with *identity* that is paramount in both queer theory and *The Lesbian Postmodern* volume, this video challenges, if not the *epistemology* of sexuality, then at least a certain time-honored notion of *lesbian* sexuality: for Linda/Les and Annie, we are told, "represent postmodern lesbian desire [as] the spectacle of *the female body becoming male*" (Judith Halberstam, "F2M" 219). At this point, there is no doubt, we are very far away from lesbian feminism. Or from any kind of lesbian desire whose object, real or fantasmatic, is indeed the female body.

In sum, it seems that a new imaginary has developed out of the progressive repudiation of femininity and, now, also the repudiation of the female body: the discourse on sexuality has moved from the impossibility of a feminine identity theorized by feminists since the late 1970s, to the alleged "subversion" of gender identity in queer/lesbian studies, to the literal becoming-male of lesbian PoMo. An announced collection of essays on "queer theory and the subject of heterosexuality" declares itself "straight with a twist."[3] Who knows, by next year's MLA, we may be reading something like "Lesbian Heterosexuality: The Last Frontier."

NOTES

1. I have elaborated the terms of this critical perspective in "Eccentric Subjects" and "Upping the Anti (sic) in Feminist Theory" (see Works Cited).

2. Leo Bersani's *Homos*, on the other hand, criticizes queer theory for suppressing the homo in homosexuality or, as he puts it, "de-gaying" the sexuality it flaunts and turning it into a matter of discourse, an issue of epistemology.

3. I am quoting from a flyer calling for proposals or papers by January 15, 1994, to be sent to Calvin Thomas at the University of Northern Iowa.

WORKS CITED

Bersani, Leo. *Homos*. Cambridge: Harvard University Press, 1995.
Burana, Lily, Roxxie, and Linnea Due, eds. *Dagger: On Butch Women*. San Francisco: Cleis Press, 1994.

de Lauretis, Teresa. "Eccentric Subjects." *Feminist Studies* 16.1 (Spring 1990): 115–50.

———. *The Practice of Love: Lesbian Sexuality and Perverse Desire.* Bloomington: Indiana University Press, 1994.

———. "Queer Theory: Lesbian and Gay Sexualities, an Introduction." *differences* 3.2 (Summer 1991): iii–xviii.

———. "Upping the Anti (sic) in Feminist Theory." In *Conflicts in Feminism.* Ed. Marianne Hirsch and Evelyn Fox Keller. New York: Routledge, 1990, 255–70.

Doan, Laura, ed. *The Lesbian Postmodern.* New York: Columbia University Press, 1994.

Feinberg, Leslie. *Stone Butch Blues.* Ithaca: Firebrand Books, 1993.

Russo, Mary. *Female Grotesque: Risk, Excess and Modernity.* New York: Routledge, 1994.

Warner, Michael, ed. *Fear of a Queer Planet: Queer Politics and Social Theory.* Minneapolis: University of Minnesota Press, 1993.

Watney, Simon. "Queer Epistemology: Activism, 'Outing', and the Politics of Sexual Identities." *Critical Quarterly* [special issue "Critically Queer," ed. Isaac Julien and Jon Savage] 36.1 (Spring 1994): 13–27.

Skin Deep

Lesbian Interventions in Language

RUTH SALVAGGIO

Beginning her essay on the possibilities of lesbian desire, Elizabeth Grosz takes notice of the "exceptionally powerful and worthwhile" mass of criticism recently emerging in the field of lesbian and gay studies. Yet in this essay ("Refiguring Lesbian Desire," in *The Lesbian Postmodern*), she wants to write something different, something "wildly speculative" and "openly experimental" that might "welcome unknown readings, new claims, provocative analyses" and the language it thrives on—critical, desirous, intensely embodied. Explaining how sexuality and desire might help us seize possibilities for relation, movement, connection, she writes:

> The sites most intensely invested always occur at a conjunction . . . they are always surface effects between one thing and another— between a hand and a breast, a tongue and a cunt, a mouth and food, a nose and a rose. (78)

Pondering such bodily "transmutations," Grosz poses these questions: "What is it that together, in parts and bits and interconnections, we can make that is new, that is exploratory, that opens up further spaces, induces further intensities, speeds up, enervates, and proliferates production (production of the body, production of the world)?" (80–81).

And, I would add, the production of language. In this essay I want to pose exactly these kinds of questions about the transmutation of lesbian bodies and language, how each is reconfigured in writing. Language has served at once as compelling subject and vehicle within feminist criticism.[1] But what peculiar nexus of body and thought emerges in lesbian critical discourse? How is it that these specific bodies materialize in language—as metaphors, as subjects of intense theoretical discussion, as conduits of erotic expression and critical thought?

In approaching these questions, I find myself turning to those "surface effects between one thing and another" described by Grosz, specifically what I take to be that crucial intersection between bodies and texts—what Judith Butler describes as the continually unfolding interchange between "language and materiality" (*Bodies That Matter* 68).[2] Far from the lesbian body, or *any* body, becoming lost in signification, I see them vibrantly taking shape within writing and, in the process, reshaping the configurations of what counts as critical thought. Elspeth Probyn might describe this interaction as an ontological and epistemological move, the way in which "the experiential may enable an enunciative position" that moves beyond fixed notions of identity and materiality (29). In what sense might the ontological sense of being a lesbian enable different modes of "enunciation," and in what epistemological directions might these writing strategies lead? Lesbian writers, staking out specific enunciative claims within feminism, have a lot to say on this matter. And how they say it, how the sheer texture of the language works, marks a crucial linguistic and epistemological turn within feminist critical thought.

Consider Elizabeth Meese's remarkably self-conscious writing as a lesbian critic, her dexterous enfolding of subject and text, lesbian and language. Distinguishing "between 'writing about' and 'writing with (or as)' one's subject," Meese invites us to become aware of "how one takes one's 'place' in language." Assuming her own place as a lesbian critic, she says that she is "interested in exploring textual erotics beyond content, acknowledging the blurred boundaries between the personal and the critical, the particular, concrete intimacy of sexual expression, and the (for some) abstract aridity of high theory" (*(Sem)Erotics* xviii). Just as she "writes about" this language, so she actually engages it as a critic, "searching for the words, syntax and grammar that can articulate the body, my body, and perhaps yours." Her criticism becomes intimate exchange, a "love letter" that loses none of its intellectual vigor yet openly indulges its physical powers of connection: "When I write my love letter to you, I want to bring myself to you, hand myself over. When I write about lesbian : writing, I take my life in my hands, as my text." Her writing moves, "when my tongue slides over the osmotic, lively breathing surfaces of your skin like words," or "as the pen makes its tracks across the body of the page, its friction and its struggle to mark the course faithfully, our passions inscribed energetically in the body of language in the mind: a love letter" (3). Language here becomes a highly charged surface effect, "your skin like words." Text carries the weight of tongue and hand, its physicality skimming the surface of the page.

When Hélène Cixous, in "The Laugh of the Medusa," called on women to "write the body" fifteen years ago, she brought to center stage a topic that had already begun to shape an enormous range of feminist criticism and theory. Some of this theory has been influenced by French traditions of *l'écriture féminine;* elsewhere it has unfolded in diverse cultural contexts. Just a few examples: Audre Lorde long invoked and enacted the powers of the body in her writing, seeking ways to fuse body and mind, feeling and intellect into literate traditions dominated by the "brain alone" (*Sister Outsider* 38). Gloria Anzaldúa describes her own writing as inextricably linked to the flesh and substance of her body, and says that when she writes "it feels like I'm carving bone . . . like I'm creating my own face" (*Borderlands/La Frontera* 73). Trinh T. Minh-ha seeks "the body in theory," writing characterized by its "physicality (vocality, tactility, touch, resonance)" that would allow theory to engage the "excess not fully contained by writing's unifying structural forces" (*Woman, Native, Other* 44). And of course Cixous: "And why don't you write? Write! Writing is for you, you are for you; your body is yours, take it" (246).

Such feminist reclamations of the body in writing undergo a peculiar kind of reworking, perhaps a complete workout, in Meese's lesbian criticism—almost exhausting the written word, forcing it to its physical limits, and then more. Literary criticism begins to sound very different. Meese's chapter on Virginia Woolf and Vita Sackville-West folds in and out of letters exchanged among all three of them. In one letter, the fur of a sheepdog becomes part of this tactile exchange: "Will you pet her when you arrive? Will you remember the feel of her fur and discover new ways to startle her? Love, V." Then Meese adds: "Dear V and V, I feel empty when I write one without the other . . ." (41). Yet for all the tactile sensation and desire that fuels this criticism, there is no lack of abstraction and analysis. Meese is thoroughly academic, thoroughly erotic, thoroughly personal. In fact, personal and erotic connections can be fused into critical ones, as Meese does when she begins her chapter "Gertrude Stein and Me": "Yes, I know Gertrude Stein too. I have known her since the day I knew I was a lesbian. I knew both at once, something about the one connecting the other. That is worth understanding in some detail—a lesbian convergence, and here for the first time I bring them together, literally, in the letter" (63). Nothing is lost in this language, not theory to pleasure nor pleasure to theory.

Is this lesbian writing? Is this peculiar tactile and bodily investment in literary criticism a peculiarly lesbian undertaking? Meese herself is reluctant to engage in such definitions, and prefers to regard lesbian writing not so much as an entity all its own but as an action, a vibrant linguistic activity instigated by certain subjects—in this case very particular subjects—who continually articulate and invent themselves in language. As she explains, "the lesbian writer seeks to intervene in language, reinvent, or better, re-work its texture, to produce an exploratory language through which we can find ourselves as subject and (of) desire." Or later, sliding down that same page: "And that word, 'lesbian.' Can you tell me whose word it is? . . . 'Lesbian' is applied to me in a system I do not control, that cannot control itself. Yet it is a word I want to embrace, re-write and re-claim, not to install it but to explode its meaning . . ." (14).

What I find especially important about Meese's "(sem)erotics" is that she shows how placing herself as a lesbian in language itself unfolds as a process, a way of continually expanding the tactile dimensions of criticism. Her language brims with the ontological sense of actually being a lesbian, and yet it hardly stops there—shifting the process, as Shane Phelan says, from one of being to one of "becoming." Phelan asks: "What relations of power are called into play when we assume a 'lesbian' subject position? Which of those relations require change, and which might be drawn upon to effect that change?" (*Getting Specific* 55). Again, I would inquire about these kinds of relations and effects as they unfold in language. How, in word and in deed, have lesbian writers made language itself a vehicle of critical reassessment and change?

I would turn here to Monique Wittig, whose critique of fixed categories of sexuality and gender make it possible for her to claim the word "lesbian" as signifying something beyond these domains. She explains how the very "categories of language" force us "to speak of ourselves and to conceive of ourselves as women and as men," and in so doing make us "instrumental in maintaining heterosexuality" (*The Straight Mind* 30). What's worse is that these categories continually inscribe themselves in discourses, so that the very language of a particular discourse reflects the unquestioned assumption "that what founds society, any society, is heterosexuality."

Wittig's own writing, both as novelist and as critic, works to construct the lesbian even as it dismantles the very categories which have nominally inscribed her existence. Thus the beginning of her novel *The Lesbian Body* is actually a farewell to the old order of inscribed bodies: "In this dark adored adorned gehenna say your farewells m/y very beautiful one m/y very strong one m/y very indomitable one m/y very learned one m/y very ferocious one m/y very gentle one m/y best beloved to what they, the women, call affection tenderness or gracious abandon.... Not one will be able to bear seeing you with eyes turned up lids cut off your yellow smoking intestines spread in the hollow of your hands your tongue spat from your mouth long green strings of bile flowing over your breast, not one will be able to bear your low frenetic insistent laughter" (15).

In *The Straight Mind,* Wittig complains of how women are written into language, already inscribed "into language through gender" (81). Her answer: "Gender must be destroyed. The possibility of its destruction is given through the very exercise of language.... To destroy the categories of sex in politics and in philosophy, to destroy gender in language ... is therefore part of my work in writing, as a writer" (80). And that is exactly what she sets out to do in *The Lesbian Body.* She explains the "bar in the *j/e*" as "a sign of excess. A sign that helps to imagine an excess of 'I,' an 'I' exalted. 'I' has become so powerful in *The Lesbian Body* that it can attack the order of heterosexuality in texts and assault the so-called love, the heroes of love, and lesbianize them, lesbianize the symbols, lesbianize the gods and the goddesses, lesbianize the men and the women. This 'I' can be destroyed in the attempt and resuscitated. Nothing resists this 'I' (or this *tu,* which is its same, its love), which spreads itself in the whole world of the book, like a lava flow that nothing can stop" (*The Straight Mind* 87). Lesbian is no longer a category, but a process, to lesbianize, to release from categorical inscription.

Wittig strikes me as being fascinated by those energies in language that keep it on the move. Perhaps this is why she is drawn to Nathalie Sarraute's writing and its preoccupation with "'l'usage de la parole' [the use of speech]" (*The Straight Mind* 91). Sarraute's works are filled, as Wittig explains, with "interlocutors," with all their "interventions," "changes of meaning," and "variations" that prevent any single interpretation. Wittig herself seizes this pace in her own critical language: "I would delight in speaking of the very substance of the text itself, of the rhythm, the sequences, and their mode of development, of the use of words dispersing between interlocutors, of the spectacular oscillations of the text at moments when shifts in point of view take place, of the interlocutory sequences, of the cliches that are orchestrated around a word, as though by baton, of the birth and deployment in counterpoint of a text" (92).

Such "spectacular oscillations" hardly provide grounds for any definition of lesbian writing, but they do account for powerful forces in writing, unleashed within texts, that transform subjects and sexualities. To return to Phelan's question "What relations of power are called into play when we assume a 'lesbian' subject position?" we could answer that for Wittig, the very power of culturally sanctioned definitions of woman, man, lesbian, heterosexual is not only questioned but also dismantled bit by bit through an incessant textual deployment. Yet while Wittig pursues this project with verve and vengeance, she is hardly alone in the effort. Marilyn Farwell brings together Wittig and Adrienne Rich in their mutual, though different, attempts to infuse lesbian sexuality into language. As Farwell puts it, "for both, the word *lesbian* provides a key term for the woman writer to posit herself anew in an alien language" ("Toward a Definition of the Lesbian Literary Imagination" 79).

For Rich, this endeavor has taken her beyond her own earlier claims for lesbian identity and into the political possibilities generated through poetic writing. In her most recent critical book, *What Is Found There: Notebooks on Poetry and Politics*, Rich does not claim poetic language exclusively for lesbians, any more than she would claim it for the diversity of feminist and multicultural poets now emerging in American culture. But what Rich has to say about the powers of poetic language and the crucial importance of poetry does come from the voice of a woman who once proclaimed: "It is the lesbian in us who drives us to feel imaginatively, render in language, grasp, the full connection between woman and woman. It is the lesbian in us who is creative . . ." ("'It Is the Lesbian in Us . . .'" 201). Explaining that she does not mean to restrict the meaning either of lesbian or the creative process in this remark, Rich acknowledges what she calls "the intense charge of the word *lesbian*" and "all its deliquescences of meaning," the way in which "the word *lesbian* has many resonances" (202).

These myriad "deliquescences of meaning" that Rich once ascribed to the word *lesbian* now come to inform her ideas about the crucial importance of the poetic word that she explores in *What Is Found There*. Like Meese's attempt to "intervene in language, reinvent, or better, rework its texture," like Wittig's "spectacular oscillations of the text," Rich wants to tap into those "extraordinary electrical exchanges" in language: "the association of thing to thing, spiritual fact with embodied form, begins here. And so begins the suggestion of multiple, many-layered, rather than singular, meanings, wherever we look, in the ordinary world" (6).

The way language can connect "thing to thing" and in so doing explode the possibilities of meaning, well beyond the dictates of the straight mind, recalls for me again those sites of conjunction described by Grosz: "they are always surface effects between one thing and another—between a hand and a breast, a tongue and a cunt, a mouth and food, a nose and a rose." I hasten to add: word and body, finger and page, tongue and theory. Certain lesbian critics, it seems to me, have invested tremendous energy in the conjunction of body and theory, especially as this peculiar "thing to thing" connection unfolds through the workings of language. Their writings occupy a distinctive place in queer theory, a discourse virtually consumed with bodies even through-out the articulation of some notably abstract and analytical theoretical writing.

What we have here is an intense dialogue about bodies and lan-guage as they promote what Judith Butler calls an "enabling disrup-tion" and "resignification" within the norms of heterosexuality (*Bodies That Matter* 23, 240). The intensity of this dialogue reveals itself at the very beginning of Butler's book. She describes her interest in ways that bodies move across boundaries and categories as posing a bit of a "vocational difficulty" for "those trained in philosophy, always at some distance from corporeal matters, who try in that disembodied way to demarcate bodily terrains: they invariably miss the body or, worse, write against it." And so the question of the materiality of the body kept emerging for Butler. Yet it kept emerging as a personal question, one, as she explains, that "was repeatedly formulated to me this way: 'What about the materiality of the body, *Judy?*'" She continues: "I took it that the addition of 'Judy' was an effort to dislodge me from the more formal 'Judith' and to recall me to a bodily life that could not be theorized away" (ix).

If, in Butler's work in particular, there tends to be much more theorizing about the body than enactments of bodily writing, the body itself is hardly theorized away. It emerges as a subject of analysis even as it becomes a subject that changes analysis. As Butler explains, the continual mutual infiltration of matter and language, body and writing, can effect crucial changes—what she calls "resignification" within the "symbolic domain." What this means is not some complete overthrow of the heterosexual order and all of its supporting discourses (which would run the risk of instituting yet another exclusive system of sexu-ality and discourses), but rather crossings and disruptions and destabi-lizations within symbolics through which bodies and what they mean can be rearticulated, reworked, continually reinvented beyond the constraints of normative heterosexuality. If we can think of theory as part of this general symbolic domain, then the task is not necessarily to overthrow theoretical discourse, but work at it—enliven it, embody it—from within. Thus Butler explains that "resignification" can take place only if we "think of the symbolic as the temporalized regulation of signification, and not as a quasi-permanent structure" (22). Symbolic structures, theory, writing—none of these are permanent, forever fixed in place. Language and bodies can move within them, can move them. Bodies most certainly "matter" in this language. They are its lively substance, its momentum, its ability to move beyond the normative boundaries of any discourse.

This conspicuous emergence of the body in lesbian and queer theory shapes a very distinctive intervention in theoretical language. In her essay in the volume *Inside/Out: Lesbian Theories, Gay Theories*, Butler expresses her own ambivalence about engaging the writing of "theory" in its traditional sense: "And what's worse, I do not understand the notion of 'theory,' and am hardly interested in being cast as its defender, much less in being signified as part of an elite gay/lesbian theory crowd that seeks to establish the legitimacy of gay/lesbian studies within the academy. Is there a pregiven distinction between theory, politics, culture, media? How do those divisions operate to quell a certain intertextual writing that might well generate wholly different epistemic maps?" ("Imitation and Gender Insubordination" 14).

Butler's concept, and I would also say her engagement, of "a certain intertextual writing" signals the breakdown of those very structures that demarcate not only such discourses as theory, politics, and poetry but also the numerous kinds of identity categories that establish what is in and out, male and female, heterosexual and homosexual. As Diana Fuss explains in her introductory essay to *Inside/Out*, "The fear of the homo, which continually *rubs up against* the hetero (tribadic-style), concentrates and codifies the very real possibility and ever-present threat of a collapse of boundaries, an effacing of limits, and a radical confusion of identities" (6). Here we encounter yet another surface effect, a skinlike rubbing together of discourses, and a resulting reconfiguration of theory. Butler's comments might well describe this transmutation: "If the political task is to show that theory is never merely *theoria*, in the sense of disengaged contemplation, and to insist that it is fully political (*phronesis* or even *praxis*), then why not simply call this operation *politics*, or some necessary permutation of it?" (14–15).

Or why not call this yet another operation of bodies in writing, in this case, the writing of lesbian or gay or queer bodies into theory? My point is simply that if bodies do matter in the ongoing symbolic production of sexualities and in the shaping of culture, then they obviously also matter in the production and reshaping of theory. These are crucial conjunctions between "thing and thing," crucial sites of crossing that have in turn come to mark some of the most important border disputes within queer theory.

And they take place on the surface terrain of writing. Introducing her most recent book *Tendencies,* Eve Kosofsky Sedgwick describes her essays as being about "passionate queer things that happen across the lines that divide genders, discourses, and 'perversions,'" not the least of which is the way her own language crosses these lines. As she explains, "I've wanted to recruit—but also where I could, to denude or somehow transfigure—the energies of some received forms of writing that were important to me: the autobiographical narrative, the performance piece, the atrocity story, the polemic, the prose essay that quotes poetry, the obituary" (xiii–xiv). Why not call it all theory? Her essay "A Poem Is Being Written" signals a radical breakdown of discursive boundaries not only because it combines poetry and criticism or because it fuses autobiographical, personal, and analytical writing, but more so because it builds and turns, crosses, the very boundaries of a fixed sexual body. Not straight but not lesbian, not male but maybe very gay, Sedgwick brings her own undefined, uncategorical body to her writing, "to the epistemological bucking bronco of a more than transsexual identification . . ." (210). What happens to theory when bodily and linguistic categories—male or female, straight or gay—begin to collapse?

Here, I would suggest, is where language moves well beyond the confines of the "straight mind" and into enticingly embodied territory. Sedgwick describes this kind of bodily-linguistic effort: "The expense, rhetorically, of spirit involved, the arduous labor of embodiment required, in 'the finger's-breath by finger's-breath' construction of meaning around a site of meaninglessness . . ." (211). Bringing the queer body to writing, "finger's breath by finger's breath," can be a personally and theoretically exhausting undertaking; it can open possibilities even as it disturbs and unsettles. In her essay "White Glasses," Sedgwick moves through the frames of a pair of white glasses belonging to a friend dying of AIDS and also through her own body as she dons these glasses and confronts the diagnosis of her breast cancer. Bodies that matter all too much. What happens when these shifting bodies work their way into theory? The world becomes destabilized, precarious, scary, and at the same time strangely full of possibilities. At one point in "White Glasses," Sedgwick describes the "dizzying array of gender challenges and experiments" that come "with the initiations of surgery, of chemotherapy, of hormone therapy" (263), challenges layered upon the already indecisive identity of one who described herself in the beginning of the essay as "a queer but long-married young woman whose erotic and intellectual life were fiercely transitive . . ." (253). Here is a body, a theory, intensely involved in the "arduous labor" of constructing meaning, putting language to work in all its possible twists and turns. Describing herself after her surgery, Sedgwick writes: "I have never felt less stability in my gender, age, and racial identities, nor, anxious and full of shreds of dread, shame, and mourning as this process is, have I ever felt more of a mind to explore and exploit every possibility" (263–64).

If Sedgwick's writing is "queer," its momentum, its seizing of linguistic opportunities for change and transmutation, connect with the charged surface of much lesbian writing. Alice Parker, for example, writing very self-consciously as a lesbian, describes her work this way: "But when I speak/write as a lesbian the (gendered) center no longer holds. The fact that I speak in the place of the Other problematizes the authorizing discourses that would like to keep me at the margins, or, indeed, invisible" ("Under the Covers" 322). Subjectivities and categories merge, cross, enfold—and all through the continual enfolding of bodies and language. In Parker's writing, as in the writing of other lesbian critics and theorists, theory bends toward poetry: "I study locations: letters, words fly off in all directions, relieved of gravity, sentences turn in/side out. . . . I am sentenced to begin again, unwrite, re-write. Under the covers are certain *sign*als: an in/tensity of the eyes, configurations of the hands. . . . Negotiations (re-claimed from the crass world of commerce): from one language to another(s) and back, transactions, texts juxta-posed, sometimes just brushing against each other, a slight pressure of the fingers. How do you line up tongues?" (324). Again we have the skinlike rubbing conjunction of words, bodies, thought.

Parker embraces the term "polymorphous lesbian body" to seize what she calls a "process metaphor" that is both "indeterminate and precise" (339), that could account for both the specificity and momentum of lesbian writing. These same kinds of claims revolving around identity and dynamism work their way through Judith Roof's book *A Lure of Knowledge: Lesbian Sexuality and Theory,* in which she theorizes lesbian sexuality in terms of "polymorphous diversity." Here lesbian theory embraces its excesses, in bodies and language. As Roof explains, "Adopting a desire for desire instead of a desire for identity or stability may enable a lesbian theory and criticism that really do exceed the singular, the patriarchal, the category lesbian, deploying the lure of knowledge beyond certainty, identity, and mastery" (254).

Something about this lure, this desire, flows from and within language. In a pivotal chapter on language, "Beginning with L," Roof follows the lure of Olga Broumas's poem "Beginning with O" and its search for "tongue-like forms / that curve round a throat / an arm-pit, the upper / thigh . . ." (128). Roof seems lured by the idea of origins, one which appears to take us back to a beginning, but ultimately remains "unlocatable." For her, the O configures this unlocatable lesbian sexuality and language: "The source of writing is evasive and circular like the 'O,' empty and full, beginning, end, middle, playing the paradox of the body as the source of the writing . . ." (129).

Yet for me, the O is not evasive, but thick with meanings; the very language of Broumas's poem is not paradoxical, but positively excessive. While Roof reads Broumas theoretically, I would read her poetically, listening for the power of language to circle and spiral around the body. For Roof, a key word in Broumas's poem is "transliteration," what she describes as translation and transmutation, "the desire to write over, a tracing that simultaneously moves through the past and the future" (139). For me, this "transliteration" happens through a crucial intervention in language that I continue to find so characteristic of lesbian writers—and their varied efforts to transpose, transmutate, connect "thing to thing."

Perhaps we are all talking about a kind of polymorphous desire in language, a desire that keeps words moving across the page as fingers move across the surface of skin—with tactile, theoretical verve. I sense this momentum in Teresa de Lauretis's recent book *The Practice of Love: Lesbian Sexuality and Perverse Desire,* a book dense in its analytical rereadings of psychoanalytic theory, yet where a desiring language keeps expanding the contours of the very theory it proposes. And that is exactly her argument: lesbian sexuality and desire are no longer attached to the phallus "but able to move on to other images and objects" which can serve as signs for the female body and continually sustain desire itself (223, 243). De Lauretis explains: "For this reason, I would argue, the lesbian subject's desire is 'limitless': in a repeated process of displacement and reinvestment, her desire is a movement toward objects that can conjure up what was never there, and therefore cannot be refound but only found or, as it were, found again for the first time [in Rich's words] ('But in fact we were always like this, / rootless, dismembered: knowing it makes the difference')" (251).

While de Lauretis's prose is thick with the subject and process of analysis, she regards her writing as the pursuit of "my own passionate fiction through a theoretical fantasy" (85n3), writing that engages the very lesbian desire she theorizes. Near the end of her book, she writes: "That my own critical practice of subjective, dialogic engagement with the texts I cite is itself a practice of love and the exposure of a passionate fiction, should be by now quite apparent: it is only by generic and rhetorical conventions that this book does not read like an autobiography" (293). I believe that "critical practice" becomes a "practice of love" through language, through words that are passionately aroused by a "subjective, dialogic engagement" with the text—like a body, like skin.

How this tactile textual practice takes shape in lesbian writing unfolds in specific contexts—for writer and reader. In saying this, perhaps I am suggesting something close to what Paula Bennett felt when she read Emily Dickinson and discovered in her poetry an intense tactile engagement with "small but precious objects" such as buds and berries and jewels. Bennett claimed this as clitoral symbology, a distinctive metaphoric mode that might help us understand a wide range of women's writing, but especially lesbian language. Among the texts that Bennett turns to is a passage from Virginia Woolf's *Mrs. Dalloway,* one that had already been the subject of Roof's inquiry into lesbian sexuality and was subsequently addressed by de Lauretis in her work. Why would this particular passage attract such intense attention from lesbian critics? The answer, I think, has everything to do with the crucial connection between language and body, text and skin. And so I turn once again to Woolf:

> ... yet she could not resist sometimes yielding to the charm of a woman, not a girl, of a woman confessing, as to her they often did, some scrape, some folly. And whether it was pity, or their beauty, or that she was older; or some accident—like a faint scent, or a violin next door (so strange is the power of sounds at certain moments), she did undoubtedly then feel what men felt. Only for a moment; but it was enough. It was a sudden revelation ... an illumination; a tinge like a blush which one tried to check and then, as it spread, one yielded to its expansion, and rushed to the farthest verge and there quivered and felt the world come closer, swollen with some astonishing significance, some pressure of rapture, which split its thin skin and gushed and poured with an extraordinary alleviation over the cracks and sores! Then for that moment, she had seen an illumination; a match burning in a crocus; an inner meaning almost expressed. But the close withdrew; the hard softened. It was over—the moment. (*Mrs. Dalloway* 46–47)

Each critical response to this image assumes a particular relationship between lesbian and language, or how lesbian desire might be configured in language. Roof reads the crocus as a kind of double phallus in its shape, resisting representation in the phallic register, evoking a kind of "representational impossibility." Bennett, however, reads the crocus as a very obvious clitoral symbol, made visible and representable in a symbology directly expressive of lesbian sexuality. De Lauretis suggests that Woolf was all too aware of Clarissa Dalloway's lack of desire, and reads the crocus passage as "brilliantly representing" that "emptiness" which Clarissa felt. Whatever interpretation one assumes, language here has hardly obscured matters of lesbian sexuality. In this text, bodies matter excessively.

So much so that de Lauretis seizes the opportunity in a footnote to offer her own assessment of a crocus:

> As I am writing this, in the city of Amsterdam and during the week of late-winter school recess that the Dutch call *krokus vakantie* (crocus vacation), I must confess that I actually went for a walk to look at the crocuses, now beginning to bloom in virtually every available bit of soil. This field research proved to me and my companion that both Roof's and Bennett's readings of the image are supported by the shape of the crocus, depending on its stage of bloom. (*The Practice of Love* 237n18)

Her observations are a "passionate fiction" indeed—at once scholarship, textual commentary, observation, reflection, tactile evocation. As critical writing, it reminds me of a different passage from Woolf, one that Rachel Blau DuPlessis evoked in *The Pink Guitar* (60) to describe her own desire to write a different kind of essay:

> I wish I could invent a new critical method—something swifter and lighter and more colloquial and yet intense: more to the point and less composed: more fluid and following the flight. . . . The old problem: how to keep the flight of the mind, yet be exact. (Woolf, *Writer's Diary* 324)

When I consider Woolf's desire for language that is swift, light, and intense, fluid yet exact, I come back to those charged "surface effects between one thing and another." And I read into these words the movement of bodies, as insistent and emergent here as they are in all the writing about a crocus.

I began my inquiry wondering, with Grosz, how we might seize these charged effects so that we can do something "that opens up further spaces, induces further intensities, speeds up, enervates, and proliferates production. . . ." This swift, intense production of language, I would say, is well in process. Yet to define it as lesbian writing would be a mistake. If bodies matter in language all the time, and it is strikingly clear to me that they matter intensely in the lesbian writers I have been discussing here, then the questions we should be asking are: how exactly do specific bodies materialize, how might they in turn be reinscribed, and—to get specific about lesbians—what does this particular tactile connection between language and bodies promise, what new spaces for desire and writing does it open?

These spaces are as wide and as expansive as the page, as beckoning as the smooth surface of skin. On this terrain, lesbian bodies are hardly lost in signification. We are moving around there with remarkable swiftness, intensity, and burning precision.

NOTES

1. See, for example, Deborah Cameron, ed., *The Feminist Critique of Language,* and Camille Roman, Suzanne Juhasz, and Cristanne Miller, eds., *The Women and Language Debate,* (New Brunswick: Rutgers University Press, 1994), for only two of the more recent delvings into this rich field of inquiry.
2. See Works Cited for publication information.

WORKS CITED

Anzaldúa, Gloria. *Borderlands/La Frontera: The New Mestiza.* San Francisco: Spinsters/Aunt Lute, 1987.
Bennett, Paula. "Critical Cliterodectomy: Female Sexual Imagery and Feminist Psychoanalytic Theory." *Signs* 18 (1993): 235–59.
Broumas, Olga. *Beginning with O.* New Haven: Yale University Press, 1977.
Butler, Judith. "Imitation and Gender Insubordination." In *Inside/Out: Lesbian Theories, Gay Theories.* Ed. Diana Fuss. New York: Routledge, 1991, 13–31.
———. *Bodies That Matter: On the Discursive Limits of "Sex."* New York: Routledge, 1993.
Cameron, Deborah, ed. *The Feminist Critique of Language.* London: Routledge, 1990.
Cixous, Hélène. "The Laugh of the Medusa." In *New French Feminisms.* Ed. Elaine Marks and Isabelle de Courtivron. New York: Schocken Books, 1981.
de Lauretis, Teresa. *The Practice of Love: Lesbian Sexuality and Perverse Desire.* Bloomington: Indiana University Press, 1994.
DuPlessis, Rachel Blau. *The Pink Guitar: Writing as Feminist Practice.* New York: Routledge, 1990.
Farwell, Marilyn. "Toward a Definition of the Lesbian Literary Imagination." In *Sexual Practice/Textual Theory: Lesbian Cultural Criticism.* Ed. Susan J. Wolfe and Julia Penelope. Cambridge, Mass.: Blackwell, 1993, 66–84.
Fuss, Diana, ed. *Inside/Out: Lesbian Theories, Gay Theories.* New York: Routledge, 1991.
Grosz, Elizabeth. "Refiguring Lesbian Desire." In *The Lesbian Postmodern,* ed. Laura Doan. New York: Columbia University Press, 1994, 67–84.
Lorde, Audre. *Sister Outsider.* New York: Crossing Press, 1984.
Meese, Elizabeth. *(Sem)Erotics: Theorizing Lesbian: Writing.* New York: New York University Press, 1992.
Parker, Alice. "Under the Covers: A Synesthesia of Desire (Lesbian Translations)." In *Sexual Practice/Textual Theory: Lesbian Cultural Criticism.* Ed. Susan J. Wolfe and Julia Penelope. Cambridge: Blackwell, 1993, 322–39.
Phelan, Shane. *Getting Specific: Postmodern Lesbian Politics.* Minneapolis: University of Minnesota Press, 1994.
Probyn, Elspeth. *Sexing the Self: Gendered Positions in Cultural Studies.* London: Routledge, 1993.
Rich, Adrienne. "'It Is the Lesbian in Us . . .'" *On Lies, Secrets, and Silence: Selected Prose 1966–1978.* New York: Norton, 1979, 199–202.

————. *What Is Found There: Notebooks on Poetry and Politics.* New York: Norton, 1993.

Roof, Judith. *A Lure of Knowledge: Lesbian Sexuality and Theory.* New York: Columbia University Press, 1991.

Sedgwick, Eve Kosofsky. *Tendencies.* Durham: Duke University Press, 1993.

Trinh T. Minh-ha. *Woman, Native, Other: Writing Postcoloniality and Feminism.* Bloomington: Indiana University Press, 1989.

Wittig, Monique. *The Lesbian Body.* Trans. David LeVay. New York: Morrow, 1975.

————. *The Straight Mind and Other Essays.* Boston: Beacon Press, 1992.

Woolf, Virginia. *A Writer's Diary.* New York: Harcourt, Brace, 1954.

————. *Mrs. Dalloway.* New York: Harcourt, Brace and World, 1925.

The White Negress and the Heavy-Duty Dyke

TANIA MODLESKI

To Geraldine Barr

This chapter was written at two different times with two different purposes in mind at the time of each writing. Initially I was interested in analyzing the work of women artists like Anna Deavere Smith who cross racial boundaries in their performances. In the course of writing about Sandra Bernhard's film *Without YOU I'm Nothing*, I happened to meet Roseanne Arnold's lesbian feminist sister, Geraldine Barr, and heard from her the story of the dissolution of her partnership with Roseanne Arnold. I thought the story intersected in an extremely interesting way with some concerns about Bernhard's persona that I was expressing at the end of my essay (Bernhard, as most readers will know, plays the part of a neighbor on the *Roseanne* show). Nobody could be more surprised than I about the turn my essay took at the end, and yet it seemed a logical one. Then two events spurred me to supplement what I had written: first, I was invited by Dana Heller to submit something for *Cross-Purposes*, and I felt that this was an appropriate piece given the conclusions it reaches; second, Geraldine Barr published *My Sister Roseanne*. Both events provided me with an occasion to expand upon issues I had only touched on at the end of the essay's original version. In particular they allowed me to look at two paradigmatic figures central to current controversies in lesbian and/or feminist thought: the lesbian feminist Geraldine Barr and the postmodern "queer" deconstructor of identities, Sandra Bernhard. While my staging of an "encounter" between the two women might appear to lock them in an antagonistic relation, my aim is not to strengthen a binary, as I hope the patient reader will come to see, but to complicate it.

In the early part of the century Virginia Woolf, in *A Room of One's Own*, praised women for their lack of colonialist ambition, remarking that a British woman could pass "even a very fine negress on the street without wishing to make an Englishwoman of her" (52; see Works Cited for bibliographical data). Recent feminist theory, much of it emanating from women of color, has challenged such self-congratulatory views, revealing the sometimes colonialist ambitions of feminism itself. All too often, it has been suggested, a white woman cannot encounter a black woman without wishing to make a certain kind of feminist out of her— a white, middle-class kind, that is.

In this chapter I would like to consider the converse of the situation Woolf depicts. Much theoretical attention is currently being devoted to the study of racial mimicry in general and blackface in particular, and for the most part this writing has tended to assume that blackface, the fantasy of becoming black, is a masculinist one. This suggestion has been explicitly advanced by Suzanne Moore and remains implicit in Eric Lott's work on minstrelsy and the blackface tradition—a tradition which, as Lott and others have argued, continues to this day "without the blackface." Lott writes, "Our typical focus on the way 'blackness' in the popular imagination has been produced out of white cultural expropriation and travesty misses how necessary this process is to the making of white American manhood. The latter simply could not exist without a racial Other against which it defines itself and which to a very great extent it takes up into itself as one of its own constituent elements" ("White Like Me" 476). But the question which seems pertinent to feminist theory today is how white womanhood might have been created out of white cultural expropriation and travesty of blackness. In other words, in what situations might we find a white woman wishing to make "a very fine negress" out of herself?

The first part of my title, "The White Negress," is, of course, taken from Norman Mailer's midcentury essay "The White Negro," which celebrated the white hipster's identification with the image of the sexually potent black man. Mailer's essay provided a literary apologia for the thievery and plagiarism of black culture that functioned, and would long after the writing of the essay continue to function, as a kind of "open secret" in American society. In this essay I want to look at Sandra Bernhard's film *Without YOU I'm Nothing*, which brings the white Negro into the nineties and makes him a woman (or at least dresses him in drag).

Before doing so, however, I want to make clear that there is certainly historical precedent for white female blackface. In the 1930s there was

Mae West, whose musical numbers in films like *She Done Him Wrong* are directly taken from the tradition of black female blues performers, as the very title of one of West's songs, "Easy Rider," suggests (see Ivanov, "Sexual Parody in American Comedic Film"). Hazel Carby has written about how black women used this music to register protest against their oppression and to express desires of their own (see her essay "It Just Be's Dat Way Sometime"). Given that one of Mae West's projects was to redefine norms of femininity to accommodate the possibility of female sexual desire, it is important to recognize how this white woman's rebellious reconstruction of womanhood depended on a masquerade of black femininity—a masquerade, needless to say, that had nothing to do with cross-racial solidarity. For while West incorporated aspects of blackness in her performance numbers in the films, the narratives tended to be as racist as most films from that day to this one. In *She Done Him Wrong*, for example, West frequently uses her black maid as the butt of her jokes, and at one particularly telling moment the maid replies to West's command for her to hurry up by calling, "I'se comin', I'se comin'," to which West responds, "Yeah, you'se comin', and your head is bendin' low. Well, get here before winter." This kind of dialogue alerts us to the film's double movement of expropriation in which the white woman not only mines and mimes the black woman's musical tradition but also, by invoking the lyrics of Stephen Foster's "Old Black Joe"—a staple of minstrel shows—situates the "real" black woman within the minstrel tradition, itself a white travesty of black art and culture. That in the song these words are spoken by a dying black *man* further dissociates black women from their own sexuality so as to secure it for the white woman.

While West's blackface was unacknowledged by her and unremarked (at least officially) by audiences, Bernhard is highly self-aware and parodistic—quintessentially postmodern—in her adoption of "blackface." The very title of her film *Without YOU I'm Nothing* (most people omit the emphasis on "you" when pronouncing the title) suggests quite clearly the postmodern awareness that the other is constitutive of the self, even though whites may believe the reverse to be the case—that the (white) "self" is prior to the (black) "other": "Without me . . .," Sandra at one point starts to say to the film's diegetic African American audience, stumbling over the title line. The film spoofs the belief in the originary (white) self in a variety of ways—for example, when Bernhard's cigar-smoking female manager, who addresses the camera directly, tells us that Sandra "doesn't have any influences.[1] She doesn't need any. And if you want my opinion, they've *all* stolen from her: Donna Summer, Tina Turner, Whoopi Goldberg, Nina Simone. And I have even seen traces of Sandra in Diana Ross." The camera cuts to Sandra on stage impersonating the "cross-over" artist Diana Ross, relating a story about crossing the country on a late-night flight from New York to L.A. to visit a depressed friend (who turns out to be Warren Beatty), interspersing the account with verses from Ross's hit songs. (Earlier Sandra had impersonated Nina Simone, insinuating a mocking tone of self-pity into the angry lyrics, "I'm awfully bitter these days / My parents were slaves.") In myriad parodic ways the film shows "whiteness" to be derivative and phantasmatic, caught up in the impossible dialectics of desire in which the wish to assimilate the other coexists with the self-canceling need for the other's recognition. The film's ending makes it clear that one cannot have it both ways: as Sandra, vulnerable and alone, stands nearly naked on the stage and stares out into the audience, the one remaining spectator, the ethereally beautiful, nameless black woman who drifts through the film, appears at first to be writing the name "Sandra Bernhard" on the table and thus providing the token of the recognition Bernhard seeks, but is then shown to have written a sort of curse: "Fuck Sandra Bernhard."

This curse, meant by the filmmakers to reveal a black female subjectivity that exists outside white appropriations of it and that exhibits nothing but contempt for those who engage in such appropriations, marks perhaps the single greatest failure on the part of the film to comprehend the position of the African American in relation to white American culture. The fact is, African Americans often do not have the luxury of complete rejection but must conduct ongoing negotiations with the dominant culture. One can point, for example, to bell hooks's discussion of the film in her book *Black Looks*, which expressed deep ambivalence toward the project but gives the film itself a highly nuanced reading that is the result of numerous conversations hooks had with "folks from various locations" as well as with students: "After weeks of debating with one another about the distinction between cultural appropriation and cultural appreciation, students . . . were convinced that something radical was happening, that these issues were 'coming out in the open'" (39).[2]

"Fuck Sandra Bernhard" is in fact a sentiment most likely to have been uttered by some of Bernhard's formerly most ardent supporters in the white lesbian community. In an article published in *Outweek* expressing great disappointment over Bernhard's failure to come out clearly as a lesbian, or even to take a public stance unequivocally supporting lesbianism, Sarah Pettit strongly criticizes the fact that in bringing her stand-up performance to film Bernhard came to focus more on race relations than on relations between women, which had been featured more prominently in her stage show. Pettit claims that in the early version of the show Bernhard revealed herself to be "a female artist clearly drawn to other women for inspiration and sustenance," but in the film this "dykeyness" has disappeared ("The Lesbian Vanishes" 39). In a postmodern rejoinder to Pettit that explicitly aims to identify the film's "challenge to a certain formulation of lesbian (feminist) identity," Jean Walton trenchantly responds to Pettit's criticism by arguing that Bernhard's numerous impersonations of black women performed before a bored and/or annoyed black (diegetic) audience points to the dubiousness of an ideal that posits being "drawn to other women for inspiration and sustenance" when it is considered in the context of a whole history of white culture's appropriation of African American culture ("Sandra Bernhard" 249).[3]

Although both essays make many valuable points, when they are considered alongside one another they reveal a familiar squaring off of positions—positions which get us right to the heart of this volume's topic. The postmodern, deconstructive, or queer critic faults the lesbian feminist for focusing too much on sameness or commonality among women: thus Walton criticizes Pettit for implying a "definition of lesbianism that relies for its stability on one's all-encompassing solidarity with women, on one's identification with them as a political group, on a demonstration of supportiveness of them, and indeed, almost an embracing of them in a kind of unconditional love" (248). For her part, the postmodern critic claims the moral and political high ground because she takes account of the differences among women supposedly ignored by most lesbian feminists. Bernhard, in constantly changing "her own 'identity' to construct a persona," becomes the postmodern heroine who is capable of showing us how racial identity is "as much a matter of drag as of skin color" (249, 252). Yet this view simplifies in its turn, for it seriously underestimates the extent to which skin color condemns a large segment of our population to a fixed position within dominant systems of representation and impedes certain people's ability to alter their "identities" and construct other "personae."

Indeed, postmodern feminism, for all the lip service it often pays to multiplicity of identities and positionalities, may neglect to see how it sometimes requires the black woman to signify little more than difference itself, which the postmodern feminist may then assert in order to differentiate herself from "white lesbian feminism," which in turn is viewed as monolithic. It thus may share in common with a great deal of American thought the tendency to see racial and ethnic difference in terms of a black/white binary. In this regard it is perhaps not surprising to see how small a role the issue of Bernhard's Jewishness plays in analyses of Bernhard's racial masquerades. At most, Jewishness in the film is referred to more or less in passing as "one of the positions from which Sandra speaks"—as if this position, particularly in its relation to the issue of blackface, did not possess a history and a tradition outside the text and a weight and an insistence within it that makes it more than one in a plethora of possible identities from which postmodern woman is invited to select (Walton 255). A whole history of popular entertainment positions Jews on a sliding continuum between the fixed poles of black and white and thus enables a certain free play of identity but inhibits others.

In a fascinating article on *The Jazz Singer* Michael Rogin observes how in the film "the jazz singer rises by putting on the mask of a group that must remain immobile, unassimilable, and fixed at the bottom." (I myself made a similar point in *Feminism without Women*, where I had also considered how the black woman in a film like *Crossing Delancey*— a film written and directed by Jewish women about a young Jewish woman living in Manhattan and distancing herself from her roots— comes to represent embodiment and sexuality and thus allows the heroine a more sublimated relation to romance.) Drawing on Irving Howe, Rogin points out that Jews "had almost entirely taken over blackface entertainment by the early twentieth century," especially in music (he refers as well to Jewish song writers who "turned to black-derived music to create the uniquely American, melting pot sound of the jazz age"), and he speculates that such "'musical miscegenation' produces the excitement of racial contact without its sexual dangers" ("Blackface, White Noise" 437, 440). Rogin stops short of the logical conclusion of this line of reasoning, but other analysts of the phenomenon of blackface like Kobena Mercer and Eric Lott allow us to see that since the "miscegenation" most often involved two male artists, the sexual excitement must have had a homoerotic dimension as well.

I want to extend this line of inquiry to account for Bernhard's blackface and to suggest that for all Bernhard's apparent sexual daring, "blackface" enables her to distance herself not only from interracial lesbian sexuality but, especially, from white lesbian sexuality (and, it follows, from lesbian identity). It is not accidental, I would argue, that the one occasion on which she "speaks" about lesbian relations in the film she is in "blackface," singing "Me and Mrs. Jones" ("The sisters are doing it for themselves," she exclaims at the end of the number). I will, then, be taking a position which is in direct opposition to several of the film's commentators who assert that the "dykeyness" which Pettit claims is lost from the film version of Bernhard's show asserts itself in

Sandra's relation to black women ("The Lesbian Vanishes" 39). To the extent that "dykeyness" is present, I maintain, it is disavowed, and in a manner not altogether unlike the way hom(m)osexuality has been disavowed in much male art and culture.

As was the case with the jazz singer, assuming blackface allows Sandra to explore her identity along a racial continuum, in which the Jew as outsider stands somewhere between the white Christian and the African American. Early in the film, following a Nina Simone impersonation, the black man at the microphone in the Parisian Lounge where Sandra supposedly is performing lauds her and calls her "our very own Sarah Bernhardt." This misrecognition—a reversal of the tendency of whites to misname blacks—invokes the turn-of-the-century performer whose Jewishness and "degeneracy" Bernhard seems to be playing on. The man at the mike then introduces the next performer: Shoshana, a Madonna wannabe who comes out on stage dressed in a sexy costume and does an extremely awkward striptease. The camera then cuts to a shot of the nameless black woman, who is walking across the screen with Watts Towers in the background. In the next sequence we see Bernhard attempting to lead an unresponsive, primarily African American audience in some Israeli folk songs and seguing into a brief comic autobiographical sketch which introduces a fantasy of growing up in an upper-middle-class Christian household. Her name would be Babe, Bernhard fantasizes, her brother's Chip, and they would sing Christmas carols in harmony on Christmas Eve. The fantasy ends with a little talk by the mother, who says, "And may all your Christmases be white," whereupon the camera cuts to three children singing in the snow, one of whom is a black boy.[4] Another cut shows the black woman standing in front of a Jewish market reading *Kabbalah and Criticism*. The wish invoked here (parodically, to be sure) seems to be that if the Jewish woman cannot assimilate herself to the dominant culture (mocked as shallow anyhow), perhaps she can assimilate *her* other, the dominant culture's more extremely marked other, to her own culture and traditions.

A similar wish appears to be present in the next sequence, which begins with Sandra as a black lounge singer (whose piano player is Jewish: "you know how well we people get along") performing the number, "Me and Mrs. Jones." This number is followed by one more appearance of Shoshana and then a shot of the black woman listening to rap music and clipping a lock of her hair—a shot that is the mirror image of an earlier one of Sandra performing the same act, also in front of a mirror. Again, then, the pathetically failed identification with the white feminine ideal, Madonna (whose Christian name is Christian indeed), appears to invite a compensatory fantasy of the other's identification with the self.

The film's fixation on Madonna is revealed in a variety of ways. Madonna is central to the Diana Ross number, for example, since the friend whom Sandra-as-Diana flies across country to cheer up is Warren Beatty, Madonna's love interest at the time. This kind of quadrangulation of identities and desires is familiar to queer theorists when it involves men as the primary subjects.[5] Indeed it has become commonplace in cultural studies to see a homoerotic dimension to these "geometric" relationships in which women function as objects between men, and no doubt something of this sort is at stake in the quadrangular relations among Bernhard, Beatty, Madonna, and Ross. Certainly it is tempting to read into the film's erotics the flirtation that developed between Bernhard and Madonna around the time of the film's release, with both women fanning speculation about the nature of their relationship but never satisfying the public's curiosity. Yet, what of Bernhard's relation to the black woman? To what extent does Bernhard make explicit the hidden homoerotic aspects of minstrelsy by revealing the white woman's desire for the black woman, and to what extent is Bernhard simply involved in the erotics of disavowal characteristic of minstrelsy?

Perhaps the fact that most critics have declined comment on the erotic dimension of Sandra's cross-racial impersonations indicates that political correctness is not to be found in this aspect of the film. Queer critics looking for less guilty pleasures than those which are so obviously shot through with relations of domination have turned to the figure of the nameless black woman in order to locate interracial lesbian desire. They point in particular to the final performance number in which Sandra, dressed in stars-and-stripes–patterned G-string and pasties, sings Prince's *Little Red Corvette,* then waits for a response from the woman who, it turns out, is the one remaining audience member. To posit such a desire would be to posit a way for lesbian desire to move, exogamously as it were, across racial, community, and psychic borders—out of white lesbian feminism.

But I confess I do not see how the film may be said even here to signify explicitly Sandra's desire for the nameless woman, if only because we assume until the end of the number that Sandra is performing before the entire audience. We aren't even aware until the end that the black woman has in fact been *in* the audience, and her presence comes as a surprise, since she has nowhere previously occupied the same space with Sandra. Sandra's expectation of applause, moreover, seems to me to bespeak not a recognition of and desire for the other in her difference but a longing for the other's recognition of the white woman's sameness.

Lauren Berlant and Elizabeth Freeman express disappointment about Bernhard's failure in the end to resolve her "feminine and sexual identities into a lesbian love narrative" (!) and actually label Sandra's final performance "lesophobic." They write:

> The film imagines a kind of liberal pluralistic space for Bernhard's cross-margin, cross-fashion fantasy of women, but shows how lesophobic that fantasy can be, insofar as it requires aesthetic distance—the straightness of the white-woman-identified woman—as a condition of national, racial, *and* sexual filiation. Her desire for acceptance from the black-woman-in-the audience perpetuates the historic burden black women in cinema have borne to represent embodiment, desire, and the dignity of suffering on behalf of white women, who are too frightened to strip themselves of the privileges of white heterospectacle. ("Queer Nationality" 173)

Interestingly, "lesophobia" indeed may be seen to surface in the film at the precise moment when Bernhard explicitly deals with *homo*phobia; in a narrative accompanying Sylvester's song, "I Feel Real," which she relates in the second person, a straight man finds himself in a gay disco, where he is brought by a friend and where he soon finds himself caught up in a homosexual encounter with a black man. As the story comes to a climax, the camera circles around the scantily clad black men who serve as Sandra's back-up singers in the number and positions itself for a moment in back of a black man dressed in leather who stands behind Sandra, subliminally suggesting her identification with the disavowing subject. When the scene ends, there is a cut to a curious shot of several white female bodies in a steaming shower; in the foreground of the image, the women pose erotically for the camera as they wash themselves and each other, while behind them, the figure of the black woman, wrapped in a white towel, walks across the frame, constituting a strikingly chaste and austere presence in the midst of what by comparison seems a sodden and undignified tangle of bodies. Not only does this scene suggest a "lesophobic" parallel to the disavowal of gayness the sequence has just registered; it enlists the black woman as agent of this disavowal and it problematically situates her outside of erotic desire—and this in marked contrast to the sexualized black man in the story Bernhard has just told. We might at this point be entitled to ask how far we are from Mae West and the double movement of expropriation of the black female performer's sexuality I noted in her work; if in stealing this sexuality West had relegated the actual black woman to the position of the debased servant in the narrative, Bernhard turns the coin over and makes the anonymous black woman in the film an exemplar of uplift: in contrast to the sexy black songstresses Bernhard portrays, the black woman has achieved class mobility in white society (at the outset she is playing Bach on the piano; later we see her as a scientist in a lab). This represents a marked and very important shift from a film like *The Jazz Singer,* which, as we have seen, depended on blacks' immobility; in Bernhard's postmodern version of minstrelsy African Americans engage in a kind of white face (as when they perform a classical ballet in the background while Sandra sings Prince's "Little Red Corvette"). Yet in reproducing and assigning to Sandra's psyche the very split experienced historically by black women in relation to representations of their sexuality (as Hazel Carby writes, "Racist sexual ideologies proclaimed the black woman to be a rampant sexual being, and in response, black women writers either focused on defending their morality or displaced sexuality onto another terrain," *Reconstructing Womanhood* 174), the film may be said to engage in the ultimate form of female blackface.

Against Walton and most other critics who see the nameless woman as the object of Sandra's sexual desire, I am arguing that this woman, as opposed to the sexualized females Sandra impersonates, signifies the white lesbian's desire to desire exogamously and is presented as a kind of fantasized way out of the dilemmas of embodiment (the awkwardness of a Shoshana), as well as dilemmas of (Jewish and white lesbian) identity. In this regard the black woman in *Without YOU I'm Nothing* might seem to perform a very different function from that described by Valerie Smith ("Black Feminist Theory" 45), who has argued that the African American woman, in keeping with historical constructions of women of color that associate them "with the body and therefore with animal passions and slave labor," serves as a means for white feminist theorists to consider "the material ground of their enterprise." Yet is it not the case that however self-consciously and parodistically, the African American woman is still "emptied of her own significance in order to become a sign in another's" and still being used to reveal "something of the content of [white women's] own subject positions," though it is true that in this case—as evidenced in the shower scene, where according to Walton the appearance of the black woman in the background indicates her "abstention" from the "sex debates of white [lesbian] feminism"—she signifies a *refusal* of some of these positions?[6] And is there not an analogue here to the practice of some deconstructive, queer white theorists who invoke black/white racial difference as the most privileged of a supposedly endless but relatively unspecified array of differences which, once posited, allows them not only to repudiate an identification with white lesbian feminism but to look away from the material realities of bodies and circumstances that limit the play of identity?

Discussing *The Jazz Singer,* Rogin observes that the Jew in blackface may by evoking "an imagined alternative communal identity" free himself "from the pull of his inherited, Jewish, communal identicalness" and become "a unique and therefore representative American" ("Blackface, White Noise" 440). While the postmodern *Without YOU I'm Nothing* suggests that the desire on the part of the white Jewish subject to imagine herself as part of an "alternative [i.e., African American] communal identity," to transcend the "communal identicalness" of Jewishness and, in Bernhard's case, white lesbian feminism, and to become uniquely and representatively American, it emphasizes the arrogance and impossibility of these goals (after all, Sandra's "alternative community" is out the door by the time she finishes her final number). In the preface to the striptease, Sandra, wrapped in the flag, delivers the "Without *you* I'm nothing" speech to the diegetic black audience, and in an exaggeratedly lyrical voice she speaks yearningly of her desire to get out of the main highways into the byways where she can be at one with the people:

> I wanted to walk through the Midwest early in the morning and watch all the farmers on their way to work in the amber fields of grain in Nebraska, to pick strawberries next to my Chicano brothers and sisters underneath the hot California sun, to watch the morning light shining off the body of the Lady of the Harbor onto all the Korean grocers as they stock their salad bars. These were the sounds, sights, and smells that I wanted to incorporate into my world view.

Needless to say, the Whitmanesque ideal of the artist communing with (and containing) the multitudes with whom he mingles in his travels across the nation is thoroughly deflated: "I never wanted to depend on Triple A," Sandra confides. Of course, the subversion of the notion of the American artist as representative is, it must be noted, especially easy to achieve via a woman artist. For when have women ever been able to sustain the remotest illusion of themselves as representative?

But this parody of the imperial American artist/subject marks a striking contrast to the number which comes right before it—a number which is uncharacteristically serious and which situates an "alternative communal identity" in the gay male disco subculture of the 1970s. Sandra, in (counter) drag as the black gay male drag disco artist Sylvester, performs a moving hom/femage to the late singer's memory and provides us with a glimpse of a vision that is, for once in the movie, not simply invoked in order to be parodied. In the number "Do You Want to Funk?" and its preface Sandra/Sylvester delivers a kind of poetic incantation extolling "the beat," which is said to span place and time and connect us all to one another throughout the world. This entire sequence begins, once again, with Sandra as Jew, in black wearing a veil and chanting. She goes on to claim her "roots" in seventies culture: "Of all the decades we've exploited—and we've exploited them all—the seventies remain the least understood, yet the most central to my aesthetic and philosophy." Here then, at last, Sandra posits a kind of community and an identity founded in a certain gay male subculture.

Given the privileging of gay male culture in the film, it is hard to agree with Berlant and Freeman, who characterize Sandra as a straight white woman-identified woman. Rather, Sandra seems most comfortable presenting herself as a queer male-identified woman. That the alliance with gay men that Bernhard quite openly declares in the film as well as in talk shows, interviews, etc. tacitly colludes in the social and cultural erasure of the lesbian feminist is clear when we remember that the seventies which Sandra says were so central to her "aesthetic and philosophy" was not just the era of gay male discos but also the decade of the lesbian feminist.[7] But the lesbian feminist is a figure Bernhard not only distances herself from, as in the film, but continually baits whenever she gets a chance to do so. For example, in an interview published in the *Advocate* and often cited by Bernhard's queer supporters as evidence that she is "out," Bernhard actually admits that she could envision herself living with a woman partner for the rest of her life, although, she hesitates, "two women can't have babies, . . . can they?" The interviewer responds:

> Well, they can, but they need to get some sperm from somewhere.
> *Sandra:* Oh, don't print that, because then they'll really come after me: "She doesn't even want to get sperm from men!" But I'm not antimen, so there's no point of even talking about it really.
> *Interviewer:* There's a big difference between being against men and preferring women. Most women have better things to do than obsess about how much they hate men.
> *Sandra:* Right on! Jesus, the *Advocate* was smart to send you. I was so afraid that they were going to send in some heavy-duty dyke who was just going to fry my ass. ("Acting Lesbian" 72)

Sandra assumes agreement between herself and the interviewer, but to me their emphases seem very different. Whereas the interviewer wants to assert the positivity of affirming and loving women, Bernhard wants to ward off the image of the man-hating dyke—an image that has, of course, long been used as a bogey to scare rebellious women.

Sandra's grounds for hesitating about living with a same-sex partner are surprising, to say the least. For all the acclaim given Bernhard as a postmodern artist who lays bare the performative nature of gender (and race) by continually "reproducing" herself into a seemingly endless variety of identities, she here hedges against lesbian identity by invoking woman's role in heterosexual reproduction. One can ask who is the greater essentialist—Bernhard, who appeals to male/female biological functions in thinking about what kind of social arrangement she will enter into, or Pettit, who in taking Bernhard to task for conversations like the above in which Bernhard affirms lesbians with one hand and slaps them with the other, asserts that Sandra plays "with the boundaries of our existence *for her work and for her own private gain.* Lesbianism is not an essentialism that blocks out the world; it is quite persistently a way of life for many women very much in the world, often in truly painful and violent ways" ("The Lesbian Vanishes" 42; emphasis in original). What this passage suggests to me, although Pettit herself doesn't make the connection, is that in her public persona "Sandra" appropriates lesbianism in a way that is analogous to the filmic Sandra's appropriation of African Americanness. Whereas the film is aware of many of the problems of such appropriation when it comes to blackface, the Sandra of the talk show circuit seems entirely insensitive to its effects on lesbian community.

If we needed more evidence that Bernhard's fame has been achieved to a certain extent at the expense of lesbian feminism, which is thereby threatened with renewed invisibility (to the extent that it has ever been visible), we can turn to some curious details behind Bernhard's assumption of a role on *Roseanne* playing a woman who came out as gay (and then qualified her declaration some episodes later by saying she was bisexual). According to a recent book by Geraldine Barr, Roseanne's lesbian-feminist sister who claims to have collaborated with Roseanne until the latter married Tom Arnold and got rid of her, in the sisters' original plan Roseanne's TV sister Jackie, the fictional surrogate of Geraldine herself, was slated to be a lesbian and eventually to have her own spin-off show. (Instead, it was Tom Arnold who got his own spin-off program, the atrocious *Jackie Thomas Show*—a title that even appropriated the TV sister's given name.) Ironically, then, Bernhard, who so anxiously disavows lesbian sisterhood, came to replace the (surrogate) lesbian sister of Roseanne Barr Arnold.

According to Geraldine Barr, Jackie's lesbianism was supposed to be revealed gradually and would therefore never be a major issue or problem. Barr's ambition to produce a television show about a woman like herself whose lesbianism would be only one component of a complex identity gives the lie to those who see the lesbianism which emerged from the woman's movement as a monolithic construction. In her biography/autobiography *My Sister Roseanne* (whose original splendid title *Behind Barrs* was dropped), Barr acknowledges her roots in 1970s feminism and details her and Roseanne's dream of building a sisterhood that would speak from, to, and about the women whose lives have been unacknowledged in the history of Hollywood entertainment. As a lesbian working-class Jew who grew up among Mormons in Utah, Barr herself occupies a site of so many intersecting differences that she would seem to be a postmodern feminist's dream, were it not for the fact that so many of her differences are unassimilable to postmodernism's favorite categories (its canonized differences, as a friend of mine put it) and that she gives these categories positive content rather than mining them strictly for their potential to subvert other categories.

Contrasting Bernhard to Barr on their relation to regional identities, for instance, we could note that Bernhard's assumption of such identities is meant to debunk the possibility of authenticity in a postmodern commodity culture—as when she sings a duet of the Hank Williams song "I'm So Lonesome I Could Cry" in front of a facade of a barn that opens onto a scene of New York City). By contrast, Barr actually believed in the possibility of bringing to the arena of mass entertainment the perspectives of actual working-class Moms who live in trailer parks in the Midwest and West. Even more striking, perhaps, is the difference between Bernhard and Barr in their attitudes toward their Jewish identities. While Jewishness for Bernhard is (in the film) a vehicle for negotiating her relation to other identities, for Barr Jewishness came to be not only something to be struggled against because of its patriarchal structures and laws but something which possessed positive meaning for her and inflected her evolving definition of lesbian sisterhood. For instance, she and Roseanne intended to give the name Beshert to their production company, which they planned to use to "help empower working class women through the arts" (Barr says she saw the obligations entailed by worldly success "in spiritual terms where, if you take vast sums from the universe, you must return vast sums in kind," 177). "*Beshert*," Barr explains, is a Yiddish word "that means that an event or a relationship is preordained. . . . [if] you meet someone, fall in love, and instinctively know that the other person is perfect for you . . . a perfect soul mate, that is *beshert*. . . . Rosey and I were sisters preordained to be Sisters" (216).

The point of this brief comparison is not to dole out political (or spiritual) correctness awards but to inform (or remind) readers that lesbian feminism consciously faced many of the issues that postmodern feminists sometimes claim to have discovered and, moreover, that it had hope and vision and risked self-affirmation even as it struggled with differences and fought against oppression. It had humor, too, and its humor was a major weapon in the fight against oppression. To take one example that bears repeating in light of Bernhard's fear of being perceived as a man-hating dyke, we might consider the famous Roseanne joke that Barr says came out of her and Roseanne's discussions at the "Woman to Woman Bookstore in Denver," where, in the sisters' early days before Hollywood, straight and lesbian women of many colors congregated and hashed out differences: "They say lesbians hate men. How can they? They don't have to fuck them" (134).

I am certainly not arguing that lesbian feminism is exempt from the charge of appropriating others' differences, engaging in its own forms of blackface. In an important article published a few years ago, "Homelands of the Mind: Jewish Feminism and Identity Politics," Jenny Bourne traces the "coming-out" process of Jewish lesbian feminists like Elly Bulkin to the black lesbian feminist statement of the Combahee River Collective. "The most profound and potentially the most radical politics," the Collective had written, "come directly out of our own identity as opposed to working to end somebody else's oppression" (2). According to Bourne, feminists like Bulkin seized upon this statement as a rationalization for their coming out as lesbians and then as Jews and to claim "commonality" with African American women in their "experiences of oppression" (12). Yet the process didn't always work that way. Geraldine Barr, for example, learned from women of color to reject the arguments of liberal white women when they argued, "We must concentrate on our similarities and celebrate our differences" (107). For Barr and the women of color she encountered on her journey to "Sisterhood" differences were the source of tension, and liberal feminism was at fault because it "rarely touched black women, rarely touched Hispanic women, rarely touched women who were raised in poverty" (110).

Roseanne seemed to share her sister's values and goals—so much so that in her first book, *Roseanne: My Life as a Woman,* she wrote in her dedication to her sister: "Where do you end and where do I begin?" Such words in retrospect seem ominous. As this chapter is meant to demonstrate, it is crucial to acknowledge and respect the boundaries and borders that exist between people even as we recognize that appropriation and assimilation are inevitable social processes. When Tom

Arnold entered the picture, Roseanne figured out the answer to her question, which turned out to be not at all rhetorical. "Sisterhood is dead," she announced just when Geraldine Barr, having voluntarily taken a back seat to Roseanne, who as a straight woman and a mother had been judged to be in the best position to speak for the majority of women, was about to realize her ambitions to become a producer and to launch her own projects. In this case, at least, the decision about "the limits of alliance" seems pretty much to have been made *for* the lesbian feminist. But now what? Where should she go? The queer "deconstructor" of identity, having "allied" herself with the straight feminist and become more than a little phobic, would prefer to have nothing to do with her. Perhaps these new "allies" need not worry about her fate: since she "can't have babies," maybe she and her kind will just die out. Then queers and straight feminists will never have to recognize the extent to which the heavy-duty dyke has given birth to *them,* the extent to which her commitment to the representation of women in the variety of their differences might in truth lead them to say, "Without *you* I'm nothing."

N O T E S

1. I use the name Sandra to designate the film's persona.
2. See also Riggs.
3. Rather than simply dismissing Bernhard because she effects a substitution of race for gender (as if these two categories did not significantly overlap), white feminists would do well to use the film as an occasion to reflect on white feminism's own relation to blackface. I can only briefly suggest how such a reflection might proceed, for it would be far more complicated than might be supposed. White feminism as it evolved in the seventies and eighties was often accused of formulating a political theory and practice around white middle-class women's issues and then inviting black women to join the ranks. Sometimes this theory sought to derive racism—and, it follows, its effects on identity formation—from sexism (Sandra influences Diana, not the other way around). "Racism is sexism extended," Shulamith Firestone wrote, or, in other words, "Without *me*" your experience of oppression would be nonexistent—or at least inexplicable (*The Dialectic of Sex* 122). Most frequently, claims to commonality with blacks on the parts of white feminist theorists of the last couple of decades were couched in the form of analogies. An impressive essay by Lisa Hogeland entitled "*Invisible Man* and Invisible Women: The Sex/Race Analogy of the 1970s" looks at the centrality of Ellison's metaphor of invisibility for racial oppression and suggests how protean cross-racial analogizing could be. In this case, white feminists' insistence that women in patriarchy shared a plight in common with African Americans shifted the terms of cross-racial masquerade from

"black like me" to "invisible like me." Finally, some of the most subtle kinds of blackface adopted by white feminists can be found in certain anthropological writings of white feminists in the seventies. To take a single example (a highly interesting one in the context because it involves a woman who perhaps more than anyone articulated—in "Thinking Sex"—the need for a shift in the alliance this book investigates): Gayle Rubin's powerful, influential, and by now classic essay "The Traffic in Women," looks to various tribal cultures that have figured largely in anthropological studies in order to understand the laws that enforce the oppression of all women: without the Trobriand Islanders we're nothing. A full analysis of the sex-race analogies that pervaded the writings of feminists (and not *only* white feminists) may be found in Hogeland's striking and finely nuanced essay already referred to.

4. Bernhard seems to have anticipated Philip Roth's discussion of Irving Berlin in *Operation Shylock:* "I heard myself next praising the greatest Diasporist of all, the father of the new Diasporist movement, Irving Berlin. 'People ask where I got the idea. Well, I got it listening to the radio. The radio was playing "Easter Parade" and I thought, But this is Jewish genius on a par with the Ten Commandments. God gave Moses the Ten Commandments and then He gave to Irving Berlin "Easter Parade" and "White Christmas." The two holidays that celebrate the divinity of Christ—the divinity that's the very heart of the Jewish rejection of Christianity—and what does Irving Berlin brilliantly do? He de-Christs them both! Easter he turns into a fashion show and Christmas into a holiday about snow. Gone is the gore and the murder of Christ—down with the crucifix and up with the bonnet! *He turns their religion into schlock.* But nicely! . . . If schlockified Christianity is Christianity cleansed of Jew hatred, then three cheers for schlock. If supplanting Jesus Christ with snow can enable my people to cozy up to Christmas, then let it snow, let it snow, let it snow! Do you see my point?' I took more pride, I told them, in 'Easter Parade' than in the victory of the Six Day War, found more security in 'White Christmas' than in the Israeli nuclear reactor" (157–58). I am indebted to Muera Shreiber for referring me to this wonderful passage.

5. In an extremely interesting article on interracial male relationships, Susan Fraiman discusses the way women operate as a kind of "switch point" in relations between men of different races. Here we see the black woman as a kind of switch point between two women, one a Jew, the other virtually an archetype of desirable white Christian femininity.

6. Probyn draws on Valerie Smith's work, quoted here, to make the opposite point from the one I am making; she argues that Bernhard exemplifies Smith's point about how the black woman signifies "material concerns" (*Sexing the Self* 156–57).

7. Of course, Madonna is another pop cultural figure who has aligned herself politically with gay men—with black gay men, in particular, in her voguing phase. On the level of academic theory, Eve Sedgwick has more consistently aligned herself, and even identified herself, with gay men than with feminism, lesbian feminism included. In this regard, it is interesting to come across a passage in *Epistemology of the Closet* in which Sedgwick compares the gay man in the closet with the Jew passing as gentile. She draws on the Biblical story of Esther, who announces her identity to the king when her people are about to be destroyed, in order to show how complex and implicating gay identity and its avowal are by comparison to Jewish identity as it operates in this story. For Sedgwick, Jewishness represents the fixed pole; it "has a solidity whose very unequivocalness grounds the story of Esther's equivocation and her subsequent self-disclosure. In the processes of gay self-

disclosure, by contrast, in a twentieth-century context, questions of authority and evidence can be the first to arise" (79). (Race is of course even more fixed in a racist society, since racism "is based on a stigma that is visible in all but exceptional cases . . .; so are the oppressions based on gender, age, size, physical handicap.") At one point in her interesting analysis Sedgwick becomes auto-biographical in illustrating how "Jewish little girls are educated in gender roles—fondness for being looked at, fearlessness in defense of 'their people,' nonsolidarity with their sex—through masquerading as Queen Esther at Purim" (82). These observations take on extra significance when we reflect on how frequently Sedgwick herself has been criticized by feminist critics—especially lesbians—for neglecting or simplifying their identity, thus in a sense exhibiting "nonsolidarity" with her sex as she identifies with the "opposite" one. While such practices may or may not account for Bernhard's lack of solidarity with women, they may explain Sedgwick's oft-remarked-upon tendency to neglect issues relating to lesbian identity. See Castle and de Lauretis for two examples of lesbian critiques of Sedgwick's work.

WORKS CITED

Barr, Geraldine (with Ted Schwarz). *My Sister Roseanne: The True Story of Roseanne Barr Arnold.* New York: Birch Lane Press, 1994.

Barr, Roseanne. *Roseanne: My Life as a Woman.* New York: Harper and Row, 1989.

Berlant, Lauren, and Elizabeth Freeman. "Queer Nationality." *boundary 2* 19.1 (1992): 149–80.

Bernhard, Sandra. "Acting Lesbian." An interview by Lily Burana. *Advocate* 619 (December 15, 1992): 66–73.

Bourne, Jenny. "Homelands of the Mind: Jewish Feminism and Identity Politics." *Race and Class* 29 (1987): 1–24.

Butler, Judith. *Bodies That Matter: On the Discursive Limits of Sex.* New York: Routledge, 1993.

Carby, Hazel. "It Just Be's Dat Way Sometime: The Sexual Politics of Women's Blues." *Radical America* 20 (April 1986): 6–13.

———. *Reconstructing Womanhood: The Emergence of the Afro-American Woman Novelist.* New York: Oxford University Press, 1987.

Castle, Terry. *The Apparitional Lesbian: Female Homosexuality and Modern Culture.* New York: Columbia University Press, 1993.

de Lauretis, Teresa. *The Practice of Love: Lesbian Sexuality and Perverse Desire.* Bloomington: Indiana University Press, 1994.

Firestone, Shulamith. *The Dialectic of Sex.* New York: Morrow, 1970.

Fraiman, Susan. "Geometries of Race and Gender: Eve Sedgwick, Spike Lee, Charlayne Hunter-Gault." *Feminist Studies* 20.1 (Spring 1994).

Hogeland, Lisa. "*Invisible Man* and Invisible Women: The Sex/Race Analogy of the 1970s." *Women's History Review,* forthcoming.

hooks, bell. *Black Looks: Race and Representation.* Boston: South End Press, 1992.

Ivanov, Andrea. "Sexual Parody in American Comedic Film and Literature, 1925–1958." Ph.D. dissertation, University of Southern California, 1994.

Lott, Eric. "White Like Me: Racial Cross-Dressing and the Construction of American Whiteness." In *Cultures of U.S. Imperialism.* Ed. Amy Kaplan and Donald Pease. Durham: Duke University Press, 1993, 474–95.

Mailer, Norman. "The White Negro." *Advertisements for Myself*. New York: Putnam, 1959, 311–31.

Mercer, Kobena. "Skin Head Sex Thing: Racial Difference and the Homoerotic Imaginary." In *How Do I Look? Queer Film and Video*. Ed. Bad Object Choices. Seattle: Bay Press, 1991, 169–210.

Modleski, Tania. *Feminism without Women: Culture and Criticism in a "Postfeminist" Age*. New York: Routledge, 1991.

Moore, Suzanne. "Getting a Bit of the Other—the Pimps of Postmodernism." In *Male Order: Unwrapping Masculinity*. Ed. Rowena Chapman and Jonathan Rutherford. London: Lawrence and Wishart, 1988, 165–92.

Pettit, Sarah. "The Lesbian Vanishes: Sandra Bernhard and Her Big Joke on the Sisterhood." *Outweek* 81 (January 16, 1991): 36–42.

Probyn, Elspeth. *Sexing the Self: Gendered Positions in Cultural Studies*. London: Routledge, 1993.

Riggs, Marlon. "Cultural Healing: An Interview with Marlon Riggs." *Afterimage*, March 1991, 8–11.

Rogin, Michael. "Blackface, White Noise: The Jewish Jazz Singer Finds His Voice." *Critical Inquiry* 18 (Spring 1992): 417–53.

Roth, Philip. *Operation Shylock*. New York: Simon and Schuster, 1993.

Rubin, Gayle. "Thinking Sex: Notes for a Radical Theory of the Politics of Sexuality." In *Pleasure and Danger: Exploring Female Sexuality*. Ed. Carole S. Vance. Boston: Routledge & Kegan Paul, 1984, 267–319.

———. "The Traffic in Women: Notes toward a Political Economy of Sex." In *Toward an Anthropology of Women*. Ed. Rayna Reiter. New York: Monthly Review Press, 1975, 157–210.

Sedgwick, Eve Kosofsky. *Epistemology of the Closet*. Berkeley: University of California Press, 1990.

She Done Him Wrong. A film with Mae West. Directed by Lowell Sherman. Paramount Productions, 1933.

Smith, Valerie. "Black Feminist Theory and the Representation of the 'Other.'" In *Changing Our Own Words: Essays in Criticism, Theory, and Writing by Black Women*. Ed. Cheryl A. Wall. New Brunswick, Rutgers University Press, 1987, 38–57.

Walton, Jean. "Sandra Bernhard: Lesbian Postmodern or Modern Postlesbian?" In *The Lesbian Postmodern*. Ed. Laura Doan. New York: Columbia University Press, 1994, 244–61.

Without YOU I'm Nothing. A film with Sandra Bernhard. Directed by John Boskovich. Management Company Entertainment Group, 1990.

Woolf, Virginia. *A Room of One's Own*. New York: Harcourt, 1957.

Part Two

COLLISIONS

Sexuality versus Gender

A Kind of Mistake?

COLLEEN LAMOS

For nearly twenty years, the conceptual axis of feminist theory has rested upon the distinction between sex and gender, typically understood as the opposition between biologically determined sex (male/female) and culturally determined gender (masculinity/femininity). Examinations of the dynamics of what Gayle Rubin first called the "sex/gender system" have often been aimed at demystifying and prying apart the conventional equation of femininity with women and masculinity with men.[1] However, with the advent of lesbian and gay studies, the sex/gender axis appears about to be displaced by the distinction between *sexuality* and *gender.* The conceptual axis of lesbian and gay studies rests upon the opposition between, on the one hand, sexuality, including sexual practices and sexual desires, and, on the other hand, gender.[2] Moreover, unlike queer theory, the investigation of sexuality in lesbian and gay studies, strictly speaking, often explicitly amounts to an analysis in terms of that familiar binary, homosexuality and heterosexuality.

The difference in analytical tools and theoretical assumptions between feminist and lesbian/gay studies has issued in sharp debates recently regarding their conceptual and institutional relations. What does juxtaposing sexuality to gender allow us to think, and what does it presuppose or foreclose? In particular, how is it now possible to conceive of the relationship between lesbianism and feminism—the pair that once went hand in hand, whose inseparability was epitomized by the slogan, "feminism is the theory; lesbianism is the practice."[3] Finally, after considering these questions, I will address some of the issues raised by the institutionalization of lesbian and gay studies, including its sometimes fractious disciplinary relation to feminist and women's studies.

First, on an abstract level the sex/gender pair is asymmetrical to that of sexuality/gender. Sexual practices and desires, in their multiple forms and directions, do not stand in relation to gender as male/female stands in relation to masculinity/femininity. As a consequence, lesbian and gay studies is not simply analogous or parallel to feminist studies. Second, in the switch from *sex* versus gender to *sexuality* versus gender, sex (as sexual difference, or female/male) seems to have dropped out of the picture or have been subsumed by one of the other terms. Indeed, recent developments in both feminist and queer theory have tended to reduce sexual difference, either to the performance of gender or to a generalized sexuality. For many, the merit of opposing sexuality to gender is that the contrast helps to expose the ways in which feminism has relied upon a substantive ontology of sex, sometimes even while denying it. Much feminist theory assumes the essential nature of sexual difference as a bedrock from which to argue for reformed gender arrangements. Shifting the focus and juxtaposing gender to sexuality foregrounds our assumptions concerning the supposedly hard core (and the ideological refuge) of biological sex.

Although the distinction between sexuality and gender is thus conceptually enabling, it may prove to be equally disabling. For if the analysis of sexuality along the axis of hetero- and homosexuality may unsettle some of our accustomed ideas concerning women and men, and femininity and masculinity, it often does so by means of another kind of mistake—that is, by naturalizing homosexuality and hetero-sexuality as fundamental orders of being. The consolidation of the homo/hetero binary as the primary division and organizing principle of human sexuality, thereby excluding or obscuring other ways of understanding sexual desire, is reinforced by many forms of popular and high culture, juridical codes, governmental and corporate policies, and—yes—lesbian and gay studies. Although the results of this consolidation are diverse and sometimes contradictory, lesbian and gay studies is severely restricted in its conceptual range by the homo/hetero binary, an opposition that is historically and theoretically derived from the binary structures of sex and gender.

As the title of *Cross-Purposes* suggests, lesbian and feminist interests do not coincide, for the conceptual relationship between lesbianism and feminism is founded upon an ineluctable continuity and an irreducible incommensurability. On the one hand, *lesbian* refers minimally to erotic passion or sexual activity between women, and possibly to a general sexual preference or orientation. Although lesbians have been considered virile inverts rather than genuine women, and while some theorists such as Monique Wittig claim that lesbians are not women, having refused that designation, lesbians have also at times occupied a privileged position within feminism.[4] As "women-identified-women," lesbian sexual desire has been understood as the epitome of gender solidarity against the seductive appeals of the patriarchy. At the theoretical level, the analysis of female same-sex desire is continuous with feminist inquiry insofar as the former retains an emphasis upon the gender specificity of lesbianism. On the other hand, *feminism* refers minimally to political activity on behalf of women and, at the theoretical level, to an analysis of sexual and gender social, economic, and symbolic relations, among others. The perverse directions of female sexual desire and the implications of those desires remain at the margins and cannot come into sharp focus through a conceptual lens that is trained upon sexual and gender difference.

To put the matter simply, lesbianism figures both as the apotheosis and as the scandal of feminism. Lesbianism can be seen, nearly simultaneously, as the purest form of female identification and as the wholesale rejection of all that is feminine. The lesbian may at once stand as the woman par excellence and as not a woman at all.

The paradoxical character of the relationship between lesbianism and feminism is made immediately evident by examining their apparently similar grammatical forms. As its linguistic form implies, feminism is an ideology comprising a loose and debatable set of political convictions concerning the oppression of women. Yet lesbianism denotes certain kinds of sexual acts between women and does not, strictly speaking, designate any political ideology at all. Therefore, to call it an -ism is a grammatical error, yet it is an error consistent both with the belief that such sexual activity constitutes a tacit feminist commitment and with the obverse, homophobic belief that lesbians are secret conspirators against the social order. Put into common usage by Havelock Ellis, *lesbianism* as a sexological term carries the lingering odor of an exotic pathology.[5] In short, the homophile and the homophobe share in equal measure the hope or fear that lesbianism is the carnal enactment of subversive ideological principles or a disruptive social pathogen.

If lesbianism and feminism are neither identical nor completely separable but are continuous yet incommensurate with each other, so too lesbian/gay and feminist studies overlap in significant ways but must be kept analytically distinct instead of subsuming or superseding each other. Thus Rubin argues that feminism "should not be seen as the privileged site for work on sexuality" or as "the obligatory and sufficient approach" to sexual issues.[6] Instead, sexuality and gender are interimplicated in historically and culturally specific ways, their precise relation dependent upon particular contexts. The instability of these two terms and the proximity between the irreducibility of lesbian and feminist inquiry render it all the more important not to eliminate their complexity by either collapsing or splitting them.

The second half of my title—"A Kind of Mistake?"—alludes to an essay by Katie King in which she discusses what she calls the "gay/straight split." King usefully recalls the several ways in which that phrase has been understood, first in the late 1960s and early 1970s when homosexual women and men shared the term *gay* and when feminists, provoked by dyke-baiting, confronted the stigmatization of feminism by the presence of lesbians in the movement. A few years later, the gay/straight split took on a different sense when, within feminism, lesbianism was privileged as a "magical sign." During this brief historical moment, lesbians were thought to be in the vanguard of feminism, beyond collaboration with the patriarchy or at least ranged somewhere on what Adrienne Rich called the "lesbian continuum" of female identification. In a third sense, the gay/straight split, according to King, today "marks a kind of mistake: the assumption that differences among women are only bipolar." Quite apart from the division between homo- and heterosexuality, "other differences that cannot be imagined as opposites may be as salient or more salient: race, class, [and] nationality. . . . All suggest that sexualities are too plural . . . to be named in a gay/straight division."[7]

King's criticism of the homo/hetero distinction as a coarsely grained analytical tool, one that fails to register equally significant determinates of sexuality, can be taken further. Besides excluding other factors, the division between homosexuality and heterosexuality has become increasingly naturalized in academic studies as well as in United States culture at large, in part through the efforts of lesbian, gay, and feminist scholars. Rather than offering critical leverage on gender difference and, as Judith Butler argues, by "working sexuality *against* . . . gender" to dismantle the conceptual structures and cultural practices that define and produce "women" and "men," as well as "homosexuals" and "heterosexuals," the homo/hetero binary is in the process of becoming normalized.[8] In short, homosexuality and heterosexuality seem to be on the verge of assuming a normative function similar to that of those other familiar binary oppositions, male/female and masculine/feminine.

The possibilities and the limitations of juxtaposing sexuality and gender or of drawing a sharp distinction between homosexuality and heterosexuality are evident in the institutionalization of lesbian and gay literary studies. The birth of this field parallels in many ways that of the study of women's literature. The debates over its emergence demonstrate the divergent implications and aims of lesbian, gay, and queer theorists as well as, more broadly, the simultaneously conserving and dispersing effects of an insistence upon the difference between gay and straight. An excellent instance of the current controversies in lesbian and gay studies or queer theory—for even the name of the field is in dispute, which may come as no surprise since, from the moment that "the love that dare not speak its name" tried to speak for itself, nomenclature has been a testy issue—is a collection of essays entitled *Professions of Desire: Lesbian and Gay Studies in Literature*, edited by George Haggerty and Bonnie Zimmerman.

This volume exemplifies the multivalent consequences of the institutionalization of lesbian and gay studies. Its publication by the Modern Language Association gives the official imprimatur to a field that has struggled for professional legitimacy since the founding of the MLA Lesbian and Gay Caucus twenty years ago. The MLA's endorsement lends the book a bureaucratic, perhaps even authoritative status and thus calls for our attention. The effort to establish lesbian and gay literary studies is subject to massive homogenizing pressures from within and without, such as the demand to demarcate a field of inquiry or a canon and the need to legitimate that field as worthwhile. *Professions of Desire* is a symptom of the effects of these pressures—indeed, it is a testimony to their triumph.

Among the questions the book raises are: What does it mean that lesbian and gay studies has become a discipline? Does its recognition as a properly academic field also mean the disciplining of inquiry into same-sex desire? The birth of lesbian and gay studies is a sign of its conformity to the academic standards that govern all literary fields, from Old English to African American literature; in turn, the institutionalization of lesbian and gay studies disciplines those who work within it into conformity to certain norms. This commonplace observation takes on some bite when we consider exactly what is at stake. For lesbian and gay literary studies, these issues include determining what is taught as a lesbian or gay text, what it means to be a lesbian or gay teacher or student, and the relation of bisexual or heterosexual teachers and students to those texts. Perhaps the knottiest problem of all is how to define lesbian and gay studies, given the historical and cultural relativity of the concept of homosexuality. In general, this disciplinary demand has been answered in three ways.

The first and most conventional method is to assert that lesbian and gay studies is a field like any other, concerned simply with the interpretation of lesbian and gay texts. This field may be broadly or narrowly defined—for instance, as comprising works written by lesbian and gay authors or those that have some sort of lesbian or gay content. Despite the often disputable and fuzzy boundaries of such criteria, this method assimilates lesbian and gay studies to accepted canons of literary scholarship as a minority literature—like that of women's studies—but at the price of refusing the most provocative questions raised by the obliquity of same-sex desire.

A variation of this approach, which tends to disrupt its orthodoxy, considers the intersection of homosexuality and other minorities, especially racial ones. The interimplication of sexual and racial difference casts doubt upon the habit of viewing lesbian and gay literature as a unified body of texts based upon the core, private truth of their authors' sexual orientation. Inasmuch as, in Yvonne Yarbro-Bejarano's words, "everyone's sex has a race and vice versa," the construction of a sexual identity is ineluctably intertwined with a racial one.[9] In a similar fashion, the introduction of racial, class, and other differences within women's studies has disturbed the confidence of many scholars in its conceptual coherence.

These insights have a direct bearing upon the second, currently more popular method of defending lesbian and gay studies as a vehicle for self-understanding. Like many teachers and students in feminist courses for whom the study of women's literature is a way of exploring one's gender identity, the study of lesbian and gay texts is often valued as a means of understanding one's sexual identity. While departing from traditional disciplinary criteria, this view of lesbian and gay studies possesses the authority and the limitations of personal experience.

The editors of *Professions of Desire* claim that "this is a field that one does not enter so much as come out in."[10] Professing lesbian and gay sexuality, especially in the classroom, thus assumes a confessional burden and justification similar to that adopted by early advocates of women's studies programs. The editors and many of the contributors assume that those doing the professing are lesbian and gay teachers of lesbian and gay students. The fruitful and painful possibilities of the straight or not-entirely-straight teacher or student confronting queer texts have no place here. Moreover, such self-discovery often amounts to a tautological confirmation of what one already knows. Setting off to explore one's identity might just be a circular trip, leading back to a subject position that, even when allied with other subject positions, leaves one boxed into predetermined categories of identity.

This conception of lesbian and gay studies as a means for self-realization is the result of the continued domination of the coming-out story as the field's master narrative. However dubious the belief that one's sexual desire determines the type of person one is, lesbian and gay studies is for many energized by the zeal of arriving at just that sort of knowledge. Although the courage of such a conviction of one's personal self-discovery has for many been hard won, the struggle to affirm a lesbian and gay identity should open rather than foreclose questions about the constraints of that identity.

The debate over what to call this field—whether "lesbian and gay" or "queer" or something else—is dominated by tiresome conflicts over the political and psychological value of asserting a subject position. These conflicts obscure the coercive force of academic institutions, specifically, of literature departments which are capable of recognizing either traditional periods and genres—say, the nineteenth-century British novel—and certain designated minority literatures, along with a handful of offshoots such as film theory. Reflecting epistemological structures in the culture at large, the disciplinary organization of academic institutions enforces and rewards the belief that lesbian and gay studies, like women's studies, will have "found itself" by occupying a niche as a minority literature. Thus is ghettoization celebrated as though it were liberation.

There is, however, another approach to the issues raised by the study of same-sex desire in literature that is not comfortably situated within a recognized discipline. Under the heading of queer theory, this third method tries to dismantle rather than to consolidate the categories of sexual identity, taking for granted neither the truth of subjective experience nor the objective existence of a corporate body of lesbian and gay literature. Questioning the naturalness of both homosexuality and heterosexuality, queer theory searches for avenues beyond the homo/hetero binary. An example of such an approach is Jeffrey Nunokawa's essay on *The Picture of Dorian Gray*, in which he argues against the view that this major text in the canon of lesbian and gay literature is a revelation of the homosexuality of its central characters. Instead, "the expression of homosexual desire" in Wilde's novel "cancels rather than clarifies the definition of the character through whom it is conducted," so that male same-sex love is dispersed or generalized rather than solidified as the defining essence of any particular individual.[11]

Queer theory and criticism offer a way out of the orthodoxy of sexual identity and the deadlock over the construction of a lesbian and gay canon. However, queer theory is by no means predominant in *Professions of Desire*, which is representative of several collections of essays published in the past four years that attest to the sharp divisions within a field that still does not know what to call itself.[12] The essays included in Karla Jay and Joanne Glasgow's *Lesbian Texts and Contexts*, Susan Wolfe and Julia Penelope's *Sexual Practice, Textual Theory*, and Sally Munt's *New Lesbian Criticism* are engaged in a productive debate over what are lesbian texts and how to read them. The editors of these anthologies all confess to their wish for a definitional core or "lesbian essence" that would provide what they consider a solid foundation for their enterprise. All of the editors and most of the essayists share an understanding of lesbianism born from 1970s feminism, which they find in conflict with poststructuralist theory and its spawn, queer theory. Their dilemma is situated on the horns of the conceptual opposition between sexuality and gender.

The demarcation of a body of specifically lesbian texts is a major preoccupation of these critics, which is no surprise given the historical difficulty of specifying female same-sexuality. Lillian Faderman's essay "What Is a Lesbian Text?" in *Professions of Desire* is one of the most comprehensive and thoughtful responses to the question posed by her title. Faderman argues for an expansive conception of lesbian literature that includes works written by women who were not or are not self-declared lesbians but in which "lesbian subject matter is somehow encoded."[13] Her criteria for lesbian texts are those that display a "lesbian sensibility," that criticize heterosexual institutions, that focus on female relationships such as romantic friendships, or that encrypt lesbian sexuality through, for instance, switching the gender of its characters (52). She thus opens the lesbian canon to Alice Walker's *Color Purple* and Toni Morrison's *Sula*.

The strength of Faderman's vision of lesbian literature is its attentiveness to the historical circumstances that have restricted or prohibited the expression of female same-sex desire; moreover, she is willing (up to a point) to face the consequences of her arguments. At the heart of her definition of lesbian literature is her assumption that it is aligned with feminist values, especially with a critical stance toward heterosexism. Where does that leave Radclyffe Hall's *Well of Loneliness*, what she calls "the prototypical lesbian novel" (51), yet one which "privileges heterosexuality" by adopting the sexological model of inversion? Faderman asks, "Must we see it as a heterosexual novel, despite its crucial role in the development of openly lesbian literature?" (54). While she dismisses such a conclusion as "absurd," it is entirely in keeping with her views.

The prospect that *The Well of Loneliness*, the cornerstone of the lesbian canon, might prove to be a heterosexual novel after all, according to Faderman's own relaxed standards, is enough to suggest that the effort to distinguish between the two is misguided. There simply are no "lesbian texts" any more than there are "heterosexual texts." The wish that such a distinction could be drawn stems from the same impulse toward ideological purity that drives some critics to distinguish between true lesbians and those corrupted by commodity fetishism or lured into an insidious alliance with gay men. Yet the purest lesbian identification typically overlooks the ways in which sexuality is bound up with other multiple and shifting identities. In short, the dilemma faced by Faderman and others who seek a ground for lesbian studies derives from the same impasse into which feminism was led when it staked its claims on the category of woman as an immutable foundation. We may as well give up the task of defining lesbianism or lesbian literature as such and examine instead the interplay among various kinds of nonessential differences, exploiting the conflicts between sexuality and gender rather than searching for a harmonious fusion.

The major fault line in this field that has no certain name is the tension between what one could call homosexual-specific and homosexual-diffuse theoretical aims and methods—between, on the one hand, determining lesbian and gay authors or identity positions and, on the other hand, analyzing same-sex desires in terms of the ways in which they intersect with or diverge from a lesbian or gay identity. In short, scholars in this field must choose between lesbian and gay studies and queer studies, just as feminist scholars continue to debate whether their field should be called gender studies (gender-diffuse) or women's studies (gender-specific).[14] This fissure, far from signaling a crisis in lesbian and gay studies or queer theory, is a sign of its health. The inability and, especially, the refusal to demarcate a discipline with a curriculum based upon a stable lesbian and gay identity prevents "us" from ever being complacently certain of who "we" are and of what "we" are doing.

The troubled experience of women's studies should instruct those who seek to institutionalize lesbian and gay studies, for the failure of the former to ground itself in "woman" as an entity of whatever status should serve as a warning that "lesbian" or "gay" will also fail, and for good reason. The shifting and sometimes contradictory discursive structures that fall under such headings are more legibly limned in their queerness by a theory that resists the easy binaries of gender or sexuality. The discomfort of refusing the homo/hetero and male/female distinctions can only be exacerbated by facing up to the inescapable continuity and the necessary incommensurability between lesbianism and feminism. Although depriving us of a grand theory, this discomfort may keep us honest.

In the current academic climate, discussions of homosexuality are forced to answer the question of whether or not they are subversive. Critics too often hasten to align themselves on the side of the angels and feel compelled to argue that their chosen text is properly radical. Whatever thinking that takes place is thus burdened by evangelical demands. Under the pressure of such circumstances, Sedgwick's conclusion to her essay on *The Importance of Being Earnest* is heartening. Sedgwick refuses to answer the question of "whether [Wilde's] play

. . . 'stabilizes' or 'destabilizes' the holy name of the family," for "to pose the question in this way" is to "reinforce the essentially theological assumption that any cultural manifestation under study must respond first and last to the moralistic questions 'Can it be saved?' and 'Can it save us?'"[15] If the bottom line of queer theory is whether or not it will redeem us from the heteropatriarchy, critical inquiry is doomed to dogmatism.

NOTES

1. Gayle Rubin, "The Traffic in Women," *Toward an Anthropology of Women*, ed. Rayna Reiter (New York: Monthly Review Press, 1975).

2. Judith Butler makes a somewhat different point in "Against Proper Objects," where she argues that "the theoretical distinction between feminist and lesbian/gay studies effects a refusal of the first term, 'gender,' through an assimilation of its elided sense, 'sex,' to the second set of terms, 'sex and sexuality.' Indeed, only by reducing feminism to 'gender,' then implicitly conflating gender with sex, i.e., 'female or male,' and then explicitly declaring 'sex' to be one of its two proper objects, can lesbian and gay studies establish itself as the proper successor to feminism" (*differences* 6.2 and 3 [1994]: 3).

3. Jill Johnston, among others, popularized the phrase.

4. Monique Wittig, "One Is Not Born a Woman," *The Straight Mind* (Boston: Beacon, 1992) 9-20.

5. Havelock Ellis, *Studies in the Psychology of Sex*, vol. 1, pt. 4 (New York: Random House, 1942) 258.

6. Gayle Rubin, "Sexual Traffic," an interview with Judith Butler, *differences* 6.2 and 3 (1994) 88.

7. Katie King, "Producing Sex, Theory, and Culture: Gay/Straight Remappings in Contemporary Feminism," in *Conflicts in Feminism*, ed. Marianne Hirsch and Evelyn Fox Keller (New York: Routledge, 1990) 83.

8. Judith Butler, "Imitation and Gender Insubordination," in *Inside/Out: Lesbian Theories, Gay Theories* (New York: Routledge, 1991) 29.

9. *Professions of Desire: Lesbian and Gay Studies in Literature*, ed. George E. Haggerty and Bonnie Zimmerman (New York: MLA, 1995) 130.

10. Introduction, *Professions of Desire* 2.

11. *Professions of Desire* 185. Nunokawa also discusses "the ubiquitous contemporary influence of the coming-out story" (184).

12. An exception to this is *The Lesbian and Gay Studies Reader*, ed. Henry Abelove et al. (New York: Routledge, 1993).

13. *Professions of Desire* 54.

14. My thanks to Dana Heller for pointing out this comparison.

15. *Professions of Desire* 206.

When *Lambs* and *Aliens* Meet

Girl-faggots and Boy-dykes Go to the Movies

MICHÈLE AINA BARALE

Even though gay studies shares some intellectual kinship with feminism, more often than not conversations between the two fields have been superficial at best. Head noddings, which is to say footnotings, are the friendly responses of each to each, although there are some exceptions, of course.[1] But more frequently, each lives its disciplinary life as if the other did not exist or, as is all too often the case, as if the other were a hostile presence. The causes for their mutual discomfort, if not downright distrust, are to be found both in theoretical differences and in the ways each understands itself to be invested in the academy.

Feminism worries that gay studies functions conservatively, its male focus effectively maintaining the marginality of both women's studies programs as well as gender scholars and their issues. No small part of feminism's distrust of queer theory arises from gay studies' entanglement with high theorists, a number of whom are gender-impaired in terms of analysis. Moreover, given the ways in which feminism has labored to maintain close and energetic ties between those outside and those within academia—a labor best demonstrated in its decades-long debates about activism versus intellectualizing—gay studies' use of densely theorized analysis seems to call for a degree of academicism in its practitioners that sets many a feminist's teeth on edge. Equally troubling is the traditional canon's compatibility with many of gay studies' purposes. It is feared that the canon-comfortable fit has accorded gay studies' concerns a far speedier and even more respectful entry into academia than women's studies has experienced.

In its turn, queer theory also suspects feminism of harboring repressive tendencies. Queer theory worries that some part of feminism's procensorship efforts can work toward the continued suppression of nonnormative sexualities—even to the point of playing into the hands of the political right wing's so-called family-value-focused attacks on homosexuality—and thus views feminism as inhospitable to queer intellectual and possibly even political agenda. Moreover, queer theory's insistence that gender alone cannot offer an adequate explanation of sexuality or its oppressions means that it has necessarily had to remove gender from its initial stages of analysis in order to better see sexuality's operation. Whether gender will be reentered into its theorizing remains to be seen, since it also has to be said that some male theorists are uninterested in working with the sorts of noncanonical literature that feminism finds so richly useful. But by its foregrounding of sexuality, queer theory has made a place for male homosexuality in discussions of oppression and, as a result, made nuanced and problematic our conceptualizing of faggotry's place in patriarchy. The bulk of queer theory's recent analytical effort has been expended in disentangling gay maleness from normative masculinity, thereby doing for itself what lesbian-feminism had begun for itself in the late 1970s. In this sense, queer theory's male-centeredness is exactly what is called for at this moment, and feminists' dismay at the seeming continuation of the same old "men first" model appears to miss the point, since what it enables is the very interrogation of maleness that feminism has been calling for over the past two decades.

Even putting such discomforts as these aside, both fields name and locate the sources of oppression in significantly different ways. Until very recently, and despite nearly a decade of highly articulated critiques by women of color, feminism has insisted on gender as not only the primary category of women's identity—hence one able to mediate the seemingly less substantial differences of race, ethnicity, class, and sexuality—but also as the primary source of oppression, the main cultural means by which unequal significations are instituted. Queer theory, on the other hand, understands sexuality as the "vector of oppression," as a system of sexual oppression that "cuts across other modes of social inequality, sorting out individuals and groups according to its own intrinsic dynamics."[2] As a result, queer theory has been thus far unable to enter gender's asymmetry into its analysis of sexuality. In a kind of impasse, feminism cannot usefully understand its own logical limitations (gender does not fully explain sexuality's operations), while queer theory seems unable to see around its self-imposed handicaps (sexuality's cultural meanings play themselves out within gender's asymmetries).

I do not mean to suggest that relationships between the two fields are solely superficial, hostile, or even merely ritualized forms of *politesse*. Some of the labor needed to allow them to make mutual use of their congruencies and divergings has already been undertaken. However, despite attempts to more comprehensively enter feminism's concerns with gender into considerations of sexuality, it remains the case that many feminists and most women's studies programs display a distinct wariness when matters of gay studies' institutionalization and queer theory's analytical uses of gender are brought up for consideration, just as it remains the case that gay studies, for reasons both good and ill, has been primarily male in terms of its focus as well as its major theorists. Even though a number of women have high profiles specifically as queer theorists—Judith Butler, Teresa de Lauretis, Jackie Goldsby, Cindy Patton, B. Ruby Rich, Gayle Rubin, Eve Kosofsky Sedgwick, Joan W. Scott, among others—and most current anthologies of queer writing attempt to balance gender offerings, the nearly complete absence of gender considerations in such highly influential theorists as Foucault has meant that gay theorizing has had to reprogram itself if it is to include lesbianism as part of its purview, since a gay male focus is its obvious default position.[3]

A perfect example of the nonresolution—the collision—of gender and sexuality can be found in Douglas Crimp's engagingly crabby essay "Right On, Girlfriend!"[4] Reflecting on gay film critic and historian Vito Russo's memorial service in 1990, Crimp's essay defends against accusations that queerdom is in any way involved in continuing its own oppression, but in so doing he makes feminism the fall guy and B. Ruby Rich Larry Kramer's demon twin.[5] Because I take Crimp's effort so seriously, I want to expend quite a bit of energy on it. My point in doing so is not to take Crimp—or, for that matter, B. Ruby Rich, who is voiced within Crimp's text—to task. I am not seeking to indict either of them for analyses unacceptable. Rather I am interested in thinking about how things would change were Crimp to more fully contemplate gender's complexity, and not just sexuality's, within feminism itself—were he to not understand feminism as monolithic, were he to take into consideration its fracturings and self-acknowledged contradictions, and therefore its richness. And I want to consider the potential reconfigurations that might emerge were Rich to align her sexual identity with gay maleness: were she to regender the ways in which we have understood and continue to understand—for good and ill reasons—the victim's role as solely female inhabited and the killer's actions as solely heterosexual. What I want, in a sense, is to make Crimp one of the dykes and Rich one of the fags.

Especially striking in this essay is Crimp's intricate tracing of the connecting forces that killed Vito Russo, that maintain the closet as a function of "compulsory and presumptive heterosexuality"(305), and that awarded Jodie Foster an Oscar for her performance as Clarice Starling in Jonathan Demme's *Silence of the Lambs* (1991). While the essay's larger project is to provide a logic for self-initiated queer visibility as an antioppressive political maneuver, whether through writing, political demonstration, or gossip, Crimp also analyzes the ways in which critical discussions of Demme's film articulate their speakers' differing political agendas. For Crimp, reactions to the film are not only split along gender lines (women, including lesbians, defend the film, while gay men "usually decry it. And Jodie Foster gets caught in the middle" [311]) but are also characterized by conflicting senses of identity's meaning: "on the one hand, the identity of Foster and, on the other, the conception of identity itself" (311).

Jodie Foster's nearly known gayness has become one of queer gossip's favorite subjects, and hence we are not surprised by the layers of conflicting meanings that necessarily surround Demme's choice of her to play the young FBI agent who hunts down—and is in turn hunted by—serial killer Buffalo Bill, *a.k.a.* Jame Gumb. As Crimp notes, Gumb's scarves, makeup, nipple ring, and murdered boyfriend mark him as queer, at least in Hollywood's deployment of homophobic stereotypes.[6] So, too, does his envy of female bodies, which he can only obtain for himself by butchery, a murderous misogyny which itself stereotypes and misfocuses on gay men as women's greatest danger. Women's, and particularly feminists', pleasure in the film, Crimp suggests, stems

> not only from the strength and intelligence of Foster's character, Clarice, but also from her independence from an array of alternately annoying or sinister patriarchal figures, although just *how* independent is a matter of contention. But Clarice does reject every attempt to put the make on her; her commitment is to the captured woman. (309; italics are Crimp's)

As Crimp correctly notes, however, Demme neglects "to follow through on his film's antipatriarchal logic," since he relocates patriarchy's pathology by "homosexualizing the psychopaths"—both Buffalo Bill and Hannibal Lecter—"whose disturbing appeal can hardly be divorced from his camp, effete intelligence" (309–10). It is a patriarchal displacement literally seen in the film's final scenes as Clarice Starling is stalked by Gumb's gaze, which becomes that of the spectator as well.

The film, says Crimp, thus polarizes, on the one hand, along the lines of gender: "For gay men, Foster is a closeted oppressor; for lesbians, she's a role model." It polarizes, on the other hand, along lines of identity: "Castigating Foster as oppressor both presumes her (closeted) lesbian identity and presumes that identity precedes and determines political enactment." In other words, for gay men, Foster's identity as a real-life lesbian who willingly takes on the role of FBI agent Starling necessarily implicates her in media-instigated attempts at gay male pathologizing. However, feminists' praise of Foster as role model, by contrast, accepts her feminism as itself constitutive of her identity (311). Both sets of viewers assume that Foster's personal commitments and politics are either aligned with those of the character she performs (feminist viewers) or are belied by that performance (gay males).

Earlier in his essay, Crimp has noted B. Ruby Rich's lack of surprise at this gender division in the film's reception, and he quotes her: "Male and female desires, fears, and pleasures in the cinema have rarely coincided, so it should come as no surprise that dyke and faggot reactions to this movie are likely to diverge as well" (311). And a paragraph later Crimp quotes Rich again: "I'm not willing to give up the immense satisfactions of a heroine with whom women can identify. Not willing to reduce all the intricate components of this movie down to the pass/fail score of one character. Please excuse me if my attention is focused not on the killer, but on the women he kills." Crimp then returns to Rich one final time: "And her defense concludes, 'Guess I'm just a girl.'" Crimp reads that girlish conclusion as indication that

> in this debate, Rich's identification, her politics, emphasizes gender identity over sexual identity. As we know from her writing, in debates *within* feminism, Rich is perfectly capable of reversing the emphasis [italics are Crimp's]. Rich's identity is not fixed, does not determine her political identification; rather her political identification momentarily fixes her identity: "Guess I'm just a girl." But where is the lesbian in this picture? *Hasn't she again been rendered invisible? And what, if not outing, will make her visible?* [italics mine] (311)

I think that we have to take those last two sentences quite seriously, since it is indeed the common case that femininity can obscure dykehood and that the clarity of public perceptions of lesbian visibility gets severely myopic if all the queers are wearing dresses. On the other hand, feminism's critics have long attempted to discredit its practitioners by casting doubt upon feminists' sexuality—if they critique male privilege then they must hate men and therefore they inevitably sleep with women—as well as their gender identity. As much as I admire Crimp's essay and his own fearless honesty, what he asks of Rich (whom he acknowledges as "an 'out' lesbian" [311]) is not only a kind of self-simplification—that she mono-tonize her identity so that her queerness comes to the fore—but impossible. Rich's, indeed, most lesbians', experiential history is twofold; it is both gendered female and sexually identified as gay/queer.

Gender and sexuality cannot be experienced separately—not by Rich and not by Crimp either. Crimp's difficulty with Rich's response to the film is indicative of the depth of the struggle that feminism and a concomitant focus upon gender and queer theory and a concomitant focus upon sexuality experience in uniting under a single rubric. Moreover, Crimp's careful analysis of Jodie Foster's problematic identity in all this—that it is precisely the invisibility of her own queer identity's gossiped fact that makes so troublesome her visible role as both the victim and the cop in the film's homosexualizing of the pathological—does not extend itself to Rich herself. After all, isn't Rich precisely playing against well-established stereotypes of feminists in naming herself "girl"? Surely the fact that B. Ruby Rich is *a.k.a.* dyke means that her gender claims have to be heard within a sexually identified context. Can she only be "out" as a *lesbian?* Hasn't she "outed" herself, in essence, as a *girl-feminist,* a claim for a hyphenated identity that feminism certainly might find politically antagonistic in those over the age of ten? No matter how post postfeminism is, the use of "girl" in reference to an adult female still gets our attention, particularly when the term is employed by a feminist for herself. I take that self-girlification of Rich's as a claim to outlawry and not as an attempt to situate herself in a virtuous niche in gender's political economy. At the very least the title is ironic. It signals that Rich knows that she is being "bad" in her gender loyalty but that to be disloyal is no better. She claims herself as a gender patriot, therefore, but does so in a diction that is self-disparaging in its self-diminution.

On the other hand, Rich appears not to see the sexuality that does indeed impel Buffalo Bill's violence: Demme removes even "the wan hints of sex or romance" present in the original novel in order to "transform the usually action-heavy police procedural into a drama made up of relationships and emotional intensity," she writes in her review of *Silence of the Lambs.*[7] And she is correct; the film does not situate Clarice as the recipient or enactor of romantic fantasies; it even edits out the novel's suggestions that Scott Glenn's character, Crawford, Clarice's superior in the Bureau, feels possibly and inappropriately attracted to her. Clarice is all FBI business at all times. However, when Rich claims that "the women who are his prey become victims of a clinical, even taxidermic interest that is not even remotely sexual" due to the film's treatment of Buffalo Bill's serial murders, as well as his "very nature" (a curiously vague phrase), Rich misses the mark (59). It is true that Buffalo Bill does not kill women in order to satisfy perverse but heterosexual desires. He kills them so that he can *not* be male, so that he can clothe his body in their skin and become the woman of some male's desire. His murders are the result of homosexual desires he can negotiate only when they are translated into a woman's body.

The casting of transvestites as killers in films allows everyone *but* the heterosexual male to be vaguely but nonetheless guiltily associated with homicide. Cross-dressing the killer makes a "woman" the visible performer of murder, even as it also makes queer the man whose repressed homosexuality is the cause of his murderous actions—something that the films would have us understand by means of implicit cues or explicit, pseudoclinical explanation.[8] Buffalo Bill does not desire women; he wants to be one. It is not that his actions are not sexually motivated. It is that they are not heterosexually motivated. Rich's relief—"Living in a culture that has conflated violence with eroticism so totally and unapologetically, I'm sick of the gender-specific horrors that inevitably result" (59)—comes at some expense, therefore, since not only are his victims still female but their deaths are brought about by queer desires. However "clinical" Buffalo Bill's interests may be, it is nonetheless the case that Rich, like Crimp, can be identifiably located on both sides of a murderous equation: Rich and Crimp are equally queer and equally likely to be the victim of another's repressed sexual desire. And both, it should be added, are equally able to imagine themselves as heroic rescuers.

Let's continue thinking about *Silence of the Lambs* for a little while longer. And let's include, as well, another film, James Cameron's *Aliens* (1986). I admit to having viewed both repeatedly, not only pleasurably but obsessively. My equal love and loathing of the two have a great deal in common, but in neither film is it the case that I find myself involved in a deep identification with only the female victims. Certainly in *Silence of the Lambs* I want the senator's daughter rescued and am greatly cheered by her toughness and guts in the face of danger. On the other hand, I am made profoundly unhappy by the ever-squealing girl-child, Newt, the object of Ripley's efforts in *Aliens*. Even though Newt, like Ripley, is every bit as courageous as the Marines, the ways in which we are to understand Ripley's rescue of her—as proof that beneath that double bandoliered breast and just behind those fire-spitting guns beats a surrogate maternity ready, any time, anywhere, to do battle with the meanest of alien hyperreproductive bitches and their daughters— makes that feisty child representative of all those cultural forces that canonize maternal selflessness. If *Silence of the Lambs* homosexualizes pathology and thereby allows patriarchy to go clean, *Aliens* pathologizes both viviparous maternity *and* penetration, thereby sanitizing that which is already squeaky clean: asexuality.

It is difficult not to see *Aliens* as a terrified response to AIDS, as grossly metaphorizing fears of contagion via not only penetration but bodily fluids. At the same time, it is also impossible not to see the film as equally terrified of what we might term "maternal urges." Our supposedly inalienable mammalian right to enwombment and live birth is made horrific and fatal, the result of a parasitic female need to penetrate the bodies of any human host in order to reproduce the species. In a powerful conflation, Cameron thus makes that which is most dangerous that which is both penetrating and monstrously fecund. In so doing, faggots and mothers come to occupy the same site—that of the alien body which itself appears in a variety of forms: dragonlike creatures of various shapes and sizes whose maturational relationship to one another remains unclear. It's as if the film cannot quite understand the ways in which maternity and faggotry are related, but remains nonetheless cognizant that they pose not only equal but distinctly related dangers. Such a maternal-fag-phobia pulls together femininity and perverse sexuality in more complex ways than does Foster-as-Starling, and suggests, possibly, the limits of Crimp's argument. But first there's still more to be said about *Aliens*.

Given the film's fears of maternity and penetration, it's not surprising that rescue comes in the form of a reconfigured family, one whose ties are neither domestic nor erotic. The new family unit is composed of three adults and a single, endlessly "gone missing" child: the kick-ass adoptive mother, Ripley; Hicks, her Marine boy companion (he takes orders, smiles appreciatively at her bravery, likes kids, and promises to kill her rather than let an alien impregnate her); and Bishop, the "synthetic person." Bishop's thin, nearly wasted body suggests disease. And his knife game with the boys in the mess room evokes obvious s/m parallels.[9] When, at the knife game's conclusion, Ripley notices that a small cut on Bishop's hand is leaking the milky semenlike fluid that serves as synthetic's blood, she suddenly recognizes his "nature" and warns him away from her. She is unwilling to let go of her mistrust of the "species" despite assurances that his "line" has now been (politically) corrected. And finally, of course, there is the lost girl-child, Newt, the sole remaining survivor of the terra-farmer families sent to colonize the planet.

Evacuated of sexuality, this new, synthetic family both resists and invites our Oedipal imaginings. Ripley, as dyke-coded a figure as one

might find short of the muscle-flexing Vasquez, does not invite speculation about the likelihood of a future romance with her Marine sidekick,
although his role as Robin to her Batman does offer us some queer
possibilities.[10] If Bishop were going to have sex we really can't tell if his
partner would be a machine, the alien body he has dissected and
studied with noticeable passion, or Hudson's, whose hand was joined
with his own in the knife game. Where sexuality does reside is in the
figure of Newt. It is her small, stringy-haired, dirty-faced body whose
danger of penetration impels the narrative of search. Hers is the body
whose capture and cocooning forces us to actively wonder if she has
already been "interfered with," since the film's frenzied pace never
allows us to clearly understand the exact series of events that lead to
birthing monster babies. It is the child body that is sexualized, wrapped
round with evocations not only of kidnapping and molestation—
though certainly that—but also with an alienated incest: those monstrous births will issue from the sexual/reproductive activities of the
same alien mother who made similar use of her parents.

What compels me to watch these films again and again is that I, like
Ripley, like Starling, can test my ability to withstand exposure to the
utterly terrifying. I can face serial killers who wish to inhabit my flesh
and creatures who cannot control their monstrous need to penetrate me.
Are such horrors gender specific? Not hardly. Males, particularly young
men and gay men, are the frequent victims of serial killers; young boys
are no less vulnerable to incest than are young girls. And I would thus
assume that men as well as women, fags as well as dykes, would
identify with Starling, with Ripley, with tough little Newt and the
senator's gutsy daughter. As Hudson's arrogance subsides into a long
whine of fear, bemoanings that are equally annoying and amusing, I
recognize myself in him even as I want to be as fearless as Ripley. When
Vasquez chins herself while clearly besting Hudson in a moment of
verbal sparring early in the film; when she takes up the role of pointman
as the Marines first enter the immense darkened and dripping structure
of the colonists; and when, at the very moment of death, she manages to
disparage male authority ("You always were an asshole, Gorman," she
tells the Captain as they mutually clasp a grenade)—at such times my
own cowardice is unwanted—and perfectly clear.

These moments in *Aliens,* when I fear my kinship with Hudson and
recognize my lack of resemblance to Vasquez, are ones when my own
dyke-identity fails me.[11] I'm not the bold Ripley; I'm not the magnificent
Vasquez: instead, I'm the miserable Hudson, quaking with fear, certain
we're all going to die. I can't even imagine myself as Bishop—coolly
competent on his computer and hence able to fly the rescue ship into an

impossibly small space with a safety margin of mere seconds. Every time I try to map myself upon a queer, brave site, I slide right off, and my valorous fantasies turn tail and join Hudson, who is off in the corner, whimpering. In *Silence of the Lambs,* as the autopsy of one of the victims proceeds, I want to turn away from that naked, female body. It is important that I refuse to identify with her, with any possibility of my own victimization, torture, murder: I do not want to situate myself within that agonized domain. And as luck would have it, I don't have to. I can align with Starling, who, having fought to be allowed to witness the autopsy, smears Vicks on her upper lip—*just like the guys*—and steels herself for the ordeal, ultimately discovering in the victim's mouth the piece of evidence that will enable the crime to be solved. I turn to Starling at this moment because she is *not* the helpless female body, dead and about to be further splayed. I attach myself to Starling because she is the alternative to death.

Gay male and girl-feminist viewers are surely as desirous of, and have as much need for, lessons in courage as I. Moreover, I suspect that the more visibly likely sites of viewers' self-mappings in the film—upon bodies similar in gender or in implied sexuality—are not the sole sites of affiliation. Other shared identities also come into play, by necessity and by choice. Both gay males and lesbians might well find that Vasquez and Bishop, Buffalo Bill and Hannibal Lecter, also provide valid sites and even desirable articulations of self-understanding or cultural insight.

For all of us, however—for fag and dyke alike—wherever it is that we enter ourselves into the films, the price of admission is that a degree of self-alienation is demanded of us. If we are to gain the benefit of tutelage in valor, we must also experience ourselves pitted against ourselves, saved from a horror which is as much a part of us as it is a threat to us. My hatred, in both films, is that I am only too aware that their pedagogical profiles in courage necessitate that an important part of my identity become the very thing that is my murderous enemy. In *Silence of the Lambs,* it is my own sexual identity that threatens me; in *Aliens* it is my biological potential that is alien. In both films, if I am to be rescued I must affiliate with institutions—the FBI, the Marines—licensed to penetrate and destroy alien threats to the national whole. That threat is precisely what I am governmentally perceived to be.

Bringing gender into an analysis of sexuality is inevitable; the two feel so knotted together in our experience. It goes without saying that gender will differentiate that experience—that's a corollary fundamental to feminism. But it also seems to go unsaid that the experience of queerness works to erase, or at least obscure and complicate, some of those sure differences. Crimp's and Rich's readings of *Silence of the*

Lambs are more intent than they need be upon specifying and polarizing their viewer's self-sitings as either gendered or queer. What's so lovely about seeing movies, about darkened theaters and dimmed rooms, is that there's just no telling how I—or you—might locate ourselves upon the screen. Whoever you long to be, for this moment, for once, wishing can make it so.

NOTES

I am much indebted to Rick Griffiths, Margaret Hunt, Janet Jacobs, Andy Parker, and Julie Willis, who have been willing to share my movie obsessions, convey some of their own, and help me work through the twists and turns of my thought.

1. For examples of queer readings employing feminist approaches, see, for instance, the following essays in *The Lesbian and Gay Studies Reader,* ed. Henry Abelove, Michèle Barale, and David M. Halperin (New York: Routledge, 1993): Tomás Almaguer, "Chicano Men: A Cartography of Homosexual Identity and Behavior" 255–73, and John J. Winkler, "Double Consciousness in Sappho's Lyrics" 577–94. For instances of gender-focused analyses in which gay (male) theory plays a part, see, in the same anthology, Teresa de Lauretis, "Sexual Indifference and Lesbian Representation" 141–58, and Michèle Barale, "When Jack Blinks: Si(gh)ting Gay Desire in Ann Bannon's *Beebo Brinker*" 604–15.

2. Gayle Rubin, "Thinking Sex: Notes for a Radical Theory of the Politics of Sexuality" in *The Lesbian and Gay Studies Reader* 3–44. Let me continue this quotation just a little further: "It [the system of sexual oppression] is not reducible to, or understandable in terms of, class, race, ethnicity, or gender. Wealth, white skin, male gender, and ethnic privileges can mitigate the effects of sexual stratification. A rich, white male pervert will generally be less affected than a poor, black, female pervert. But even the most privileged are not immune to sexual oppression. Some of the consequences of the system of sexual hierarchy are mere nuisances. Others are quite grave. In its most serious manifestations, the sexual system is a Kafkaesque nightmare in which unlucky victims become herds of human cattle whose identification, surveillance, apprehension, treatment, incarceration, and punishment produce jobs and self-satisfaction for thousands of vice police, prison officials, psychiatrists and social workers" (22).

3. Judith Roof, for example, points out that "in a recent issue of the respectable *South Atlantic Quarterly,* titled *Displacing Homophobia,* of the thirteen articles only one, Eve Sedgwick's 'Across Gender, Across Sexuality: Willa Cather and Others,' even purports to treat lesbian sexuality, and it rather spectacularly takes the same male homosexual route as Freud. The rest of the articles are written by men, mainly about men. Somehow in displacing homophobia the editors have also displaced lesbians, manifesting a kind of sapphophobia." Judith Roof, *A Lure of Knowledge: Lesbian Sexuality and Theory* (New York: Columbia University Press, 1991) 213.

4. Douglas Crimp, "Right On, Girlfriend!" in *Fear of a Queer Planet: Queer*

Politics and Social Theory, ed. Michael Warner (Minneapolis: University of Minnesota Press, 1993) 300–20.

5. The occasion that puts him on the defensive—and it must be said that his defense feels wonderfully offensive—is a speech Larry Kramer delivered at the memorial service. As Crimp transcribes it, Kramer rhetorically asks "Who killed Vito?" so as to answer: "As sure as any virus killed him, we killed him. Everyone in this room killed him. Twenty-five million people outside this room killed him. Vito was killed by 25 million gay men and lesbians who for ten long years of this plague have refused to get our act together. Can't you see that?" 301). Kramer then goes on to "name names—mostly those of closeted gay men and lesbians in the entertainment industry" (301). It is Kramer's listing of names that allows Crimp to undertake his own "short archeology of 'outing'" (305), concluding in a defense of Michelangelo Signorile's column "Gossip Watch" in *Outweek* and an attack upon the straight media's creation of "outing": "Signorile's initial impulse was . . . to 'out' enforcers of the closet, not to reveal the 'secret' of homosexuality, but to reveal the 'secret' of homophobia. For it is only the latter that is truly a secret, and a truly *dirty* secret. As for the former, the speculation about the sexuality of celebrities, gossip is a privileged activity for queers, too" (308).

6. Notes Crimp: "Maybe these features don't have to add up to a homophobic stereotype within the complex alignments of sexuality and pathology represented in *The Silence of the Lambs,* but they most certainly do within the history of their deployment by Hollywood, the history Vito Russo wrote" (309).

7. B. Ruby Rich, review of *Silence of the Lambs,* in *Village Voice,* March 5, 1991, 59.

8. And here I am thinking of *Dressed to Kill* and *Psycho.*

9. Bishop carries out a knife demonstration on Hudson's hand, which has been forcibly coupled to his own; this is followed by jokes about the great "poontang" found on the last mission, "poontang" which, so the mess room jokes go, turned out to be *male* in Hudson's case.

10. It is interesting that the film's out-takes include a brief scene in which romance is a hazily flirtatious but distinct possibility between the two.

11. Thanks to Julia K. Willis, who figured this out for me after a scary-movie-filled weekend in a cheap motel.

AUTOBIOGRAPHY CANNOT BE SEPARATED FROM THE HISTORY OF
INSTITUTIONS AND THE CONSTRUCTION OF SUBJECTS WITHIN
THESE INSTITUTIONS; IN OTHER WORDS, MY STORY IS
"MY OWN" ONLY TO A DEGREE.

—THOMAS PIONTEK[1]

Where Experience and Representation Collide
Lesbians, Feminists, and the AIDS Crisis

KATIE HOGAN

In 1988 feminist cultural theorist Paula Treichler wrote: "Given the intense concern with the human body that any conceptualization of AIDS entails, how can we account for the striking silence, until very recently, on the topic of women in AIDS discourse?" ("AIDS, Gender, and Biomedical Discourse" 193). Feminists, with a few remarkable exceptions, have been slow to recognize both the impact of AIDS on women and the implications of HIV for feminist theory.[2] Lesbians, unless they identify as feminist or as "political," are often indifferent and ignorant.[3] Complicating the situation is the fact that feminist and queer theorists often reject writing about women and queers in terms of their bodies and "experiences" for fear of reinscribing the biological essentialism that has, throughout history, been used to control and persecute them. As feminist philosopher Elizabeth Grosz explains, "Where patriarchs have used a fixed concept of the body to contain women, it is understandable that feminists would resist such conceptions and attempt to define themselves in non- or extracorporeal terms" (*Volatile Bodies* 14).

I believe that there are multiple costs for women and queers, and for feminist theory, in this tendency to privilege a non- or extracorporeality. Women's health, bodies, and deaths, and the health, bodies, and deaths of queers, clash with postmodern feminist and queer theory's often unexamined inclination to subordinate the body to the mind. As Grosz puts it, "Feminist theory . . . has tended, with some notable exceptions, to remain uninterested in or unconvinced about the relevance of refocusing on bodies in accounts of subjectivity" (*Volatile Bodies* vii).

AIDS theorist John Erni reframes corporeality in the light of the HIV/AIDS pandemic by arguing that bodies are both "text and anti-text": "Personal encounters with suffering, disease, and death tend to reveal a dimension of [AIDS] . . . that exceeds representation: they foreground the material or corporeal dimension of the epidemic. . . . For many, the body cannot be easily deferred or ignored" ("Intensive Care" 53).

The work of Donna Haraway and Linda Kauffman, for example, continually pushes against traditional notions of bodies as inert and passive and explores bodies in terms of the exciting and fast-paced changes in technology, medicine, and science. Kauffman, for instance, examines how performance artists Bob Flanagan and Orlan disrupt fixed categories of meaning by weaving the practices and discourses of critical theory, technology, science, medicine, and sexuality into cultural intervention/expression. And Haraway repeatedly argues that techno-logical developments have the liberatory potential to usher in what anthropologist Emily Martin calls "the end of the body" in this "post-human" moment.

My focus in this chapter is not the future or even the present "post-human" moment, but the recent past. I want to explore, to quote from feminist/queer/AIDS theorist Cindy Patton, "the underlying assump-tions which simultaneously made woman both a radiant figure of sexual purity and a magnet for blame during the pandemic's first decade" (*Last Served?* 2). The numerous constraints that affect what and how AIDS will be talked about in terms of gender are saturated with cultural beliefs and histories that many queer and feminist literary critics rarely consider in today's contemporary critical scene: the para-doxical image of woman as both fleshy demon and abstract, disembod-ied symbol, as either the force of nurturance and social order or the source of pathology and destruction.

"EXPERIENCE"

My experiences in trying to write about my sister's struggle and death from AIDS in a feminist context made clear to me that academic writing connected to women's bodies, health, emotions, and experiences was suspect. As one of my peers, now a professor, remarked, "Your work is too immediate; too real." In addition to the threatening immediacy of my project are the ways in which HIV/AIDS is still conceptualized as a male disease, with women figuring in only as "the partners of men," the mothers of HIV-infected innocent children, or reckless and pathetic drug abusers.[4] Even some well-known cultural studies on AIDS include short blurbs about women and statistical risk, but the reluctance to theorize women's bodies and gendered experiences and deaths in terms of HIV suggests that the corporeal complexities of the pandemic may be in conflict with the practices of academic theorizing, even theorizing that proposes fundamental epistemological reconceptualizations. It should come as no surprise that in mainstream and popular discourse women are construed in the languages of statistics, gender and racial stereotypes, and, sometimes, activist rhetoric. In general, these representations offer little critique or resistance. By and large, grassroots feminists and queers have been peculiarly alone and isolated in their fight to have their voices heard. As HIV-positive Rebecca Denison writes,

> One of the biggest disappointments of my life was when I realized that the women's movement that I had been a part of for years couldn't help me. I had been involved in International Women's Day marches, Take Back the Night marches, and others. But I realized that, in the six years since my first women's studies class at UC Santa Cruz, no one had ever addressed AIDS as a women's issue. Never. Furthermore, of all the women I had met as an activist, only a few called me after word got out that I was HIV-positive. They weren't avoiding me. They just didn't know what to say. I thought to myself, "Where the hell have we been." ("Call Us Survivors!" 195–96)

For several years I have been obsessed with stories such as Rebecca Denison's and with my own experiences. I have been asked disturbing questions by academics regarding my evolving feminist-queer literary dissertation on AIDS. For example, in addition to my peer's observation that my work is too immediate, too "real," I have been asked the following: How is silence about women in AIDS discourse an academic argument? Is there much literature written by or about women with AIDS? Aren't most of the women with HIV straight, poor, and women of color? Are lesbians really at risk for HIV? and Do people ever question your right to speak about AIDS? As bell hooks writes, perceived nonconformity in graduate school and in the academy at large—in my case, trying to write about my experiences using various academic language—is "viewed with suspicion, as empty gestures of defiance aimed at masking inferiority or substandard work" (*Teaching to Transgress* 5).[5] Most of these questions are asked with little or no deliberate aggressiveness or hostility, and often out of unacknowledged ignorance. However, no matter how well-meaning, they always anger me. Why is it inconceivable that literary writing on AIDS cannot possess a transgressive sensibility and still occlude, distort, or constrain the experiences of women?

Today, with women and teenagers around the globe becoming HIV-infected at alarming rates, it is more difficult to read AIDS as coded male, although it is still associated in homophobic cultural mythology with representations of promiscuous, irresponsible, deviant, urban white gay men. Representations of women and AIDS are showing up in novels, poetry, and testimony, on television, in magazines, and in commercial films such as the recently released *Boys on the Side*. Women's organizations, for example, the New Jersey Women and AIDS Network, have placed women, gender, and race at the center of their policy, outreach, and services since the late 1980s. The Gay Men's Health Crisis has a Lesbian AIDS Project, now three years old. Medical research and policy paradigms are changing, although slowly, to meet the needs of women. And Elizabeth Grosz's call for a more "corporeal feminism" is an encouraging trend for academic queer feminists like myself who are working on the corporeality of women and AIDS.[6] While this "new" visibility of woman is hopeful, it alone cannot challenge, expose, or historicize the underlying gendered assumptions of the epidemic and the blind spots in feminist theorizing. The new visibility of women cannot erase the gendered narratives and assumptions that created women's initial invisibility and stereotypical presentations.

AIDS AND VICTORIAN IMAGES OF WOMEN

The late philosopher and cultural theorist Linda Singer argued in *Erotic Welfare: Sexual Theory and Politics in the Age of Epidemic* that the cultural anxiety and crisis mentality associated with HIV/AIDS is revitalizing entrenched cultural fears over women's sexuality and economic autonomy. In order to ward off threatening breakdown and ease the moral panic that many conservative discourses on AIDS predict, the notion of white, middle-class, virtuous femininity is held up as the norm. Similarly, Elizabeth Grosz observes that in AIDS prevention rhetoric, women alone are "the ones urged to function as the guardians of the purity of sexual exchange" (*Volatile Bodies* 196). In addition to targeting women as responsible for the transmission of HIV to men and innocent children (lesbian transmission is rarely addressed), this construction of woman as "guardian of purity" reinforces the pervasive belief that women's health counts only in terms of its impact on other people. In other words, the intensity of suffering, loss, and panic that ensues because of AIDS creates nostalgia for supposedly less ambiguous times—when women were always available to nurture the afflicted. Early twentieth-century lesbians, as Lillian Faderman has argued, gained prominence "because what they did could often be seen as housekeeping on a large scale—teaching, nurturing, healing—domestic duties brought into the public sphere" (*Odd Girls and Twilight Lovers* 23). The desire for this ministering angel can overwhelm our ability to read AIDS as a disease of women.

As Catherine Warren's research suggests, "many feminists stood by and silently watched women being dressed in tight red sheaths and stiletto heels or in Victorian white with a lamp held out in protest" ("The Empress's Old Clothes" 3).[7] Meanwhile, predictions of chaos and moral decay are exploding in a variety of public discourses, unleashing a cultural nostalgia for the disease-free heterosexual family, a rhetoric that has been historically linked to the regulation and control of all women's sexual, political, social, and economic expression.

LITERARY BODIES/LITERARY AIDS

When I turned to the outpouring of AIDS literature in 1990, the year my closeted brother-in-law died of AIDS-related conditions, I found in novels, poems, and plays few HIV-positive female characters, which did not surprise me. I have learned from people with personal experience that the publishing world is still largely controlled by white upper-middle-class people, and that many of the gay men writing on HIV and getting published were fortunate to have access to that world. I am grateful that these men were able to get their work published, for texts such as William Hoffman's *As Is*, Paul Monette's *Halfway Home,* and especially Alan Barnett's *The Body and Its Dangers* helped me to feel less alone. I read these works with a desperation that matched my furious reading of *The Second Sex* when I was twenty or lesbian and queer writing when I first came out in my late twenties and early thirties. I found in these books an alternative discourse, one that resisted the mass-media mythologizing and disembodied New Age rhetoric. I rarely found representations of women's complicated experiences in these gay texts or an awareness of the gendering of the HIV pandemic, but this seemed to match the mainstream cultural discourse, although nonliterary books such as *Women, AIDS, and Activism, AIDS: The Women,* and *Women and AIDS* had been published by small presses between 1988 and 1990.

But what did surprise me about these texts was not the number of absences or presences of female characters but the kinds of representations of women and gender relations that I encountered: conservative, traditional conceptions of femininity and gender, and, in some instances, outright misogyny. It has been extremely difficult to invent a language to describe my ambivalence toward this AIDS writing without being perceived as an antitheoretical, inflexible, simple-minded separatist. As bell hooks writes, "It is difficult to find a language that offers a way to frame critique and yet maintain recognition of all that is valued and respected in the work" (Introduction 49).

Victoria A. Brownworth's article "Someone Has To Say No: Women in Gay Male Writing," published in the *Lambda Book Report*, cracks open some of the tensions among communities of gay men, lesbians, feminists, and AIDS. Brownworth begins with a brief history of gay male writing in terms of literary representations of women. While never questioning the literary merit of gay male texts—in fact, Brownworth argues that some of these books are examples of great creative talent— she argues that female characters are constructed in gay writing just as they are in heterosexual texts: as either threats to male development and expression or as peripheral walk-ons. For example, "If one looks at the history of writing by gay men—Oscar Wilde, Jean Genet, and John Rechy are some examples that come to mind—their writing is parallel to the mass culture as far as the female characters are concerned: it is only the male characters who are different" (7). Female characters' basic literary function in gay and straight literature is either to hinder or serve the male hero; they lack contradiction, conflict, ambiguity, and complexity:

> Most often women are the good mommy or bad mommy, the anti-sex lesbian or feminist, the straight friend who is merely a foil and who ultimately either wants sex from a man he wants sex from, is the revolting older straight woman who wants sex from young men, or simply an ugly, fat, irritating, or repellant female walk-on character. (7)[8]

Unfortunately, a similar pattern of second-class citizenship emerges in the outpouring of AIDS fiction. "Nowhere have women been discarded more abruptly than in the literature of AIDS," Brownworth writes (8). "In these books the women exist to thwart or to serve—just as they do in heterosexual male fiction" (42).[9] In texts such as *Angels in America* and *Halfway Home*, one can discern a subtle glorification of traditional gender relations accompanied by imagery of women as nursemaids and servants.[10]

The character of Harper Pitt in Tony Kushner's prize-winning *Angels in America*, for example, despite her engaging eccentricity, her childlike imagination, and her exquisite sensitivity, seems more like a symbol or force that tempers the multiple stigmas associated with HIV infection than a complex character. In fact, in an entry on AIDS literature in the recently published *Heritage of Lesbian and Gay Literature*, the author observes that playwright Tony Kushner uses his heterosexual female character in the same way that he uses spectacle and the super-natural: to distance his work from the realities of AIDS. However, in contrast to female characters in Larry Kramer's *Normal Heart* and the late David Feinberg's novel *Eighty Sixed*, in which lesbian and straight female characters are depicted as cruel, self-absorbed, flakey, and indifferent to HIV, Harper Pitt is the ideal empath: she intuits Prior Walter's feelings and fears of death even before he himself can articulate them. Even her sexual longing, "I miss Joe's penis," could be seen in terms of the "straight woman hopelessly in love with gay man" plot, a plot device that Brownworth says reinforces the shallow and peripheral treatment of female characters.

I turned to novels written by women and found similar conservative sensibilities. For example, Alice Hoffman's highly publicized and best-selling novel, *At Risk*, tells the story of an eleven-year-old girl named Amanda Farrell who contracts HIV through an emergency blood transfusion. As a result, she and her family are ostracized by their suburban neighbors. This plot choice deliberately stirs up "compassion for every AIDS victim regardless of how he or she contracted the virus," argues literary critic Judith Laurence Pastore ("Suburban AIDS" 40). It is true that the novel tries to send a clear message that anyone can become infected with HIV, that AIDS, as many public health announcements claim, is a "democratic" disease. It is also true that the novel devotes considerable space to the mechanics of how one contracts HIV and dramatizes the fears that HIV induces. Yet a competing discourse threatens this humanitarian message.

According to the heroine's father, "Amanda's been murdered" (65). Amanda's Boston AIDS specialist, Dr. Ellen Shapiro, reminds Mr. Farrell that "this is nobody's fault" (69). The underlying assumption throughout the novel is that some people with AIDS deserve more sympathy than others, a formulation that has shaped public understanding of AIDS from the start. For while Hoffman clearly wants to contest, educate and reform, it seems more likely that her always already innocent girl heroine, her stay-at-home mom, and other markers of traditional gender and familial relations, ultimately reassure readers, who are assumed to be citizens of the so-called uninfected "general population," that AIDS will not destroy their families and social cohesion, even if one of its members becomes infected. As critic Joseph Dewey explains, *At Risk* is "not about AIDS. The virus seems less the subject than an occasion to test a family's resilience" ("Music for a Closing" 28).

When Hoffman's novel was presented in 1988 at the American Booksellers Association conference under glitzy lights and with a glossy cover, best-selling novelist David Leavitt rightly complained that *At Risk's* favorable public reception was linked to homophobia and the politics of the innocent victim. Other gay male writers echo Leavitt's feelings and point to *Newsweek's* mixed review of Paul Monette's memoir *Borrowed Time* while praising Hoffman's *At Risk* for its heartfelt, family qualities. "I fell in love with this book. I fell in love with this family," cheered the young-adult book writer Judy Blume.

Curiously, however, while Leavitt exposes the cultural politics of Amanda's character in terms of gay male sexuality and health, he seems unaffected by the novel's use of feminized innocence or by its refusal to imagine the complex ways in which gender and sexuality get constructed in relation to HIV. In other words, Leavitt and other critics seem oblivious to the implications of how idealized notions of femininity silence information and expression of women's sexuality and health.

The effects of the angelic sentimental girl in a contemporary AIDS novel significantly determines the presentation of several adult female characters. From the New Age, asexual, blonde, gothic Laurel Smith who intuitively guides Amanda to the next world to the creation of Polly Farrell, Amanda's defeated and long-suffering mother, Hoffman casts her female characters as women without ambivalence or needs. The novel breaks this pattern when Amanda's contentedly married mother collapses into Ned Reardon's (Amanda's doctor's) arms, at which time the two exhausted grownups kiss and notice that their body heat is steaming up the car windows.

But my interpretation of this scene is that here Hoffman clearly wants her readers to understand Polly's desire as irregular, as caused by the enormous stress and depletion associated with her child's dying from AIDS. The embrace and kiss is portrayed as warm, cuddly, affectionate, nonthreatening: it both unleashes and contains our culture's unconscious belief that AIDS is linked to every imaginable form of chaos—the demise of traditional families, the rise of nonmonogamy, promiscuity and deviant sexual practices. Traditional notions of gender relations and femininity are portrayed as the only defense against the chaos of HIV and AIDS.

At Risk is not interested in presenting complicated women characters who experience sexual arousal, let alone conveying in fiction the unglamorous, tedious, intricate experience of grief. It renders women's sexuality almost invisible and fails to consider the fact that women have HIV infection and AIDS, never mind presenting a female character with the disease. That is, the objections to *At Risk* and other examples of literary AIDS have been mostly articulated from a still patriarchal perspective, with hardly any commentary from feminists.

In short, adult female characters in many literary representations, especially if they are depicted as HIV-negative, white, and middle class, are portrayed as emotionally open, loving, even gifted and intuitive caretakers, yet their emotional service to others overshadows their own corporeality or transformations. In other words, as Linda Singer predicted, the fears associated with HIV—fears about engaging in gay sexual practices, sex work, belonging to a "minority" culture, using injecting drugs, to the fact of having a mortal, marked body whose discharges and fluids are conflated with death and shame—are tempered by an asexual, idealized conception of benevolent womanhood that will protect us from the chaos, disorder, and meaninglessness of AIDS. This desexualized femininity champions the individual rights of the stigmatized male; and it often helps to liberate gay male characters from being cast as symbols and signifiers of evil and sickness; but at the same time, this traditional notion of woman as "feminine" force and guardian of sexual purity is a form of silence that is linked to the regulation of women's sexual, political, social, and economic autonomy. The spectacle of angelic, benevolent femininity serves as a decoy for the broader cultural denial and distortion of women's experiences with HIV infection, in particular, the experiences of poor women and women of color.

Representations of HIV-infected female bodies in other venues, such as popular magazines and commercial film, reveal a similar construction of gender. For example, when Elizabeth Glaser died of AIDS in December 1994, *People* magazine placed her photograph on its cover and writer David Ellis compiled a list of quotations from friends and celebrities under the heading "Remembering an Angel of Hope." Glaser was called a "camp counselor," "a mother bear," and "just a mother who happened to have two children with AIDS." Her own experiences as an adult woman with AIDS were strategically overshadowed by this presentation of her as the devoted, asexual mother who bravely launched the first Pediatric AIDS Fund after the death of her young daughter.

Similarly, HIV-positive Mary Fisher, who spoke at the 1992 Republican National Convention, is described in *POZ* magazine by journalist Maureen Dowd as "the planet's most famous mommy with AIDS" and as "the Christmas angel." Fisher, observes former NGLTF executive director Torie Osborn, brings a "feminine force, a maternal fierceness, into AIDS," an image that Fisher consciously reinforces (Dowd, "Proud Mary" 35). For example, Fisher intersperses pictures of her two HIV-negative young sons throughout her recently published collection of speeches, a book whose subtitle emphasizes her maternal work: *A Mother Challenges AIDS*. One of Fisher's essays rejects the angry, feminist assertion that women have been "invisible" in AIDS, that they have not been given their "place":

More than a century ago, before radios and telephones and fax ma-
chines; before Dorothea Dix humanized mental health and *Uncle Tom's
Cabin* shook the morality from slavery; before many American women
had learned to read, there was the quilting bee, the weekly community
of women. . . . When, a century later, some San Francisco friends
decided that each name of lost loved ones should be captured on a
Quilt, the history of women was woven into the history of AIDS in
America.

Therefore, we women need not fight to find our place. It has been
given to us. We need only be true to who we are, women; to do what
women have done through the centuries: Wrap the family in the Quilt.
(*Sleep with the Angels* 56–57)

Fisher frames U.S. women's relationship to HIV by evoking the language of women's historical roles as caretakers and quilters, a political
strategy that middle-class white and black women have used brilliantly
in this country. When poor women of color have AIDS, however, it is
often impossible for them to weave this narrative of "woman" as
feminized quilt. Unlike Fisher, a wealthy, well-educated, socially connected white woman, poor women are often pegged as either bad
mothers/prostitutes or as IV drug users; or they are ignored by the
media altogether, unless they "repent" and start living their lives for
their children.[11] The color of a woman's skin as well as her socioeco-
nomic status often determines which slot in the representational hierarchy of HIV she will occupy: the maternal angel, the quilter/volunteer,
the bad mother, the swinging single, or the dangerous prostitute. In
other words, unless they are able to graft the sentimental figure of the
"good white mother" onto the limited representational narratives available to them, their complex histories and experiences are silenced.

I am not arguing that feminists and queers should reject these
representational strategies of Fisher and Glaser or accuse these women
of withholding the "truth." Instead, a careful analysis of their self-
presentations emphasizes the disturbing gendered and racialized narratives that structure the discourse of AIDS. Conventional ideas of
women, the "maternal," and the good citizen offer a smooth way to
mediate the stigmas.[12]

RACE, SYMPATHY, AND AIDS

A pattern of what cultural critic Wahneema Lubiano calls
"racialized gender" structures aspects of the relationship between
Whoopi Goldberg's and Mary Louise Parker's characters in the film
Boys on the Side.[13] For U.S. women of color between the ages of fifteen
and forty-four, AIDS is the third leading cause of death, yet this film

showcases an HIV-infected white middle-class woman.[14] In "Missing Persons: African American Women, AIDS and the History of Disease," Evelynn Hammonds observes that "when the threat of AIDS to women is discussed, no mention is made of African American women. When African American women are discussed, they are relegated to the drug abuser category or partners of drug abusers or bad mother category for passing AIDS onto their children" (8–9). These stereotypes of black women haunt *Boys on the Side*; its often straightforward use of the imagery of white women with AIDS, which, on average, is associated with innocence and tragedy, is problematic.

The film possesses all of the elements of the standard AIDS narrative: a nurturing, female helpmate/servant—in this case, a black woman—who is assumed not to be at risk and whose sexuality is dematerialized or erased; a celebration of heterosexuality; an infant, in this case, two children—the dead child who communicates with his sister, the Mary Louise Parker character, and the infant who is born just before Parker's character dies of AIDS. But most important, *Boys on the Side* focuses on an educated white middle-class woman with AIDS who adores sentimental romance films. This character choice brings into view the way in which notions of granting sympathy are intertwined with the politics of racialized gender.

In contrast to *Boys on the Side*, Perri Klass's complicated novel *Other Women's Children* presents a white pediatrician and novelist who, as a child and as an adult, is an avid reader of nineteenth-century fiction by women. Dr. Amelia Stern obsessively compares the life of one of her patients, a three-year-old African American boy dying of AIDS, to Harriet Beecher Stowe's Little Eva from *Uncle Tom's Cabin*. In a powerful chapter called "Has There Ever Been a Child Like Eva," Stern wonders why Little Eva, the well-cared-for child, dies, while the servant child Topsy escapes death. Stern comes to the awful realization that the rhetorical excess and flourish of a sentimental death is the privilege of white Christian children:

> Topsy is surely statistically the child in that book who should not have lived to grow up, but then, can you imagine Topsy in that death scene? Topsy is too bad to die; she lies and steals and could not be presumed to be going straight to heaven. . . . One child will survive, but not the one who has every reason to—good food, medical attention, love and gentleness surrounding her. That one will die. (98)

Klass's text outlines the rigid notions of who gets to be the sentimental heroine. It makes clear that Little Eva's spectacular death distances us from Topsy's overworked and undernourished body. By comparison, the HIV-infected white female character in *Boys on the Side*, also an avid "sentimentalist," is, like Little Eva, an always already innocent victim. The black female character played by Goldberg is a desexualized, lesbian ministering angel who acts as a surrogate therapist to the two straight white women in her life. Her identity and activities revolve around her service to them. Meanwhile, the harrowing experiences of women with AIDS, most of whom are poor women of color, are erased.

BODIES AS GIFTS

Given these disturbing images and distortions of women and AIDS in popular culture and in several examples of literature, it is remarkable to read Rebecca Brown's novel, *The Gifts of the Body*, in which Brown portrays the lives of men and women who are HIV-positive, including two female characters, one who is dying of AIDS. These two female characters are white and middle class, but their race does not function as an ideal standard of innocence or moral superiority. They are not held up as norms against which all other women, especially poor women and women of color, are judged.

The female character dying of AIDS, Mrs. Lindstrom, has lived all her life in an orderly middle-class neighborhood in a small neat house with a mailbox "painted red to look like a barn" (13). Her story, like all the stories in this novel, is told from the perspective of an unnamed lesbian home health aide who changes sheets, does laundry, makes meals, and bathes the ill. In describing the home health aide's tasks as interactions with her patients, Brown creates an embodied writing that neither reduces her characters to mere biological functions nor dissolves their bodies into a New Age ethereality stripped, as Beth Brant argues, of "physical evidences."

The gradual changes in the caretaker's relationship with Mrs. Lindstrom show the tender building of intimacy that happens through the connections and activities of bodies. Mrs. Lindstrom asks the home care aide to call her Connie. Then Connie asks her to help her take a bath, something Connie wouldn't allow her own children to do: "she wouldn't let her kids take care of her body, like feeding and bathing . . ." (15). While undressing Connie for her bath, the home health aide discovers that Connie has had a mastectomy. She bathes her, careful of her scar, dries her with a towel and helps her into her night clothes: "We walked her to her room. She pulled my arm around her waist and leaned on me to walk" (22). It is significant that Brown's characters always act in unison—"We walked her to her room"—the two women treating Connie's scarred, ill body as sacred.

Brown's style attends to the here and now of bodies, to the unsolved mysteries of death, the taboo of noises, sounds, eruptions, fluids, and languages. Her eleven chapters, with titles including "The Gift of Sweat," "The Gift of Tears," "The Gift of Hunger," "The Gift of Skin," "The Gift of Death," "The Gift of Mobility," and "The Gift of Hope," are never cynical, coy, saccharine, or overly abstract. Her writing escapes the potential traps of disembodied sentimentality. In her spare, detailed records of her characters' bodies as they live, lose bodily functions, and die, she provides, in fiction, a model of embodied theory. She sketches a way, as bell hooks might say, "to integrate feminist thinking and practice into daily life" (*Teaching to Transgress* 70).

The historical and social specificities of female bodies and queer bodies in relation to HIV are not inevitable theoretical burdens, destined to be invoked and then continually displaced. Bodies are historical effects and contestations. In Grosz's view, "Bodies have all the explanatory power of minds" (*Volatile Bodies* vii). Unfortunately, for many feminist and queer theorists, HIV and women is still perceived as a "single issue," a painfully transparent, "materialist," and potentially "essentialist" example of oppression that is often constructed *against* the very questions and concerns of feminist, cultural, and queer theory. Yet it is clearly *not* women and HIV that is reductive, essentialist, single-issue, transparent, or suspiciously accessible. Feminist silences on AIDS point to both blind spots in theories—feminist, lesbian, gay and queer—and to the underlying cultural assumptions that feed constructions of HIV. AIDS has always been a site of multiple contaminations, and it has always been in contact with a wide variety of feminist concerns, although the nature of this contact has yet to be fully written, historicized, described, named, and theorized, a project that several queer-feminist-activist scholars are just beginning.[15]

NOTES

1. See Thomas Piontek, "Unsafe Representations."

2. Paula Treichler and Catherine Warren of the University of Illinois at Champaign are in the process of theorizing why, even in the mid-1990s, feminists haven't taken on HIV/AIDS as a crucial theoretical/political issue. Warren and Treichler's article, "The Empress's Old Clothes," provides an analysis of representation and/or silence on women and AIDS in "the biomedical press, the mainstream women's and feminist press, and the alternative feminist press" (4). The article provides content analysis of mainstream

women's and feminist publications, from *Ms.* magazine to *New Woman* to *Vogue,* and lesbian and gay publications, including the *Advocate, Gay Community News,* and *Sparerib.* Warren's research suggests that lesbians who identified as "activists" (most of whom lived in cities such as New York and San Francisco) seemed to understand HIV/AIDS as a women's issue.

3. As Biddy Martin explains in "Sexual Practice and Changing Lesbian Identities," lesbians who identify as "political" and who have been active in AIDS movements have transformed their sexual practices through their experience. They do not interpret their involvement as "taking care of gay men": "Over the past several years, lesbians' involvements in AIDS activism and AIDS education have converged with the courageous work of sex radicals to challenge the rigid constructions of identity and to open curiosity about those fantasies and practices that cut across identity categories." Ruth L. Schwartz makes a similar argument in "New Alliances, Strange Bedfellows."

4. See Evelynn Hammonds, "Missing Persons."

5. Adolph Reed would undoubtedly read my use of bell hooks as exemplifying the traditional relationship between the "white liberal" and an "exceptional" black individual who serves to explain the black experience to the skittish, well-meaning, white liberal. Reed's *Village Voice* essay "What Are the Drums Saying, Booker?" offers a scathing review of the success of the "black, public intellectual," a category of thinkers that includes Cornel West, bell hooks, Henry Louis Gates, Michael Dyson, and others. For instance, Reed dismisses hooks and Dyson as "little more than hustlers, blending bombast, cliches, psychobabble, and lame guilt tripping in service to the 'pay me' principle" (35). But bell hooks's unflinching critique of white academic feminism and the academy at large cannot be dismissed as narcissistic, self-indulgent, capitalist sermon. I appreciate Reed's analysis of the academic star system, as well as some of his criticisms of postmodernism, but I think his characterization of hooks as commercial fluff embodies one of the academy's most cherished patriarchal rituals: a sadistic, mean-spirited dismissal of other scholars'—especially women's—work.

6. There has been an abundance of theoretical work on "essentialism" by such diverse theorists as Gayatri Chakravorty Spivak, who has called for a "strategic essentialism"; bell hooks, whose essays "The Politics of Radical Black Subjectivity" and "Post-Modern Blackness," in her book *Yearning: Race, Gender and Cultural Politics,* rethink essentialism from a black feminist perspective; Diana Fuss's popular *Essentially Speaking;* and political theorist Shane Phelan's article "(Be)Coming Out: Lesbian Identity and Politics," in which she argues that lesbian and queer academics need to refuse "the temptations to cloak crucial differences" with the discourse of "universality and to deny generalities for fear of essentialism" (786). The point I am trying to make here in relation to women and AIDS is that the possibility of having one's writing dismissed as "essentialist" has induced far more fear, intellectual conformity, and political complacency than has the possibility of having one's writing dismissed as too removed from complexities of women's lives. For example, Judith Butler and Joan Scott's collection, *Feminists Theorize the Political,* might be a very different, and I would argue a more nuanced book, if it were reframed as "the political theorizes the feminist." Spivak's "risk of essentialism" is an attempt to correct the privileging of philosophical musings, no matter how brilliant and learned, at the expense and subordination of feminist and lesbian and gay liberation movement histories and experiences. The fear of essentialism, and especially the fear of being dismissed by one's peers and professors as "essentialist," and therefore as

theoretically unsophisticated, may explain why feminists—queer and straight—have denied and repressed the enormous corporeal complexities of women and AIDS in the context of feminist, queer, and lesbian and gay theory.

7. In addition to Paula Treichler's and Cindy Patton's writings on the subject of women and HIV, Gayle Rubin's 1984 essay, "Thinking Sex," warned that AIDS hysteria would unleash legislative threats to civil liberties. Simon Watney makes a similar argument in *Policing Desire.*

8. The attitude toward women and HIV infection in nonfiction is less subtle in its misogyny than in fiction. In an April 1995 article in *Mirabella,* "A Dangerous Woman," David France interviews a gay man who refers to Brenda Jensen, an HIV-positive woman who has been jailed for having sex with a man, and who is the "dangerous woman" of the article's title, as "a cow who can't control herself" (96). In "New Alliances, Strange Bedfellows," Schwartz describes her complex experiences with men in the "AIDS industry." She writes that "the roles of class, race, and gender in people's lives . . . were brand-new and highly disputed concepts for gay men. The AIDS Foundation scheduled what was to have been a series of antiracism workshops for staff; during the first of the workshops, some white gay men were so offended by the suggestion that any of their actions could be racist that the remainder of the sessions were canceled" (237). In "Lesbian Involvement in the AIDS Epidemic," Nancy E. Stoller writes, "when I went to my supervisor, a gay man (and Southerner) who was director of the education department, to show him the text [of a brochure on lesbians and AIDS] and get formal permission for printing, for the first time in my work at the foundation I was told that my brochure would not be approved for printing because, in this case, unlike others, 'Lesbians are not at risk for AIDS.' Needless to say, I was shocked by his response" (278).

9. My dissertation (Katie Hogan, "'The Angel in the House': Gender, AIDS, and the Politics of Sentimental Representation") examines AIDS novels that either reinscribe or resist the literary tradition of sentimentality. While literary sentimentality in the United States is most often associated with nineteenth-century women writers, I argue that sentimentality is one of the most prevalent languages used in the construction of women in AIDS literature and popular culture. The sentimental figure of woman as guardian and symbol of purity and caregiving is pervasive in AIDS discourse and is, in fact, one of the only ways the subject of women and AIDS has been allowed to surface. I argue that this sentimentalization of women in the context of AIDS is both cultural silencing and social control. I also challenge the feminist scholarship that reclaims the sentimental in the name of oppressed women by showing how this feminist project is itself based on a white, Christian, middle-class, bookish experience.

10. An exception to this pattern is the last story in Allan Barnett's collection, *The Body and Its Dangers,* in which the focus is on the life of a lesbian with breast cancer, her life partner, and their daughter.

11. It is still common for federally funded researchers and medical practitioners to speak about women's health only in terms of how it affects *other people*—namely the fetus, babies, and men. (See Gena Corea, *The Invisible Epidemic* 40–51.) The few research studies designed for women and AIDS have been named "Pediatric AIDS" and "The Prostitute Study," hence the bad mother and the whore (Corea, *Invisible Epidemic* 44, 49).

12. See Beth E. Schneider and Valerie Jenness, "Social Control, Civil Liberties, and Women's Sexuality."

13. I am using Wahneema Lubiano's term *racialized gender* as articulated in "Black Ladies, Welfare Queens, and State Minstrels."

14. A similar reading could be applied to the films *Forrest Gump* and *Reality Bites*.

15. See Nancy Roth and Katie Hogan, *Gendered Epidemic: Identity, Theory, Policy, and Practice,* forthcoming. The collection brings AIDS into contact with a wide variety of feminist, lesbian, gay, and queer issues from the perspective of scholar-activists.

WORKS CITED

Barnett, Allen. *The Body and Its Dangers.* New York: St. Martin's, 1990.

Brown, Rebecca. *The Gifts of the Body.* New York: HarperCollins, 1994.

Brownworth, Victoria A. "Someone Has to Say No: Women in Gay Male Writing." *Lambda Book Report* 2.7 (October–November 1990): 6–8, 42.

Butler, Judith, and Joan W. Scott. *Feminists Theorize the Political.* New York: Routledge, 1992.

Corea, Gena. *The Invisible Epidemic: The Story of Women and AIDS.* New York: HarperCollins, 1992.

Denison, Rebecca. "Call Us Survivors! Women Organized to Respond to Life Threatening Diseases (WORLD)." In *Women Resisting AIDS: Feminist Strategies of Empowerment.* Ed. Beth E. Schneider and Nancy E. Stoller. Philadelphia: Temple University Press, 1995, 195–207.

Dewey, Joseph. "Music for a Closing: Responses to AIDS in Three American Novels." In *AIDS: The Literary Response.* Ed. Emmanuel S. Nelson. New York: Twayne, 1992, 23–38.

Dowd, Maureen. "Proud Mary." *POZ,* October–November 1994.

Ellis, David. "The Defiant One." *People,* December 19, 1994, 46–53.

Erni, John. "Intensive Care: Mapping the Body-Politics of AIDS." *Praxis* 3 (1992).

Faderman, Lillian. *Odd Girls and Twilight Lovers: A History of Lesbian Life in Twentieth-Century America.* New York: Penguin, 1991.

Fisher, Mary. *Sleep with the Angels: A Mother Challenges AIDS.* Wakefield: Moyer Bell, 1994.

France, David. "A Dangerous Woman." *Mirabella,* April 1995.

Fuss, Diana. *Essentially Speaking: Feminism, Nature, and Difference.* New York: Routledge, 1989.

Grosz, Elizabeth. *Volatile Bodies: Toward a Corporeal Feminism.* Bloomington: Indiana University Press, 1994.

Hammonds, Evelynn. "Missing Persons: African American Women, AIDS and the History of Disease." *Radical America* 24 (July 1992).

Hoffman, Alice. *At Risk.* New York: Berkley, 1988.

hooks, bell. *Teaching to Transgress.* New York: Routledge, 1994.

———. *Yearning: Race, Gender and Cultural Politics.* Boston: South End Press, 1991.

Klass, Perri. *Other Women's Children.* New York: Random House, 1990.

Lubiano, Wahneema. "Black Ladies, Welfare Queens, and State Minstrels: Ideological War by Narrative Means." In *Race-ing Justice, En-gendering Power.* Ed. Toni Morrison. New York: Pantheon Books, 1992, 323–61.

Martin, Biddy. "Sexual Practice and Changing Lesbian Identities." In *Destabiliz-*

ing Theory: Contemporary Feminist Debates. Ed. Michele Barrett and Anne Philips. Stanford: Stanford University Press, 1992, 93–119.

Martin, Emily. Flexible Bodies: Tracking Immunity in American Culture from the Days of Polio to the Age of AIDS. Boston: Beacon, 1994.

Pastore, Judith Laurence. "Suburban AIDS: Alice Hoffman's At Risk." In AIDS: The Literary Response 39–49.

Patton, Cindy. Last Served? Engendering the HIV Pandemic. London: Taylor & Francis, 1994.

Phelan, Shane. "(Be)Coming Out: Lesbian Identity and Politics." Signs, Summer 1993, 765–90.

Piontek, Thomas. "Unsafe Representations: Cultural Criticism in the Age of AIDS." Discourse 15.1 (Fall 1992).

Reed, Adolph. "What Are the Drums Saying, Booker? The Current Crisis of the Black Intellectual." Village Voice, April 11, 1995, 31–36.

Rubin, Gayle. "Thinking Sex: Notes for a Radical Theory of the Politics of Sexuality." In Pleasure and Danger: Exploring Female Sexuality. Ed. Carol S. Vance. Boston: Routledge, 1984.

Schneider, Beth E., and Valerie Jenness. "Social Control, Civil Liberties, and Women's Sexuality." In Women Resisting AIDS 74–95.

Schwartz, Ruth L. "New Alliances, Strange Bedfellows: Lesbians, Gay Men, and AIDS." In Sisters, Sexperts, Queers: Beyond the Lesbian Nation. Ed. Arlene Stein. New York: Plume, 1993, 230–44.

Singer, Linda. Erotic Welfare: Sexual Theory and Politics in the Age of Epidemic. New York: Routledge, 1993.

Spivak, Gayatri Chakravorty. The Post-Colonial Critic: Interviews, Strategies, Dialogues. Ed. Sarah Harasym. New York: Routledge, 1990.

Stoller, Nancy E. "Lesbian Involvement in the AIDS Epidemic: Changing Roles and Generational Differences." In Women Resisting AIDS 270–85.

Treichler, Paula. "AIDS, Gender, and Biomedical Discourse: Current Contests for Meaning." In AIDS: The Burdens of History. Ed. Elizabeth Fee and Daniel M. Fox. Berkeley: University of California Press, 1988, 190–226.

Warren, Catherine A., and Paula Treichler. "The Empress's Old Clothes: Feminist Silence on AIDS, 1982–88." In Gendered Epidemic: Identity, Theory, Policy, and Practice, forthcoming.

Watney, Simon. Policing Desire: Pornography, AIDS and the Media. Minneapolis: University of Minnesota Press, 1987.

"Feminism without Women"

A Lesbian Reassurance

ANNAMARIE JAGOSE

The relationship between feminism and lesbianism has never been easy, less because it has at times been structured by mutual hostilities than because it has been difficult to specify with any precision. While such imprecision is seldom productive, it is interesting to note the ways in which the historically different formations of the categories "women" and "lesbian" are comparable. Recently, the category "women" has been a site of feminist dispute, both denounced as falsely ontological and reinstated as the proper ground of feminism. Some feminists have argued that any allegiance to what was previously understood as feminism's grounding category is a totalizing gesture which misrecognizes the effects of political action as its prerequisite. Other feminists register their suspicion that the recent poststructuralist critiques of identity are recuperative attempts on the part of dominant subjects to protect themselves against the increasingly effective, identity-based political formations being made by marginalized groups. Many argue that the category "women" must be used strategically, that is, deployed for tactical effect in full knowledge of its incoherences. Jane Gallop suggests such a position when she asserts that "identity must be continually assumed and as immediately called into question."[1] Others, such as Judith Butler, warn that such provisional mobilizations of identity terms have effects in excess of their intended strategy, that even the subscription to "a false ontology of women as a universal in order to advance a feminist political program" maintains a regulatory gender coherence to which it ostensibly has no commitment.[2] It is possible—and worthwhile—to make an intervention in these debates by drawing a connection between the category "women" and that category with which it has had its most troublesome relation, the category "lesbian." For the uncertainty—celebrated by some, mourned by others—which has recently marked mobilizations of the term *women* becomes more nuanced through an examination of the recent history of the term *lesbian*. Such an intervention does not promise to resolve for feminism its crisis in relation to the category "women." Nevertheless, *lesbian*—long the subject of contentions and ongoing negotiation over its limits and precise constituency—provides a template for an identity that is not organized by notions of coherence and consistency.

Tania Modleski's book, *Feminism without Women: Culture and Criticism in a "Postfeminist" Age,* is a convenient text around which to rehearse these connections, given both its overt insistence on the necessity of the category "women" for feminism and its covert discounting of the category "lesbian."[3] Perhaps I should explain at this initial point that Modleski's is not a homophobic argument in any conventional sense of that word. Insofar as the argument of *Feminism without Women* delegitimates a lesbian perspective, it can be said to work against its own avowed and inclusionist position. In reading *Feminism without Women,* I am taken by the rightness, even the deftness, of its argument, and yet I am also troubled by the way in which its unarticulated implications exceed its avowed and carefully negotiated agenda, an agenda to which I am otherwise committed. Modleski makes valuable and productive interventions entirely consistent with the project of gay studies. For instance, her reading of the popular cop/buddy film *Lethal Weapon* as explicitly homoerotic while everywhere marked by hysterical attempts to safeguard the integrity of white heterosexual masculinity or her focus on the repressed gay sexuality that underwrites the fantasy of *Dead Poets Society* demonstrate in the field of popular culture what is by now axiomatic for gay studies, that the "canon as it exists is already . . . a [male-homosocial] canon, and most so when it is most heterosexual."[4] Moreover, *Feminism without Women* is a text which defends the position of the lesbian, which argues, for example, that one of the postfeminist dangers of gender studies is "the silencing of the lesbian perspective" (12). Yet I hope it will be clear by the end of this chapter how Modleski's defenses double back on themselves. For her argument—like the category "women" it vigorously defends—demonstrates a culpable lack of solidarity with the category "lesbian," a category which, as we will see, returns to destabilize the grounds of the argument that would exclude it.

The radical disparity between the intent and the effect of Modleski's argument is largely determined by her figuring of postmodernism as inimical to feminism. For Modleski, postmodernism's antiessentialism is apolitical and opposed to a feminism whose politics are somehow self-evident in its commitment to grounding, identificatory categories. Since such an antiessentialism critiques the notion of a politics proceeding as if unproblematically from any foundational identity and since Modleski reinstalls the category "women" as a counter to what she considers the damaging excesses of such postmodern logics, any adjudication between the two positions seems impossible. Contradicting each other, they demonstrate a resilient self-sufficiency, every point in favor balanced by a comparable point against. However, the category "lesbian"—both awkwardly invoked and carelessly laid aside at different points in *Feminism without Women*—affords a possibility of adjudication by clarifying to a certain extent what is at stake in taking up or opposing Modleski's position.

The main title of this chapter, then, is also and first Modleski's. In her book, Modleski contextualizes her title in relation to both the rise of an avowedly male feminism and feminism's destabilization of its foundational category, the category "women":

> The debates over female essentialism, along with the rise of gender studies, are the major contextualizing events of this book: thus, "Feminism without Women" can mean the triumph either of a male feminist perspective that excludes women or of a feminist antiessentialism so radical that every use of the term "woman," however "provisionally" it is adopted, is disallowed. (14–15)

Modleski's oxymoronic title in part ironizes a certain anxious moment in contemporary feminism which finds itself politically motivated in the name of a foundational category in which it no longer believes. As Modleski explains in her opening chapter, she did not mean that title literally but "as an exaggeration of certain trends in contemporary feminist studies" (12). In direct proportion to the extent to which I am interpellated by Modleski's arguments about not simply the value of feminism but the ways in which an indifference or hostility to it are negotiated in its name, I am resistant to her positing the problematizing of the category "women" as just another postfeminist moment. For in assimilating the projects of male feminism and feminist antiessentialism, Modleski argues simply that both are conservative reworkings of "the once exhilarating proposition that there is no 'essential' female nature" (15). In making this connection, she elides from consideration the most cogent, the most denaturalizing—the still exhilarating—implication of the recent destabilization of "women." For the radical problematization of the category "women" goes further than pointing out "the historical variability of definitions of women" (17) or "dissuading feminists from claiming commonalities across class and racial lines" (18). It argues that the category "women" is a regulatory fantasy whose deployment inadvertently reproduces the normative relations between sex, gender, and desire which naturalize heterosexuality (Butler, *Gender Trouble* 17). Feminism without women might not seem such a bleak or even oxymoronic prospect given the heterosexual imperative which ensures the cultural intelligibility of the category "women." Consequently, like Modleski's title, the subtitle of my chapter, "A Lesbian Reassurance," is ironic, but only in part. That is, in the kind of double talk in which feminism is increasingly eloquent, it offers a reassurance that, as Irigaray might say, is not one.

Modleski aligns the destabilization of the category "women" with what she calls "postfeminism." For Modleski, postfeminism marks not the point of feminism's satisfaction but its betrayal; it is, she writes, "engaged in negating the critiques and undermining the goals of feminism—in effect, delivering us back into a prefeminist world" (3). Moreover, she understands the allegedly "postfeminist" destabilization of the category "women" to effect a kind of political paralysis, which follows logically from her belief that a shared identificatory category is a prerequisite for feminist resistance: "It is not altogether clear to me why women, much more so than any other oppressed groups of people, have been so willing to yield the ground on which to make a stand against their oppression" (15). In expressing her bafflement at the apparently counterproductive latest turn of feminism, Modleski assumes that an identification with the category "women" is a prerequisite for feminist political intervention.

Certainly the recent critique of the category "women" does not understand itself as yielding the ground on which to make a stand against oppression. Judith Butler, for instance, has argued persuasively that the dissolution of feminism's foundationalist category, the category "women," does not mark the end of feminism but enables its new possibility: "The deconstruction of identity is not the deconstruction of politics; rather, it establishes as political the very terms through which identity is articulated."[5] It is clear, then, that feminist interest in antifoundational politics is neither antifeminist nor apolitical. In establishing foundational identificatory categories as not the conditions for but the consequences of specific identity claims, feminist antifoundationalism provides a set of potential positions which rearticulate what "politics" and its related terms—"identity," "agency," "community"— might mean.

Moreover, careful attention to the category "lesbian" might figure what Modleski advocates as a resistance to yielding ground as less a plucky gesture of insurgency than an act of territorialization which would dispossess others of their equal claim. For while she suggests that there is a correlation between a willingness to problematize the category "women" and positions of privilege—she describes the advocacy of female antiessentialism as "a luxury open only to the most privileged women" (22) and even allows that it "may well be the latest ruse of white middle class feminism" (21)—there is an available counternarrative that suggests a correlation between the former and the figure of the lesbian, who historically has occupied a subject position which interpellates her partially or incompletely. While there is plenty of evidence of individual lesbians being securely and thoroughly interpellated by the category "lesbian," the unembodied history of that category demonstrates a contrary and persistent instability. Even since the development of second-wave feminism, the category "lesbian" has been the subject of definitional debate, the progress of which has been more frequently marked by deferral than closure. The outlines of this debate are suggested in the juxtaposition of Jane Gallop's confident assertion that "lesbians are, obviously, a subset of all women" and Monique Wittig's once controversial declaration that "lesbians are not women."[6]

In 1981–82 several articles, many of which cross-referenced one another, were published which attempted to provide a conclusive definition of the category "lesbian" and to critique other theorists' definitions. The major outlines of the debate are articulated in Adrienne Rich's now classic "Compulsory Heterosexuality and Lesbian Existence"; Ann Ferguson, Jacquelyn N. Zita, and Kathryn Pyne Addelson's collective response, "On 'Compulsory Heterosexuality and Lesbian Existence': Defining the Issues"; Wittig's "Straight Mind" and "One Is Not Born a Woman"; and lesbian literary surveys such as Catharine R. Stimpson's "Zero Degree Deviancy: The Lesbian Novel in English" and Bonnie Zimmerman's "What Has Never Been: An Overview of Feminist Literary Criticism."[7] The discursive field constituted by these essays does not consolidate some monolithic definition of "lesbian," but rather generates complementary and conflicting definitions.

It is not that the largely modernist anxieties about identity, truth, and determinacy which circulated around the definitional intractability of the category "lesbian" in the academic debates of the early 1980s are the same as those poststructuralist articulations of the category "women" which subsequently problematize that category's claims to fixity and closure. I am not arguing here for a standpoint politics, a particular political position derived from a specific identity. After all, lesbian theorizing and politics have often represented themselves as securely grounded in stable identity categories. However, it has largely been recent lesbian theory that has recognized and disseminated the implications for feminism of the antifoundationalist position, in part because it allows a retrospective explanation for the tenacity with which "lesbian" has resisted definitional closure.

In the late 1980s and early 1990s various feminist theorists critiqued the seemingly coherent relations between chromosomal sex, gender, and sexual desire naturalized in the category "women." Modleski suggests that the new uncertainty of the previously dependable category "women" is the effect on feminism of "the tendency within poststructuralist thought to dispute notions of identity and the subject" (15), that is, a spillover from a male subjectivity in crisis. While there is no doubt that the wider frame for these speculations is a poststructuralist reworking of modern notions of the self and subjectivity, the source of disquiet is closer to home than Modleski thinks, not outside but within feminist theory. The recent destabilization of "women" equally inherits its uncertainty from "lesbian," an identity widely theorized as incoherent and discontinuous *before* poststructuralist paradigms refigured the overwhelmingly humanist/empiricist register of its field.

Even while the category "women" had been considered self-evident, prefatory gestures which indicated the fundamental uncertainty of the category "lesbian" were virtually de rigueur in lesbian criticism and theorizing. The reason why the category "lesbian" resisted definition at a time when formulations of the category "women" were regarded as unproblematic proceeds from the former's disruption of that regulatory fiction which appears to be underwritten by, but actually constitutes, the latter. The category of "lesbian," then, is problematized by, and renders problematic, the illusory coherence of gender whereby anatomical sex determines gender which determines sexual desire. So the demonstrated difficulty of fixing the category "lesbian" within a system of interdependent genders and sexualities does not only illustrate the structuring incoherences of that category. Equally, it demonstrates that the apparent coherence of the category "women" is a fiction produced by, and in the service of, that matrix of regulatory structures which constitutes compulsory heterosexuality. The incoherences which have visibly structured the category "lesbian" structure the category "women" no less, albeit less obviously.

Modleski's call for the reinstallation of the category "women" problematically and covertly—indeed, problematically *because* covertly—assumes a fundamental but largely unexamined heterosexuality which structures the heart of that category. For the destabilization of the ontological foundations of the category "women" is effected in large part through the scrutinizing of the previously naturalized relations between chromosomal sex, gender, and sexual desire. Jane Flax poses some of the questions which follow such a scrutiny:

> What is gender? How is it related to anatomical sexual differences? How are gender relations constituted and sustained (in one person's lifetime and more generally as a social experience over time)? How do gender relations relate to other sorts of social relations such as class or race? Do gender relations have a history (or many)? What causes gender relations to change over time? What are the relationships between gender relations, sexuality, and a sense of individual identity? What are the relationships between heterosexuality, homosexuality, and gender relations? Are there only two genders? (627)[8]

These questions foreground the instability of the category "women" through their denaturalization of the categories of gender. They demonstrate that the category "women," far from being a fixed and stable entity, an identity always already in place and preceding its mobilization in any oppressive or emancipatory articulation, is marked by instability, fluctuation and indeterminacy. Rather than assume gender as axiomatic, as a self-evident category, Flax's questions focus on the ways in which gender has come to occupy such a naturalized position. They problematize the seemingly logical coherence of "women" by drawing attention to its delimitations, its historicity, its reinforcement and disruption of anatomical sex and sexual desire. Consequently, they call into question any unexamined assumption of "women" as the subject of feminism, as feminism's foundationalist category.

When the category "women" is understood as unstable, as changing not simply from one historical period to another but also from one articulation to another, any call for collectivity and solidarity on the basis of an allegedly shared "womanhood" is bound to be problematic. The efficacy of that category is questionable when "women" is understood to be unavoidably implicated in the naturalized structures of compulsory heterosexuality which feminism ostensibly resists. Such a sequestering of "women" within quotation marks, with its suggestion that the category "women" ought not nor can be feminism's foundation, has prompted accusations that theoretical explorations of this category's instability and inconstancy eliminate the possibility of its functioning as a site of feminist identification and solidarity and, consequently, are more properly complicit with an antifeminism. Modleski makes such an accusation when she describes herself as "worr[ied] that the complicated belief structure [antiessentialist feminists] counsel us to adopt as a *female* form of disavowal . . . might be said not so much to counter masculine disavowal as to participate in the same phobic logic" (22). However, an exploration of the fundamental instability of the category "women" does not find against feminism but, in resisting the urge to foreclose prematurely that category, licenses new possibilities for a feminism that constitutes "women" as the effect of, not the prerequisite for, its inquiries. Indeed, the reification of the category "women" does not secure a safe space from which to consolidate a feminist initiative. Rather it simultaneously limits the field of those subjects it purports to represent while reimplicating them, in the name of their liberation, in the very apparatus of oppression by which they have been constituted.

Just as it is no coincidence that the implications of poststructuralist destabilizations of identity categories resonated strongly for lesbian theorizations of gendered identity, so it seems no coincidence that attempts to revalidate the category "women" for feminist initiatives do so at the expense of the category "lesbian." In her chapter "Postmortem on Postfeminism," Modleski provides an account of the relation between lesbianism and feminism:

> I would hope that in correcting its habit of neglecting the lesbian perspective (which, revisionist histories notwithstanding, held sway in the women's movement for only a brief moment in time with only a segment of its members) feminism will not fall into an error of equally serious postfeminist consequence, and see lesbianism as existing at the same political and theoretical level as other so-called marginalized groups. (13)

It is difficult at first to grasp what distinction Modleski is making between lesbianism and "other so-called marginalized groups." Partly this is because her description of marginalization as "so-called" suggests a critically sophisticated account of the processes and effects of social diversification. Yet her eagerness to keep lesbianism separate from other "so-called marginalized groups" seems to exceed the by now commonplace feminist assertion that different oppressions should not be conflated or regarded as analogous, having less to do with maintaining the specificities of various groups than minimizing the extent to which lesbianism as a social formation is marginalized in comparison with those other groups. For in an instance of that kind of hierarchizing of oppression she might at first be taken to oppose, Modleski argues that race and sexuality are incomparable categories not because they cannot be compared but because when compared the latter is somehow so much less consequential than the former: "There seems to me to be a crucial difference between telling, say, a white woman she should be aware of her racial privilege and telling her she should be aware of her privilege as a heterosexual female" (13).

The history of race and sexuality has been at least as fraught, as energized by misunderstanding, as the history of lesbianism and feminism. It is worth pointing out then that my objection to Modleski's attention to issues of race privilege in the passage above is not a minimizing of the importance of race but entirely dependent on the extent to which her mobilization here of race—or elsewhere of the black woman—not only licenses a neglect of the lesbian perspective but does so through a legitimation of the centrality of heterosexuality for feminism. While agreeing with Modleski that a feminism indifferent to race is barely a feminism at all, I am suspicious that the inaugural gesture which enables a heterosexual feminism to sort out its internal race relations is the sidelining of the lesbian on the grounds that she does not merit the attention due "other so-called marginalized groups."

Indeed, when Modleski theorizes the relation between "lesbian" and "women" it is to say that since feminism has "emphasized from the beginning the *oppressiveness* of the ideology of compulsory heterosexuality" the lesbian occupies some dubiously privileged position in relation to heterosexual women (13). It seems that the position of privilege and the figure of the lesbian are in Modleski's argument synonymous. For in her account it is heterosexual women who are figured as feminism's beleaguered group:

> The special difficulties faced by lesbians under such a system are analogous to those of a prisoner who has escaped incarceration and, being "at large," faces more extreme punitive measures than many of the more docile inmates. The hazards faced by lesbians cannot be overestimated, but we might remember the time when feminism deemed it no great "privilege" to be a wife in patriarchy. (13)

While allowing that feminism has long maintained—theoretically, at least—that heterosexuality is an institution oppressive to women, it does not follow that it is "no great 'privilege' to be a wife in patriarchy," in part because this would require taking up a position so internal to feminism that "patriarchy" would constitute an almost imaginary structure; in part because, despite Modleski's slippage, being a heterosexual woman is not necessarily the same as being a wife.

In a later chapter, "Cinema and the Dark Continent: Race and Gender in Popular Film," Modleski again figures two women separated from each other by a locked door. This image occurs at the end of the chapter as Modleski offers a reading of the film *Ghost* which counters that film's "participat[ion] in an old tradition of forcing black women to serve the function of embodiment" (133). In Modleski's resistant reading, the black psychic holds hands with the white woman who is her client not as a conduit for the spirit of the dead white male lover but for the symbolic feminist promise of that same-sex, interracial handclasp. Although the black and white women's union is offered in contradistinction to "the white heterosexual romance," its lesbian character is more properly a metaphor for the coming together of black and white women, race issues being the major concern of this chapter. Perhaps this reading would be unremarkable—and entirely analogous to the gay male readings Modleski produces elsewhere in the book—except that its interest in sexuality is entirely and oddly limited to heterosexuality. In imagining a scenario in which a black and a white woman come together, it replicates the figure of the (white) heterosexual woman as without privilege with regard to her sexuality, all the privilege of heterosexuality accruing to her masculine counterpart:

> If in the film the black woman exists solely to facilitate the white heterosexual romance, there is a sense in which we can shift our focus to read the white male as, precisely, the obstacle to the union of the two women, a union tentatively suggested in the image of the black and white hands as they reach out toward one another. I like to think that . . . a time will come when we eliminate the locked door (to recall an image from *Ghost*) that separates women (a door, as we see in the film, easily penetrated by the white man), a time when we may join together to overthrow the ideology that, after all, primarily serves the interests of white heterosexual masculinity and is *ultimately* responsible for the persecutions suffered by people on account of their race, class, and gender. (134)

I cite this passage at length because of the way in which it has a periphrastic lesbianism—"the union of the two women"—negotiate a safe passage for a heterosexual femininity which exists only as the object, never the subject, of persecutory ideology. Although Modleski invokes a culpable but notably masculine (and white) heterosexuality, it turns out that people suffer persecution on account of their race, class, and gender while sexuality, presumably on account of its being ranked at some second order "political and theoretical level," is not listed.

While Modleski's attention to axes of race, class, and gender is productive, her insistence that sexuality—and, more specifically, lesbianism—does not take up a position on the same level is extremely problematic. Her attempt to bring together, in the name of feminism, black and white women in a scenario that is, by her own account, a utopian fantasy is undone in the end by the very figure she excludes, the lesbian whose metonymic presence is alluded to by the union of the two (heterosexual) women but whose position in networks of power Modleski cannot account for. Despite her own resistance to theorizing lesbians as a marginalized group, Modleski historicizes feminist neglect of the lesbian perspective as something which "revisionist histories notwithstanding, held sway in the women's movement for only a brief moment in time with only a segment of its members." Nevertheless, when the category "women" is recuperated in the name of feminism, when it is represented as unproblematically accessing and enabling a feminist practice, it is possible to charge that feminism with neglect. For the category "women" only maintains its apparent coherence and representational universality for as long as its naturalized heterosexism goes unquestioned, as long as the always already heterosexual mappings of chromosomal sex to gender to sexual desire are regarded as unproblematic.

Modleski figures the lesbian as a prisoner on the run while her heterosexual sisters languish obediently behind bars. Rather than figure the divide between lesbians and women across the locked gate of a prison cell, I would like to refigure that relation across a less violent threshold. For the relation between the categories "lesbian" and "women" is less one of untransactable difference than one of unacknowledged similarity. This, then, is the reassurance my chapter offers feminism: that the seemingly dependable category "women" shares a similar formation with the historically hesitant category "lesbian." Given the reluctance with which Modleski, for one, admits to a similarity between the categories "women" and "lesbian," this is hardly a reassurance, if we think of the reassurance's function as a dispelling of apprehension or a restoration of confidence. Perhaps then what the figure of the lesbian offers feminism is better seen as an antireassurance given its sinister reworking of that familiar gesture of hospitality—everything I have is yours.

NOTES

Thanks to Marion Campbell and Linda Hardy for reading earlier drafts of this essay when I no longer could and for making generous sense of my proto-argument.

1. Jane Gallop, *The Daughter's Seduction* xii.
2. Judith Butler, "Gender Trouble, Feminist Theory, and Psychoanalytic Discourse" 325.

3. Tania Modleski, *Feminism without Women*. Henceforth, page references will be incorporated in the text.

4. Eve Kosofsky Sedgwick, *Between Men* 17.

5. Judith Butler, *Gender Trouble* 148.

6. Jane Gallop, "The Problem of Definition" 118, and Monique Wittig, "The Straight Mind" 110.

7. Adrienne Rich, "Compulsory Heterosexuality and Lesbian Existence"; Ann Ferguson, Jacquelyn N. Zita, and Kathryn Pyne Addelson, "On 'Compulsory Heterosexuality and Lesbian Existence': Defining the Issues"; Catharine R. Stimpson, "Zero Degree Deviancy"; Bonnie Zimmerman, "What Has Never Been"; Monique Wittig, "One Is Not Born a Woman." These articles are by no means an exhaustive survey of the theorizing about the category "lesbian" produced at this time but they suggest the most general outlines of that debate.

8. Jane Flax, "Postmodernism and Gender Relations in Feminist Theory" 627.

WORKS CITED

Butler, Judith. *Gender Trouble: Feminism and the Subversion of Identity.* New York: Routledge, 1990.
———. "Gender Trouble, Feminist Theory, and Psychoanalytic Discourse." In *Feminism/Postmodernism.* Ed. Linda Nicholson. New York: Routledge, 1990, 324–40.
Ferguson, Ann, et al. "On 'Compulsory Heterosexuality and Lesbian Existence': Defining the Issues." *Signs* 7 (1981): 158–99.
Flax, Jane. "Postmodernism and Gender Relations in Feminist Theory." *Signs* 12 (1987): 621–43.
Gallop, Jane. *The Daughter's Seduction: Feminism and Psychoanalysis.* Ithaca: Cornell University Press, 1982.
———. "The Problem of Definition." *Genre* 20 (1987): 111–32.
Modleski, Tania. *Feminism without Women: Culture and Criticism in a "Postfeminist" Age.* New York: Routledge, 1991.
Rich, Adrienne. "Compulsory Heterosexuality and Lesbian Existence." *Signs* 5 (1980), 631–60.
Sedgwick, Eve Kosofsky. *Between Men: English Literature and Male Homosocial Desire.* New York: Columbia University Press, 1985; rpt. 1992.
Stimpson, Catharine R. "Zero Degree Deviancy: The Lesbian Novel in English." *Critical Inquiry* 8 (Winter 1981): 363–79.
Wittig, Monique. "One Is Not Born a Woman." *Feminist Issues* (Winter 1981): 47–54.
———. "The Straight Mind." *Feminist Issues*, Summer 1980, 103–11.
Zimmerman, Bonnie. "What Has Never Been: An Overview of Lesbian Feminist Literary Criticism." *Feminist Studies* 7 (1981): 451–76.

Supermodels of Lesbian Chic

Camille Paglia Revamps Lesbian/Feminism (while Susie Bright Retools)

KARMAN KREGLOE AND JANE CAPUTI

In the spring of 1993, *New York* magazine put k. d. lang on its cover, announcing a new era of "Lesbian Chic." To some, that coupling might seem at best oxymoronic. Yet throughout the year the trend gathered momentum. On June 21, 1993, *Newsweek* featured a story on lesbianism. The cover image was of two young, white, conventionally attractive, and affluent women (one wore pearls) in an affectionate embrace. The headline read: "Lesbians Coming Out Strong: What Are the Limits of Tolerance?" One implicit message was that if a lesbian were not young, white, conventionally attractive, affluent, and normatively coupled, there would be no tolerance. And even then, who knows?

Then in August 1993, *Vanity Fair*'s cover sported a Herb Ritts photograph, camping up standard Norman Rockwell iconography. Here a men's-suited k. d. lang leaned back, eyes closed in a barber's chair, her face slathered with lather, while a barely clad (and similarly shut-eyed) Cindy Crawford wielded a straight-edged razor, preparing to shave her. (To recuperate any insult to heterosexist gender delivered by this camp image, *Vanity Fair* blew up this statement of lang and featured it on an inside page: "I have a little bit of penis envy. They're ridiculous, but they're cool.") Whether Ritts intended it or not, a subtext of this overtly sexy cover image is that one woman, the (often presumed lesbian) "supermodel," is about to cut the avowed dyke's throat!

Significantly, these motifs of (glamorized and eroticized) lesbian-on-lesbian violence and a de rigueur genuflection to phallic power are much reiterated in the varied texts that make up "lesbian chic" (from

Single White Female, to Madonna's racist "Girlie Show," to cheap poster art, and to the works of Camille Paglia and Susie Bright).[2] As several lesbian commentators, including Victoria Brownworth, Sue O'Sullivan, and Kathy Miriam, have noted, one of the central motivations behind this media-generated phenomenon is to play the old game of divide and conquer, "good girls" against "bad girls."[3] First label as cool a generation of young, sexy, glamorous lesbians. Then use that image to deride 1970s-style lesbians—bad, scary, hairy, unfashionable, and "ugly," that is, feminist dykes. As Miriam sees it, "A notion of lesbianism as the rage of all women, once celebrated as the embodiment of women's resistance to male supremacy, has given way to an new era of 'hot dykes': of 'sex rebels'" who are "all the rage."

Camille Paglia and Susie "Sexpert" Bright, two notoriously un-1970s lesbians (or bisexuals, depending on to whom they are speaking) are now functioning as supermodels of "lesbian chic." Paglia (who rages only against other women, mostly lesbians) and the rageless Bright both have enjoyed inordinate indulgence from sources as varied as *Esquire, 60 Minutes,* CNN, *On Our Backs,* the *New York Times,* and the *Advocate.* Each may be found speaking about, around, and sometimes against lesbians in any number of lesbian, gay, and mainstream publications. Paglia, of course, regularly extols the endless glories of white male Western civilization, deploring the lack of lesbian contributions to culture, beauty, and eroticism and railing against lesbian diminishment of women's minds. Simultaneously, Bright urges us to "reclaim" our sex lives from the clutches of the "anti-sex" lesbian/feminist[4] movement, suggesting that the most effective (and entertaining) form of lesbian activism might be to have as much sex with as many people as possible.

While quite different—in age, style, and emphasis—what the two have most in common is their willingness to blame any "lack," real or spurious, in lesbian lives not on the blights of heterosexist culture but on the stultifying influence of lesbian/feminism. Certainly radical lesbian/feminism is subject to criticism, change, revision, and renewal. It is a movement that can survive and learn from criticism on race and class oppression, as well as the emergence of even widely divergent views on issues such as erotic agency, sexual representations, and gender identity. Yet these new "supermodels," particularly Paglia, have no interest in enriching or enlivening lesbian/feminist philosophy, but only in silencing it. In the careers of both Paglia and Bright, it is evident that disrespecting and disavowing the politically threatening aspects of lesbianism (while stroking the phallic ego) is the token demanded for entry into the world of lesbian chic.

REVAMPING: A NEO-ATHENA ASSAULTS THE GORGON

> NOW THAT TWENTY-FIVE YEARS HAVE PASSED, IT'S TIME TO ADMIT THAT
> LESBIAN FEMINISM HAS PRODUCED ONLY THE GHETTOIZATION AND MINIATUR-
> IZATION OF WOMEN. NO GREAT WORKS OF ART OR INTELLECT HAVE EMERGED
> FROM IT. ON THE CONTRARY, IT HAS ASPHYXIATED YOUNG WOMEN WITH
> PROPAGANDA AND STUNTED THEIR TALENT BY LIMITING THEIR VISION AND
> CONSTRICTING THEIR EMOTION. WOMEN NEVER GROW FROM THE MOMENT
> THEY ENTER THE LESBIAN WORLD.
>
> —CAMILLE PAGLIA, *VAMPS AND TRAMPS*[5]

> IF BOOKS COULD KILL, HER SECOND, *SEX, ART, AND AMERICAN CULTURE,* WOULD
> WIPE OUT ANY TRACE OF FEMINISM IN THE LAST 20 YEARS.
>
> —MIMI=FREED, "INTERVIEW WITH AN UZI"[6]

When the *Advocate* ran a story on Camille Paglia in October 1994, it was headlined "The Attack of the 50-Foot Lesbian." Paglia's gigantism here is meant to refer to her powers of intimidation, yet it is crucial to recognize that she enlarges herself specifically by making other women, particularly lesbians, small. Camille Paglia is, to put it simply, a token—a woman who achieves position and power because of her willingness to cut down other women, to punish lesbians and/or feminists for transgressing against the law of the father. Heroes of patriarchal myth frequently become legendary by the one defining act of slaying a monster who signifies female powers (a serpent, dragon, sea monster, or Gorgon). Paglia's cultural movement is similar: in the act of revamping radical lesbian/feminism, that is, in mocking, refuting, and attempting to kill off lesbian/feminist thought, she achieves hero (celebrity) status.

There have been several biting lesbian/feminist critiques of Paglia's role in the patriarchal counterattack against feminism, notably by Teresa L. Ebert in the *Women's Review of Books*, B. Ruby Rich in the *Village Voice*, and, more recently, S. Elaine Craghead in the anthology *Lesbian Erotics*.[7] Writing in 1991, Rich still held out some hope that Paglia would discover aspects of lesbian/feminist culture that belie her caricatures (e.g., Amber Hollibaugh, Sue-Ellen Case, Cheryl Clarke, Jewelle Gomez, the theater of Split Britches, *On Our Backs*) and then expand her views. Yet, four years later, it is most obvious that Paglia has no real interest in anything but (self-serving) service to those whom Rich dubs those "lords of doublespeak who rule America."

Paglia's work reeks with (self-) loathing for the lesbian body. She not only regularly describes lesbians as hideous, drab, inert, and boring, but she consistently promotes misogynist, male- and white-supremacist biological determinism. In this view, women are ineluctably bound to chthonian nature, bloody, overwhelming, and repulsive: "The historical repugnance to woman has a rational basis: disgust is reason's proper response to the grossness of procreative [female] nature."[8] The male genitals, on the other hand, "have a mathematical design, a syntax," from which all cultural achievement, art, beauty, purposiveness, concentration and civilization are released in a precisely aimed flow. Paglia contends that it is not males who politically dominate women, but the other way around. Anyone who thinks otherwise is a deluded "victim feminist." Indeed, the glories of Western civilization are directly rooted in man's need to defend himself against the suffocating, consuming presence of the primal, universal dominatrix-woman.

Paglia's work is steeped in a politics of a new manifest destiny which, like the old, is firmly rooted in commingled racism and sexism. Curiously, on her 1992 speaking tour, Paglia traveled, as she proclaimed, "under the aegis of African-American culture." Literally, this meant that she was flanked on stage by two large and muscular African American male bodyguards, whom James Wolcott described in *Vanity Fair* as "macho bookends in matching shades and black leather."[9] Why are human beings so casually equated with objects and African American culture with mute, bought, staged brutishness? Paglia, like Madonna, uses African American men as props, positioning their ("inferior") blackness to contrast with her ("superior") whiteness.[10] Here her favorite script of the ascendancy of so-called reason/civilization/order over so-called savagery/nature/chaos is visually enacted in neoplantation theatrics.

In a speech in September 1995, presidential candidate Bob Dole slammed any notion of multicultural education and declared that "Western tradition and American greatness must be taught in our schools."[11] Paglia would be first in line for that job. Her entire body of work is a love song to European high culture and American popular culture. In her reading of "high" culture, there are virtually no references to people of color as creators, artists, and thinkers, save the dynastic Egyptians. Here, as bell hooks wryly observes, Paglia gets "downright Afrocentric." Moreover,

> when it came down to really talking about changing canons and curricula and divesting of some white supremacy, all Miss Camille could say was, "African Americans must study the language and structure of Western public power while still preserving their cultural identity, which has had world impact on the arts." Oh, we so hurt! Miss Camille, you mean all you think we can do is dance and sing? We read and write now, yes ma'am.[12]

Well, along with dancing and singing, Paglia does think that men of color also can fuck: "The powerful, uncontrollable force of male sexuality has been censored out of white middle-class homes. But it's still there in black culture, and in Spanish culture."[13] Adopting, as hooks reads it, the vernacular flair of the Black Queen, Paglia uses that stolen voice to trot out the most clichéd tenets of sexual racism.

Who can't fuck (or think, or dance, or sing, or play sports with any flair), it turns out, are lesbians, presumably of any color. "Lesbianism, seeking a lost state of blissful union with the mother, is cozy, regressive, and, I'm sorry to say, too often intellectually enervating, tending toward the inert."[14] And "I conclude that to my regret exclusive lesbianism is emotional retardation. . . . When lesbians cut themselves off from men, the end result [is] that the middle-aged lesbian personality is childish. It's infantile."[15] Since men are the source of all dynamism, it turns out that even the most "real" butch women, in Paglia's eyes, are *straight* women.[16] Lesbians just can't do anything right!

Despite a great deal of waffling about her sexuality,[17] when it suits her purposes Paglia speaks out as a "lesbian" (elsewhere she is bisexual or in a state of limbo). For example, speaking in a *Playboy* interview, Paglia forthrightly identifies with rapists in that, she contends, both lesbians and heterosexual men view women with predatory eyes. Indeed, she tells *Playboy*, had she been born a man, she might have been a rapist. Paglia justifies the stalking of women as sexual prey and sympathizes with the rage of men who kill women who reject them sexually. She relates an incident when she left a public event with a woman who had invited her to go to a lesbian bar, and, after that, out for coffee. When the woman did not subsequently offer sex, Paglia went ballistic: "I can't tell you the rage. . . . All I can say is, if I had been an 18-year-old street kid instead of a 45-year-old woman, I would have stabbed her. I was completely humiliated and furious. If I had been a guy with a hard-on, I would have hit her."[18]

As a self-proclaimed "feminist," Paglia sagely reveals that women who do get beaten in these and similar situations are secretly loving it. In her view, what whining "victim feminists" see as male battery is really consensual S&M, especially for "working-class relationships where women [who] get beat up have hot sex."[19] How deliciously "savage" and sexual the working class is (especially if they are black or Latino) in Paglia's middle-classist fantasies!

Apologists for rape and even rape-murder characteristically legitimate these atrocities by mystifying them as the inevitable outcome of male anatomy and an imperative sex drive. Radical lesbian/feminists instead point to a cultural climate of misogyny and sexual objectification that encourages and even demands rape. Sexual violence— from harassment through battery, rape, and femicide—is a political use of a particularly sexual terror in the ongoing construction and maintenance of male supremacy. Paglia simply dismisses that hard won insight and reiterates the old line: "Rape-murder comes from the brutish region of pure animal appetite."[20] Feminists, she rants, have done a great disservice by hiding this "truth" from young women and hence are partially responsible for these women being raped by acquaintances or while on dates. The rest of the responsibility lies in the young woman's "stupidity" and middle-class naiveté!

Everywhere, Paglia's identification is with the rapist, the batterer, even the incestuous abuser. As such, her very "lesbianism" seems rooted in heterosexist politics. Continually she tells us that straight women and men, gay or straight are far more compelling, dynamic, and sexy than lesbians. She boasts that she is equally attracted to men, but complains that sexual relations with men don't work out for her because they can't tolerate her aggression and independence. Clearly, Paglia reserves her greatest respect, admiration, and longing for men and phallocentric culture. Hence it seems that she practices lesbianism out of male-identification, since lesbianism allows her to take on the heterosexist role of lording it over women. In doing so, she embodies and perpetuates the most homophobic stereotypes of lesbians in a heterosexist culture. It seems that Paglia wants to divorce lesbianism from feminism only to marry it to patriarchal politics.

Paglia prides herself on her sense of mythic significance and declares the Greek goddess Athena to be one of her heroines. No surprise here. Lesbian/feminist/womanist thinkers such as Phyllis Chesler, Mary Daly, Alice Walker, and Catherine Nicholson all have offered up the story of Athena as a mythic model of the token woman, in Alice Walker's words, a "flunky of the order that created her."[21] Like much of Greek myth, Athena's origins are in Africa. According to Barbara Walker, the Egyptians revered "Isis-Athena, which meant 'I have come from myself.'"[22] In Greece, Athena's legend was distorted to serve an emerging system of male supremacy. She was revamped as a virgin warrior who was not of woman born, but who sprang full grown and armed from the head of the father-god Zeus.

As a born-again daddy's girl, Athena not only totally forgets her origins, but provides essential assistance to those who would ghettoize, miniaturize, mutilate, and destroy female powers. For example, as Aeschylus details in *The Furies*, it is Athena who casts the deciding vote absolving the matricidal Orestes. Declaring herself "all for the father," Athena rebukes the raging Furies and orders them to cease hounding Orestes for his crime. Athena also supplies crucial guidance to the hero Perseus in his quest to behead the Gorgon Medusa, the snake-haired goddess whose all-powerful gaze turned men to stone. Athena then fastens the severed and bloody head of Medusa to her aegis, flaunting her murderous betrayal of female powers.

So too Paglia's reputation is founded upon her willingness to parade her allegiance to the father and her avid collaboration in attempting to discredit and destroy gynesophical[23] philosophies. When reading her words, one continually experiences déjà vu: we have heard all of this before—whether in reading de Sade or in viewing *Natural Born Killers*. Paglia's rhetoric acquires its *frisson* in contemporary culture not because she is saying anything new, but because a self-proclaimed lesbian and feminist is, with great rhetorical flair and cocksure confidence, reciting patriarchal "pop" mythology.

Such clichés would never be noteworthy, would never have catapulted this author into the realm of celebrity, unless that author were functioning as a token. With the (very temporal) authority of her femaleness and her lesbianism, this neo-Athena attempts to decapitate the Gorgon of radical lesbian/feminism and defuse the Furies of twenty-five years of resistance. Perhaps here is at least part of the source of Paglia's fathomless loathing for lesbian/feminism: in her heart, she knows that without it she would be nothing.

Radical feminism/lesbianism aspires to immunity to the seductions of chic, media spotlighting, and "sexpertise." To symbolically communicate its resistance, numerous lesbians/feminists have put forth the Gorgon Medusa as an emblem of repulsion for and resistance to male supremacist culture and behavior. Elana Dykewoman put the Medusa's wide-eyed, fanged, and snake-haired face on the cover of her 1976 book of poetry, *They Will Know Me by My Teeth*. Emily Culpepper claims Medusa as "guardian and promise of the female power within" and "a face for contemporary women's rage." Medusa is the inspirational muse (May Sarton). She is "the unfaceable within ourselves [granting] . . . access to the powers we require" (Chela Sandoval). The Gorgon Medusa is guardian of the sacred, of taboo, the one who stops snools[24] from "boldly going where no man has gone before" (Jane Caputi). As Hélène Cixous sees her, she is the beauty, not the horror of the dark. In Alice Walker's recognition, she is "the black female Goddess/Mother tradition and culture of Africa." Finally, according to Gloria Anzaldúa, Medusa, like the Aztec Coatlicue, is "a symbol of the fusion of opposites: the eagle and the serpent, heaven and the underworld, life and death, mobility and immobility, beauty and horror."[25]

With her relentless loyalty to oppositional hierarchy, which she mystifies as natural and inevitable, Paglia is incapable of understanding the deeper character of either Medusa or Athena. To her, Medusa is horrific, chthonian female nature whom men must defeat and escape in order to create civilization. Paglia rejects lesbian Jane Ellen Harrison's recognition of Athena as a collaborator with the father/oppressor, the goddess who "on principle forgets the Earth from which she sprang." Rather, Paglia applauds Athena's targeting of nature and Gorgon as the hideous enemy and celebrates Athena as giving "man control over capricious nature."[26]

This, of course, blatantly legitimates elite men's domination over women and anybody else who can be associated with demonic nature. It also mandates the fissioning of female powers. Nowhere can Paglia grasp that Athena and Medusa are really aspects of a chaotic unity that has been forcibly severed in a culture hooked on control and bound to ordering perception through oppositional hierarchies.[27] Invoking Coatlicue, the gorgonish Aztec goddess, Gloria Anzaldúa understands the core need to demolish that paradigm:

> The work of *mestiza* consciousness is to break down the subject-object duality that keeps her a prisoner and to show in the flesh and through the images in her work how duality is transcended. The answer to the problem between the white race and the colored, between males and females, lies in healing the split that originates in the very foundation of our lives, our culture, our languages, our thoughts. A massive uprooting of dualistic thinking in the individual and collective consciousness is the beginning of a long struggle, but one that could, in our best hopes, bring us to the end of rape, of violence, of war.[28]

Paglia might well dismiss Anzaldúa's hopeful vision as mere "Betty Crocker feminism . . . naively optimistic . . . a childlike faith in the perfectibility of the universe."[29] In her view, it is much more civilized and grown-up to see rape as inevitable and to equate nature with savagery, barbarism, primitivism, and living in "grass-huts"[30] —all rather transparent sexist and racist references. Paglia's sophisticated pessimism is what Paula Gunn Allen might see as "part of the plot" to squelch any resistance to the white man's civilization by annihilating all cultural memory of the historical reality of nonhierarchical, gynocentric cultures, including those that flourished on this continent before the European genocidal conquest.[31]

Paglia identifies with the hollow, man-made Athena, who retains the Medusa's fierceness, flair, and independence but has lost her memory, her origins, her soul. As such, she participates in the ongoing quest to defame, split and murder the dark/female powers. Perhaps one day she will find herself able to face the Medusa. But perhaps not. Ironically, when Paglia's media moment fades, she probably will be remembered only as a token, fanatically soliciting the mass media, selling out the lesbian body.

PIMPING THE LESBIAN BODY

> LESBIANS KNOW FEMALE SEXUALITY FROM BOTH SIDES, AND SO WE HAVE AN
> INTERNAL, ALMOST INCESTUOUS INTIMACY WITH THE SUBJECT. IT GIVES US A
> WISDOM THAT CAN'T BE MEASURED. BUT IT CAN BE SHARED.
>
> —SUSIE BRIGHT, "HOW TO MAKE LOVE TO A WOMAN"[32]

Unlike Paglia, Bright is no Athena; she simply lacks the substance. Rather, she reminds us of a figure usually associated with Athena—Pallas. According to Barbara Walker, stories of Pallas are conflicting: "Some said Pallas was identical with the Goddess Athene. . . . Some said Pallas was a wooden image of a female warrior. . . . A majority believed Pallas was a phallic god and his Palladium [fetish] was . . . 'in the likeness of a male sex organ.'"[33] Whether Bright's larger-than-life sexpert persona turns out to be made of wood or silicone has yet to be determined, but one thing is certain: her celebrity status is no proof of greater acceptance of lesbians in heterosexual culture; it perhaps represents only an opening up of what Ruthann Robson would call "domestication" of lesbianism in a way that makes it more accessible to appropriation, consumption, and incorporation by heterosexist culture.[34]

At first glance, it might seem unfair to couple Susie Bright, the self-proclaimed lesbian "sexpert" of our time, with venom-spewing, lesbian-loathing Camille Paglia. After all, Bright's writing and performance art/lectures have equipped many lesbians with the language with which they might discuss sex more freely. They also have helped to eliminate much of the guilt lesbians and women in general have felt when thinking about and discussing their sexuality. However, since the publication of her first book, *Susie Sexpert's Lesbian Sex World* (1990), Bright's work has become more commercial and more geared to a nonlesbian audience. While she continues to write about lesbian sex and other lesbian-specific topics, she has become more likely to pit lesbian/feminist women against queer women who identify as sex-radicals and to offer solace to straight men.

In *Susie Sexpert's Lesbian Sex World,* Bright explains the origins of her "sexpert" persona. The sexpert was born in the pages of the lesbian sex radical magazine *On Our Backs* in 1984, out of anger with the old lie "that lesbians don't have sex."[35] Bright attributes this idea in part to "dumb straight people," but clearly her greatest frustration is with lesbian/feminists whom she believes to be defining themselves more by "what they won't do" in bed than their actual sexual practices. Apparently in order to counteract this overbearing lesbian/feminist influence, Bright has appointed herself the primary Goodwill Ambassador (or Lesbian Sex Missionary) of the Lesbian Nation, and she's busy spreading the gospel on what lesbians will do in bed (and with whom). Unfortunately, Bright is more concerned with selling lesbian sex to the heterosexist culture— the one that actually *has* been responsible for the attempted annihilation of lesbian self-expression, sexual or otherwise (while simultaneously commercially exploiting and consuming lesbian sexuality).

The September 1995 issue of the *Advocate* reports that Susie Bright served as a consultant for the makers of the film *Bound,* a "lesbian thriller" written and directed by two heterosexual men (Larry and Andy Wachowski). The writer/directors saw no justice in the charge that they were exploiting the current "killer lesbian" stereotype, explaining that they were "not bogged down by what it's like to be a lesbian." So cool are these guys with the subject that they hired Bright to give the leading lesbian (played by Gina Gershon) a "crash course on butch etiquette." Bright's input was most needed when it came time to shoot the scene that would portray "sweaty, slippery, body-grinding, bed-squeaking lesbian sex." Here was Bright's advice:

> You've got a butch-femme couple here. . . . They've got a really stormy, suspenseful relationship. When they have sex—unlike most lesbian sex scenes—you don't want to be implying cunnilingus, you want to be implying penetration. You want to be implying that they're fucking, and that's crucial to understanding their sexual relationship.[36]

Despite promoting herself as "like a *Good Housekeeping* seal of approval [for] . . . lesbian sex," and much to her chagrin, Bright was excluded from the set when the scene was shot. The *Advocate* reports that after producer Dino De Laurentis viewed the completed sex scene, he told his cast and crew, "The price of the film has just gone up." But to what audience, straight male or lesbian, is this sweaty scene pitched? Clearly, to a mainstream, heterosexist audience. As lesbians know, femme-butch sexuality, including cunnilingus, dildos, and penetration, can be outrageously transgressive and thoroughly subversive of normative heterosexuality, as vividly portrayed in Leslie Feinberg's *Stone Butch Blues*.[37] Yet we suspect that Bright's version of "real" lesbian fucking is one that will translate as "just like us" to the heterosexist public—hence the enthusiasm of the straight, and profit-conscious, directors and producer.

Bright implies that penetration alone defines the act of having sex for the couple in *Bound* and, ostensibly, for "couples" everywhere. This is an outrageous endorsement of phallocentric sexuality. Here and elsewhere, Bright foregrounds penetration as the most passionate and meaningful sexual practice available to lesbians. In this context, as in Madonna's *Sex*, as bell hooks observes, lesbianism "may well appear as merely an extension of heterosexual pleasure, part of that practice and not an alternative or fundamentally different expression of sexual desire."[38] De Laurentis was probably correct in his financial prediction. The manner in which Bright envisioned the sex scene in *Bound* guarantees that a heterosexual audience could recognize and accept it as "real." Similarly, *Bound* will probably appeal to a lesbian and female bisexual audience as well, an audience so hungry for images of ourselves that we will, like Bright on the movie set, tolerate being virtually shut out of them.

Bright's belief that representations of lesbian sex are innately revolutionary and transgressive is simply incorrect. Her inability and refusal to interrogate the politics of sex and sexual representation is evident not only in her own writing and "consulting," but also in her educational performance pieces. Former *Out/Look* editor Jackie Goldsby writes of attending Bright's illustrated 1989 lecture, "All-Girl Action: A History of Lesbian Erotica":

> it took only one film clip, a two-minute snippet from a Russ Meyer sex spectacle, to alienate me from the pro-porn agenda Bright had, up until that point, persuaded me to accept.
>
> The opening shot showed the blond-haired Eve-type wedged in the forked trunk of a tree. Her black fuck-buddy's long, overly long tongue flicks and darts across Eve's precious torso (is this a re-vision of the Fall from the Garden? Black dyke as evil serpent?). Then the black woman straps on a larger-than-life dildo and proceeds to ram Eve to a fascistic orgasm—the scene concluded with a tight frame of

Eve's feet, rhythmically striking out and up to the roar of mass cheers (I can't remember now: did the noise come from the soundtrack, or were blood-red anger and a blues-based sadness ringing in my ears?).

Goldsby notes that "Bright was thrilled by the thrusting potential of the sex toy (the dildo or the dyke?)," but that she was thoroughly alienated due to Bright's lack of any recognition of pornography's racial politics. As she puts it, "How has Black sexuality been historically constructed so that its representation in porn is never not racist, if the presumed gaze is either male and/or white. What modes of narrative and production would upend that power dynamic?"[39] In Bright's world, power can be eroticized in a sexual context (as with s/m) for fun, but the not-so-fun relationship between sex, desire, and political oppression is hotly denied.

Goldsby's review of the sexpert's show also exposes Bright's inability to differentiate between appropriated "lesbian" pornography created by and for heterosexual men (e.g., Russ Meyer films) and lesbian-produced and -consumed sexual scripts and images. In fact, Bright often has difficulty in differentiating between appropriated and authentic lesbian identities. Nowhere is this more evident than in her essay "How to Make Love to a Woman: Hands-on Advice from a Woman Who Does," originally published in the notorious "Do-Me Feminism" issue of *Esquire* and reprinted in Bright's third book, *Sexwise*.

Bright writes that she often notices men eyeing her and her latest girlfriend with looks that combine "envy, bewilderment, and titillation." It is for these men that Bright writes her partially tongue-in-cheek pickup guide. She advises men to relate to women as lesbians do, which can be boiled down to three simple steps: the Look, the Touch, and the Surrender. Under each of the three headings Bright describes how lesbians practice each technique and how men might best practice the techniques themselves. Bright falls all over herself pandering to her male readers, assuring them that men should have better results than lesbians themselves: "Lesbians are certainly outmaneuvered by straight men—in numbers, influence, and earning power. And of course, you have penises."[40]

Bright "lite-ens" lesbian identity by equating it solely with sexual practice. As indicated in her statement opening this section, she caters to a historic porno-abusive sensibility by identifying lesbian sexuality as "incestuous." She simultaneously commodifies lesbian sexuality by reducing it to a set of practices that can be marketed to and practiced by anyone—even and especially men; in Bright's (sex) world, lesbian identity is not only depoliticized, it is dismembered—separated from the lesbian body.

MAKING ROOM FOR DADDY

YOU KNOW I'M NOT TELLING LESBIANS TO STOP SLEEPING ONLY WITH WOMEN,
BUT I THINK IF THEY LEAVE OPEN A PART OF THE BRAIN TOWARD MEN AND
ACCEPT MALE LUST AND FIND MEN EXTREMELY ATTRACTIVE AND GET HORNY IN
RELATION TO MEN AND OGLE THEIR BODIES AND DO SOMETHING WITH THEM,
THEN SEX WITH WOMEN WILL BE HOTTER.

—CAMILLE PAGLIA TO SUSIE BRIGHT, OUT/LOOK[41]

Both Paglia and Bright are ever intent on displacing the "mother" (lesbian/feminism) of contemporary feminist thought and practice, continually pointing to its irrelevance if not its downright harmfulness. At the same time, in their own unique ways, both are especially eager to open up some space for "daddy" (cockocratic[42] thought, practice, and presence) in the lesbian (political, cultural, and sexual) world.

In "Men Who Love Lesbians (Who Don't Care for Them Too Much)," Bright assures lesbians that most heterosexual men share a common, and decidedly nonpatriarchal, interest in lesbian pornography. The men who are attracted to lesbian erotica, she tells us, are "lesbian-identified men," whom she affectionately terms "dyke daddies."[43] She continues: "Most men who like this kind of erotica don't want to save the lesbians, they want to be the lesbians." Why? Because "lesbian lovemaking is soft and slippery and it never, ever ends" and because "lesbians are free."[44] Are these "dyke daddies" who Bright claims to be enviously imagining themselves as lesbians having sex with other lesbians also imagining themselves being dyke-bashed? Do they fantasize about job and housing discrimination? Are they lobbying their legislatures to ensure lesbian rights? Or are they engaging in a completely colonizing practice, what bell hooks terms "eating the other":

> Encounters with Otherness are clearly marked as more exciting, more intense, and more threatening. The lure is the combination of pleasure and danger. In the cultural marketplace the Other is coded as having the capacity to be more alive, as holding the secret that will allow those who venture and dare to break with the culture anhedonia . . . and experience sensual and spiritual renewal.[45]

Bright does not even entertain any possibility that an exploitative use of lesbian imagery—based in the sexualized, colonial practice of appropriating, owning, and controlling Otherness—is what drives many heterosexual men's affinity for lesbian porn. In so doing, she happily positions lesbians as objects of a voyeuristic, appropriating gaze, asking lesbians, even in lesbian erotic space, to continually "make room for daddy."

The problem, as Bright sees it, is not with heterosexist men using lesbian porn, but with uptight lesbians who object to this. According to Bright, these dykes are plagued with an aversion to "male attention." Moreover, they have an unhealthy fear of bodily fluids (here male ejaculate), they are overly protective of lesbian privacy, and ridiculously fearful, in a Victorian feminine kind of way, of any portrayal of lesbianism that foregrounds the sexual. Nowhere does she entertain the possibility that lesbians are justifiably leery about the appropriation of lesbian sexuality by men. Not unlike Camille Paglia, Bright roots lesbians' oppression in lesbian retrograde thinking. When she predicts that the motto for sexual liberation in the 1990s will be "Get Over Yourself,"[46] Bright is addressing such "repressed" and unduly concerned lesbian/feminists.

In her introduction to *Susie Bright's Sexual Reality*, Bright gets downright ontological: "I have been captivated by the idea of 'virtual reality,' by the recognition that our fantasies and fears—especially the sexual ones—are more real than the 'real' forces we have reckoned with historically."[47] This sentiment is given full treatment in the "Dan Quayle's Dick" essay of *Sexwise*. Forget his role in denying women access to birth control and abortions, forget his support of the "family values" platform whose proponents declared an open war on queers. Bright asks us to join her in exploring her own sexual fantasies about the former vice president and writes of her imagined tryst with Quayle, "Geez Louise, his cock is such heaven. I mean, what are the qualifications of a great fuck? Spelling ain't one of 'em. Neither is any kind of brains, let alone progressive politics." After several pages of descriptive fucking, Bright explains the purpose of her fantasy: "C'mon, I don't want him anywhere near the White House. But wet dreams like this don't visit that often. I only want Dan Quayle sweat-soaked, the cum drained out of him, chained to my bed, just a heartbeat away if I need him."[48] One way to read this fantasy is that Bright is suggesting that all Quayle needs is the proverbial "good fuck." (Speaking as daddy's perfect little mouthpiece, she has prescribed the same for Andrea Dworkin and Catharine MacKinnon.)[49]

While we respect the power of radically transgressive dreams, visions, and mythmaking as modes of conjuring power and shifting realities, Bright's fantasy is by no means transgressive. Her attempt to turn the tables on the right wing fails because she refuses to address the eroticization of hierarchy and power that underlies and bolsters the male supremacist system (perhaps she should reread Dworkin and MacKinnon).[50] Imagining oneself in a sexualized relation to men in power (even if one is however fantastically "on top") is a response subliminally suggested, even required, by the endemic sexualization of phallic power. When subjected peoples find irresistible, even sexually irresistible, that which oppresses us, the success of power is ensured. In a nutshell, Bright is not rebelling against but acting out a (wet) version of the "American Dream."

Bright's piece on Quayle is a vivid example of the sort of "political" agenda suggested by lesbian chic. Fuck your enemies, dazzle them with the sizzle of "lesbian" sex and watch all of your political troubles melt away in the afterglow. It is unlikely that Quayle would be threatened by Bright's fantasy, and why should he be? Bright's naughty girl image isn't really meant to overthrow political and sexual systems, only to (sex)toy with them. Her books are less a call to arms than a call to beds, suggesting that lots of hot and heavy lesbian sex—at home and on the silver screen—can replace activism. Her prediction for the 1990s is that "we're going to start talking about what we do instead of who we supposedly are."[51] Identity politics are out, and lesbian sexual celebrity is in. Bright's fame reveals the dirty little secret behind lesbian chic: they like us, they really like us—as long as we're only rocking the bed and not the boat.

REVENGE OF THE STEPFORD DYKES

In 1972, Ira Levin published his novel *The Stepford Wives* (which later proved the basis for three films, including *Revenge of the Stepford Wives).*[52] The plot of the novel concerns a group of affluent white suburban family men who have bonded into a "Men's Association." The underlying purpose of this malevolent association is the manufacture of glamorous, robot replicas of the members' wives. The first act of the robot is to kill off the real wife. The Stepford wives are programmed for compatible personalities, totally accommodating sexual performances, superior housekeeping abilities, and a penchant to perpetually praise their men.

The careers of both Paglia and Bright are based in bizarre variants of these Stepford behaviors (nonthreatening if flamboyant personalities, superior hegemonic upkeep capabilities, and, well, that same penchant to perpetually praise men and waste women). They also, oddly enough, are rooted in a desire for revenge. Despite their righteous rantings against "victim feminists," Paglia and Bright at root present themselves as "victims," as having been banished from the Lesbian/Feminist Nation. When Bright questioned Paglia about her assault on lesbian feminism, Paglia admitted, "there is also an element of revenge in it—no doubt about that—because I am pissed that I spent the best years of my sex life in misery."[53] Bright herself refers to lesbian feminists and other "fundamentalists" when she writes that "frankly, I'm sure my sex life could be better—so much better than I could possibly imagine—if their hands had never been around my throat."[54] Despite their "feminism," both resort consistently to the most basic sexist stereotyping, reducing lesbian/feminists to "prudes."

Indeed, throughout their works is an inordinate amount of name-calling, nasty personal attacks (even against other women's bodies), and social climbing over the (intended broken) backbone of lesbian/feminism. Some feminist critics continue to hope that Paglia, particularly as the "academic," will read such scholars as Judith Butler and Teresa de Lauretis, who write extensively on queer bodies and identities. But that would require Paglia to be genuinely moved by lesbian thought or feminist academia. She manifestly is not. Her role as Supermodel/Stepford Dyke is to target and discredit the radical thought which has had the most sociopolitical impact and which is the most profoundly transgressive (hence Paglia and Bright's studied attention to Dworkin and MacKinnon).[55]

As tokens, Paglia and Bright both emerged from and continue to exploit political and community fissures around issues of sexuality and sexual practice. A founder of the lesbian feminist movement, Julia Penelope, has admitted that the lack of lesbian feminist conversation about actual lesbian sex practice has "created a vacuum around sex and how to 'do it.'"[56] Because this accurate information has never been available from mainstream sources either, Penelope argues that sex radicals (particularly proponents of sadomasochism) have "made the totality of Lesbian sexuality their 'domain,' virtually without challenge."[57] Paglia, who implies that lesbian sexuality is a contradiction in terms, and Bright, who accuses anyone who doesn't share her vision of lesbian sexuality of being "sex negative," have thus arrogantly staked their claims to that "domain." Yet many of us who are "antipornography" (in the Dworkin-MacKinnon sense of pornography as the sexualization of hierarchy, inequality, domination, and subordination) know that we root that opposition in profoundly sex-positive and radical sensibilities. Lesbian and bisexual feminists should explore, both privately and in public discussion, our sexual practices as they are infused with our feminist desires. We should publicize and promote our insights with as much vigor and confidence as our detractors, including through the creation of sexual stories and pictures.

Paglia, Bright, and their entrepreneurial successors market to the mainstream the polarizations within lesbian/feminist communities and among lesbians of every political orientation. Indeed, they bank on "proving" the continually reported demise of lesbian/feminism. Yet, at the same time, they fail to recognize that even they are included in the lesbian reality that journalist Victoria Brownworth identifies: "We are media fodder, trivialized and minimized as a group." She shrewdly continues: "The *Newsweek* piece . . . [described earlier in this chapter] is the most disturbing. The subhead of the article reads WHAT ARE THE LIMITS OF TOLERANCE? This confirmed all my worst fears about the mainstream perception of dykes: Gay men might be worrisome, but lesbians are scary. When *Newsweek* did its cover story on gay men, there was nothing about the limits of tolerance; after all, gay men are still part of the mainstream. They aren't feminists."[58]

Mythically, killing the Gorgon signifies the opening up of territory (physical or psychic) to violation and exploitation with no limitations or restrictions by taboo.[59] By helping, to whatever extent, to attack and "kill" the Gorgon of radical feminism/lesbianism, Paglia and Bright pave the way for an increased targeting of lesbians/feminists, which, inevitably, would include even them. In October 1995, *Playboy* ran a nasty article on lesbian chic naming Paglia, Bright, and Dworkin the "Best Marketed Lesbians." In the eyes of the mainstream, each of these women, however radically different, is a freak, a joke, a transgressor, an enemy. The bitter irony is that, for all Paglia and Bright's catering and collaboration, the unleashed intolerance of that meanstream would undoubtedly include them in its sweep.

NOTES

1. bell hooks, "Camille Paglia: 'Black' Pagan or White Colonizer," *Outlaw Culture: Resisting Representations* (Boston: South End Press, 1994) 83-90.

2. In *Single White Female* (a film directed by Barbet Schroeder, 1993), the not so subtextual lesbian, when thwarted, becomes a knife-wielding psychopath. An act from Madonna's tour, "The Girlie Show," shown on the MTV 1993 Video Music Awards, shows Madonna in butch drag, pantomiming beating and raping a lingerie-clad Asian woman; cheap poster art, for example that of Geoffrey Hargrave Thomas, regularly features lingerie-lesbians with knives or razors aimed at other women.

3. Victoria Brownworth, "More than Just a Trend," *Advocate*, July 27, 1993, 80; Sue O'Sullivan, "Girls Who Kiss Girls and Who Cares?" in *The Good, the Bad, and the Gorgeous: Popular Culture's Romance with Lesbianism*, ed. Diane Hamer and Belinda Budge (San Francisco: Pandora, 1994) 78–95; Kathy Miriam, "From the Rage to All the Rage: Lesbian-Feminism, Sadomasochism, and the Politics of Memory," in *Unleashing Feminism: Critiquing Lesbian Sadomasochism in the Gay Nineties*, ed. Irene Reti (Santa Cruz: HerBooks, 1993) 7–70.

4. We use "lesbian/feminist" to signify the attack of Bright and Paglia on lesbian feminisms and, indeed, all radical feminisms.

5. Camille Paglia, "No Law in the Arena: A Pagan Theory of Sexuality," *Vamps and Tramps* (New York: Vintage, 1994) 19–96.

6. Mimi=Freed, "Interview with an Uzi: Camille Paglia Talks at Mimi=Freed," *On Our Backs* 9.4 (March–April 1993): 16–20, 40.

7. Teresa Ebert, "The Politics of the Outrageous," *Women's Review of Books* 9.1 (October 1991): 12-13; B. Ruby Rich, "Top Girl," *Village Voice*, October 8, 1991, 29–33; S. Elaine Craghead, "Camille Paglia and the Problematics of Sexuality and Subversion," in *Lesbian Erotics*, ed. Karla Jay (New York: New York University Press, 1995) 85–100.

8. Camille Paglia, *Sexual Personae: Art and Decadence from Nefertiti to Emily Dickinson* (New York: Vintage, 1991) 12.

9. James Wolcott, "Power Trip," *Vanity Fair*, September 1992, 299–303.

10. See bell hooks, "Madonna: Soul Sister or Plantation Mistress," in *Black Looks: Race and Representation* (Boston: South End Press, 1992) 157–64.

11. Anthony Jewell, "Dole: Make English Official Language," *Albuquerque Journal*, September 5, 1995, A4.

12. bell hooks, "Camille Paglia," *Outlaw Culture* 85.

13. Paglia, "No Law in the Arena" 63.

14. Camille Paglia, *Sex, Art, and American Culture* (New York: Vintage, 1992) 23-24.

15. Wolcott, "Power Trip" 302.

16. Paglia, "No Law in the Arena" 81.

17. Craghead, "Camille Paglia" 87–89.

18. *Playboy*, May 1995, 51–64.

19. Paglia, "No Law in the Arena" 65.

20. Ibid. 33.

21. Alice Walker, *The Temple of My Familiar* (San Diego: Harcourt Brace Jovanovich, 1989) 269; Phyllis Chesler, *Women and Madness* (New York: Avon, 1972) 23; Kate Millett, *Sexual Politics* (New York: Touchstone, 1990) 114–15; Mary Daly, *Gyn/Ecology: The Metaethics of Radical Feminism* (Boston: Beacon, 1978) 13; Catherine Nicholson, "How Rage Mothered My Third Birth," *Sinister Wisdom* 1.1 (July 1976): 40–45.

22. Barbara G. Walker, *The Woman's Encyclopedia of Myths and Secrets* (San Francisco: HarperSan Francisco, 1983) 74.

23. *Gynesophical* is a word invented by Paula Gunn Allen.

24. *Snool* was first used and defined by Mary Daly in *Pure Lust: Elemental Feminist Philosophy* (1984; reprint San Francisco: HarperSan Francisco, 1992). There she tells us that snools, who are "the rule," are characterized by "sadism and masochism combined" and are "the stereotypic saints and heroes of the sadostate."

25. Elana Dykewoman, *They Will Know Me by My Teeth* (Megaera Press, 1976); Emily Culpepper, "Gorgons: A Face for Contemporary Women's Rage," *Woman of Power: A Magazine of Feminism, Spirituality, and Politics*, no. 3 (Winter–Spring 1986): 22–24, 40; May Sarton, "The Muse of Medusa," *Selected Poems of May Sarton* (New York: Norton, 1978) 160; Chela Sandoval, "Feminism and Racism: A Report on the 1981 National Women's Studies Association Conference," in *Making Face, Making Soul/Haciendo Caras*, ed. Gloria Anzaldúa (San Francisco: Aunt Lute, 1990) 55–71; Jane Caputi, *Gossips, Gorgons, and Crones: The Fates of the Earth* (Santa Fe: Bear and Company, 1993) 172–73; Hélène Cixous, "The Laugh of the Medusa," in *New French Feminisms*, ed. Elaine Marks and Isabelle de Courtivron (New York: Schocken, 1981) 245–64; Walker, *Temple of My Familiar* 269; Gloria Anzaldúa, *Borderlands/La Frontera* (San Francisco: Spinsters/Aunt Lute, 1987) 47.

26. Paglia, *Sexual Personae* 87.

27. Caputi, *Gossips, Gorgons, and Crones* 275–90.

28. Anzaldúa, *Borderlands* 80.

29. Paglia, "No Law in the Arena" 25.

30. Ibid. 26.

31. Paula Gunn Allen, *The Sacred Hoop: Recovering the Feminine in American Indian Traditions* (Boston: Beacon, 1986) 262.

32. Susie Bright, "How to Make Love to a Woman: Hands-on Advice from a Woman Who Does," *Esquire*, February 1994, 108.

33. Walker, *Woman's Encyclopedia of Myths and Secrets* 764.

34. Ruthann Robson, *Lesbian (Out)Law: Survival under the Rule of Law* (New York: Firebrand, 1992) 18.

35. Susie Bright, *Susie Sexpert's Lesbian Sex World* (Pittsburgh: Cleis, 1990) 11.

36. Alan Frutkin, "Bonnie and Bonnie: Behind the Scenes of *Bound*," *Advocate*, no. 689 (September 5, 1995): 55–57.

37. Leslie Feinberg, *Stone Butch Blues* (New York: Firebrand, 1993).

38. bell hooks, *Outlaw Culture: Resisting Representations* (New York: Routledge, 1994) 16.

39. Jackie Goldsby, "What It Means to Be Colored Me," *Out/Look*, no. 5 (Summer 1990): 15.

40. Susie Bright, *Sexwise* (Pittsburgh: Cleis, 1995) 19.

41. Susie Bright, "Undressing Camille Paglia," *Out/Look*, no. 16 (Spring 1992): 14.

42. *Cockocratic* is a word invented by Daly in *Pure Lust*.

43. Susie Bright, *Susie Bright's Sexual Reality: A Virtual Sex World Reader* (Pittsburgh: Cleis, 1992) 94.

44. Bright, *Sexual Reality* 94.

45. bell hooks, *Black Looks: Race and Representation* (Boston: South End Press, 1992) 26.

46. Bright, *Susie Sexpert's Lesbian Sex World* 137.

47. Bright, *Sexual Reality* 10.

48. Ibid. 70.

49. Ibid. 66.

50. See Andrea Dworkin, *Pornography: Men Possessing Women* (New York: Dutton, 1989), and *Intercourse* (New York: Free Press, 1987); Catharine A. MacKinnon, *Feminism Unmodified: Discourses on Life and Law* (Cambridge: Harvard University Press, 1987), and *Toward a Feminist Theory of the State* (Cambridge: Harvard University Press, 1989).

51. Bright, *Susie Sexpert's Lesbian Sex World* 139.

52. Ira Levin, *The Stepford Wives* (New York: Random House, 1972). The films are *The Stepford Wives* (1974), *Revenge of the Stepford Wives* (1980), and *The Stepford Children* (1987).

53. Bright, *Sexual Reality* 83.

54. Bright, *Sexwise* 15.

55. See Paglia, "The Return of Carry Nation: Catharine MacKinnon and Andrea Dworkin," *Vamps and Tramps* 107–12, and Bright, "The Prime of Miss Kitty MacKinnon," *Sexwise* 121–27.

56. Julia Penelope, *Call Me Lesbian: Lesbian Lives, Lesbian Theory* (Freedom, Calif.: Crossing Press, 1992) 117.

57. Penelope, *Call Me Lesbian* 114.

58. Brownworth, "More Than Just a Trend" 80.

59. Caputi, *Gossips, Gorgons, and Crones* 169–93.

Part Three

COALITIONS

"Confessions" of a Lesbian Feminist

BONNIE ZIMMERMAN

I

I title this piece "confessions" for a number of reasons. Superficially, it may read as a kind of autobiography or memoir, a text in which an individual posits her personal history and experience as a model or cautionary tale for present-day readers. As such, it ostensibly offers a life history as a transparent window into the self, and into the self as an embodiment of social forces. But I am not so naive as to think that confessions do any such thing. As constructed texts, confessions reveal only as much as the author wishes, and for those purposes with which the author sets out to write in the first place. And, of course, the author of a confession or memoir is no more in control of the discourses shaping her thoughts and memories than is any other author. In fact, as this text will show, I have no intention at all of "revealing" my self through anecdote and storytelling. My use of the confessional instead plays with the juridical or religious meaning of confession as the acknowledgment of culpability in a crime or sin. I confess here to the "crime" of being a lesbian feminist.

This may sound a very odd way to begin an essay. What natural or social order do I believe I have transgressed? What crime do I consider myself accused of? Who are my accusers? What Kafkaesque fantasy leads me to assume that I am—or that my theoretical position is—on trial? I will spare the reader a detailed recitation of the accusations I believe to have been made against lesbian feminism, possibly as early as the "sex wars" of the early 1980s and at least as recently as the end of that decade. Most readers of this volume will be familiar with them: essentialism, ethnocentrism, separatism, puritanism, political correctness, and so forth. Let others engage these issues theoretically. I wish here to "defend" lesbian feminism through a deliberately, unabashedly subjective revelation of individual history. My point in this chapter is simply this: lesbianism and feminism never have been separate or unconnected in my life. Coming to feminism provided the basis for my coming out as a lesbian; living as a lesbian has shaped my life and work as a feminist. For me, the "crossing" between lesbianism and feminism has created a large shaded area in which to develop my particular subjectivity, perspective, politics, and—dare I use this word in the 1990s?—identity.

For this reason, I will evade the problems posed by grammar and punctuation. Is the proper term *lesbian feminist* or *lesbian-feminist?* Or, for that matter, *feminist lesbian,* which is, after all, grammatically more correct? For the sake of simplicity, I will use *lesbian feminist* throughout, but with the conscious intention of invoking the explosive potential in the gap between two nouns, rather than the hierarchical modification of one signifier (the noun, the substance, the essence) by another (the adjective, the quality, the difference).

When I say that my subjectivity—my sense of self—has been shaped by my experiences as a lesbian and feminist, I am drawing upon the writing of Teresa de Lauretis and Elspeth Probyn, specifically their articulation of the function and workings of experience. It is through experience—or, in Probyn's words, "the felt facticity of material being"—that we come to understand ourselves as human beings. Or, as de Lauretis puts it, experience is "a *process* by which, for all social beings, subjectivity is constructed. Through that process one places oneself or is placed in social reality."[1] Subjectivity, she argues, is the effect of experience, which is itself the interaction between the self and the world. In other words, experience is neither internal nor individual, but an interaction between self and society. That is how I attempt to approach my own experiences as a lesbian feminist: not as a justification for any particular theoretical statement nor as irrelevant delusions of a unified humanist Self, but as evidence requiring investigation and interrogation. I confess to being a lesbian feminist, but I demand a dispassionate inquiry and a fair trial by a jury of my peers.

My subjectivity, then, is the effect of my experiences, which are themselves the interaction between my individual being and the social world of the second half of the twentieth century. For me, and probably for many other lesbians of my generation and location, those experiences were shaped powerfully by both lesbianism and feminism. It is not possible to separate these out. I came to understand myself as a lesbian through feminism and as a feminist through lesbianism. I have also come to understand that this has not been the experience of all lesbians of my generation, nor of lesbians of subsequent generations. Or, if I narrow my focus specifically to lesbian critics and theorists, that the kind of feminism that shapes their consciousness may differ substantially from that which shaped mine. So my first argument in this chapter would be that we must stop generalizing and essentializing *feminism* and *lesbian feminism,* just as we have learned not to essentialize *lesbian.*

What is feminism? Some of the questions that arise around the relationship between lesbianism and feminism are complicated by the manner in which feminism is used as a generic category. But at the initiation of the second wave of the (white) women's movement in the late 1960s, there were many varieties of feminism: liberal, radical, cultural, lesbian, Marxist, and socialist, primarily. Women of color soon added more inflections, such as womanist, to these white-constructed variations. But by the 1990s these differences had been largely boiled down to two binary oppositions: cultural feminism and poststructuralist feminism.[2] Cultural feminism is perceived to be essentialist, simplistic, racist, etc.—in short, "bad" feminism. Poststructuralist feminism, on the other hand, is socially constructed, sensitive to difference, sophisticated—"good" feminism. Anyone who does not wholeheartedly ascribe to the theoretical assumptions of postmodernism (e.g., the instability of identity categories, the primacy of language) is identified and prosecuted as a cultural feminist. It has caused me much bemusement (I wish I could write amusement) that while I was once called a critic of cultural feminism, I am now labeled a cultural feminist myself.[3] In fact, I have been in my time a Marxist feminist, and briefly a radical feminist on my way to lesbian separatist, and now prefer to call myself simply lesbian feminist, but "I am not now nor have I ever been" a cultural feminist, nor have I written anything (including *The Safe Sea of Women,* despite reviews to the contrary) that could be fairly characterized as cultural feminism.[4] Cultural feminism, as I understand it, is based upon the belief in an essential gender difference, the superiority of the feminine principle, the existence of a transhistorical women's culture, and creativity as a path toward liberation. Cultural feminism was a popular variation especially in the late 1970s, and often appealed to radical lesbians, but the entire history of second-wave feminism cannot be reduced to it.

To understand the varied and particular crossings between lesbianism and feminism, it helps to pay attention to the theoretical and political differences among feminisms. Similarly, there may be many different ways in which we understand lesbianism: for example, as gender inversion, sexual behavior, intense bonding, or resistance to patriarchy. Some of these may be congruent with particular varieties of feminism, even dependent upon them. Other ways may not seem congruent, but upon investigation and examination it may still turn out that there is a "special relation" between lesbianism (no matter how one defines it) and feminism (of any sort).

II

As we explore how lesbians attempted to situate themselves historically in relation to feminism, and against it, we might begin with some of the classic texts and statements from the late 1960s and early 1970s, one particularly potent site of radical discourses throughout Western societies. Rather than a close reading of these texts—which is beyond the scope of the project I have set for myself and may instead be done in other chapters in this volume—I present here an experiential reflection upon these texts and times. The point I wish to make here is that lesbian feminism grew out of the particular conditions of its moment in history, conceived of itself as a political theory and strategy, and has subsequently come to be caricatured in ways that need to be reevaluated and, ultimately, rejected.

Every historian of the early women's liberation movement begins with the infamous words of radical feminist Ti-Grace Atkinson to characterize the "unhappy marriage" between lesbianism and feminism. According to Alice Echols, "Some [feminists] even came to regard lesbians as the vanguard of the women's movement. For instance, Ti-Grace Atkinson, who had earlier declared that 'feminism is a theory, lesbianism is a practice,' now contended that 'feminism is the theory, lesbianism the practice.'"[5] In other words, Atkinson's earlier scorn for the lesbian as a mere practitioner in contrast to the feminist as high theorist "now" mutates, by means of a crucial change of article, into high praise for lesbians as the living avatars of feminist thought. Echols is substantially correct that many lesbian and heterosexual feminists did come to believe that lesbians *experienced* in the "felt facticity" of their "material being" what other feminists only spun out as insubstantial theory, or discourse. But there are other unexplored assumptions and implications at work in this statement that further illuminate this relationship.

I decided to return to the original source to see what Atkinson might have meant by the switch from "a" to "the." Significantly, Echols led me back not to any text written by Atkinson herself, but to two contemporaneous texts attributing these statements to her.[6] Wondering if perhaps

Atkinson had been convicted on hearsay evidence, I turned to her own *Amazon Odyssey*. And there I found a curious fact: at least in writing, she never had declared feminism to be a/the theory and lesbianism a/the practice. What she had written is even more interesting: first, that "lesbianism is a 'sexual' position, whereas feminism is a 'political' position"; and second, that "lesbianism is to feminism what the Communist Party was to the trade-union movement."[7] Now these do correspond roughly to the interpretations Echols gives to Atkinson's more famous apocryphal statements. But how much richer and more evocative of the history of the times they actually are.

The first statement points to the separation between the discursive position of feminism (theory) and material experience of lesbianism (practice) that characterized the earlier women's liberation movement and necessitated the establishment of a theoretical position of lesbian feminism. It illustrates how in its earliest articulation second-wave feminism did not yet incorporate a political understanding of sexuality, positing political and theoretical feminism as a rejection of the assignment of women to the category of sexuality. Given the association of woman/sex/body that seemed so clearly marked in capitalist patriarchy, it was not surprising that lesbians, and other women who upheld this association in their material existence, should be accused of treason, or a mortal sin. Those women, among them myself, who insisted upon politicizing sex and sexualizing politics could be seen as initiating the processes that necessarily and ironically resulted in the sex wars a decade later.

The second quotation from *Amazon Odyssey* supports Echols's contention that, in a relatively short time, some women came to see lesbians as the vanguard of the women's movement. Atkinson's own analogy, however, reminds us that the word *vanguard* belongs to the Marxist lexicon, and thus illustrates a currently underanalyzed dimension of the early women's and lesbian movements: the powerful influence of Marxism over radical discourses. Marx was to 1970s feminism what Freud is to feminism in the 1990s. It may well be that the reason why many of us who were shaped by the politics of the sixties and early seventies hesitate to accept wholeheartedly the premises of poststructuralism is due to our early education in dialectical materialism.

At this point, I will turn to what to me was among the most influential writings of the early 1970s: *The Furies*, a newspaper published for several years by a lesbian-separatist collective including, among others, Charlotte Bunch and Rita Mae Brown. In its first issue, Bunch published a manifesto, "Lesbians in Revolt," that argued the basic premises and programs of lesbian feminist separatism at that moment in history. Readers can find it reprinted in Bunch's collection, *Passionate Politics*,[8] but without the rich context provided by its place within the newspaper, surrounded by articles on the myth of the Furies, coming out, physical strength, economics, and the life of Queen Christina (complete with photo of Greta Garbo). *The Furies* combined Karl Marx, Valerie Solanis, Hothead Paisan, and Lesbian Avengers into one punch in the balls of patriarchy.

"Lesbians in Revolt" argued one powerful and uncompromising principle: because sexism is the root of all oppression and heterosexuality upholds sexism, feminists must become lesbians and lesbians must become feminists if we are to effect a revolution. Here, in breathtaking and audacious simplicity, is the unification of lesbianism and feminism that subsequently has been broken asunder. But we should note that Bunch is positing a constructionist, not essentialist, argument. Feminists are not essentially lesbians, any more than lesbians are necessarily feminists. To state that feminists must become lesbians assumes that lesbianism is a matter of choice and conviction, not biological conditioning or sexual behavior. Moreover, lesbians must also become feminists; that is, they must ground their sexuality in a political discourse if any social change is to occur.

It is easy today to dismiss statements such as these as totalizing, utopian grandstanding. To a certain extent, that was exactly their intention. They were based upon an analysis of sexism as the source of all other oppressions, a discredited notion that often forms the basis for dismissing radical lesbian analyses. But we need to place lesbian separatism (or lesbian feminism) and *The Furies* in historical context. Because of the hegemony of Marxist theory over the left at that time, all political movements defined themselves in relation to the notion of "primary contradiction"—either to demonstrate how and why their issues were part of the primary contradiction of class (the approach taken by Marxist feminists) or to posit a different primary contradiction such as race or gender. Replacing Marxist theory with postmodern, typically Foucauldian, theory has changed all this, of course. But to some extent, the difficulty of holding multiple oppressions in relation to one another may be a legacy of Marxism—indeed, of all the grand totalizing metanarratives of the past. To the extent that lesbian feminism established itself as another metanarrative, its overthrow is salutory. But we should not ignore its valuable insights: the interconnections between sexism and heterosexism, the centrality of these to social systems in general, and the need to develop a political program to undermine them. Even if that political program was, is, and ever will be utopian.

One of the current indictments of this lesbian feminist utopianism is that it often led to acrimonious battles to define the perimeters of community. It is certainly true that lesbian feminists struggled over definitions and that these struggles led to a series of exclusions. But at least at the beginning, the excluded category was men, which does not seem inappropriate to the project of defining lesbian politics and communities. I confess to being puzzled that this has become an indictment of lesbian feminism. All political movements involve a certain degree of exclusion, of self-identification through separation. Perhaps the queer movement (if it is a movement) or postmodern "lesbianism" (if that conjunction of terms makes sense) does not or will not; however, Andrew Parker's half-humorous comment that "there are no queer republicans" suggests an identity based on exclusion as well.[9]

But the lesbian feminist movement also attempted to define community in terms of inclusion. The struggles around class and race that began as soon as lesbian feminism first articulated itself—read issues of *The Furies* or *Ain't I a Woman* or any of the many ephemeral publications from the early to mid-1970s—were framed in terms of inclusion, not exclusion; that is, how do we create and conceptualize communities that potentially include all women who call themselves lesbians (of any sort)? Our very real failures ought not completely erase the history of our worthy intentions.

Much of what I hear and read these days about lesbian feminism is written by women who criticize it without apparently having had much firsthand experience of the movement and era they condemn.[10] So, increasingly, young women learn about lesbian feminism through parodic representations of it. These representations construct the stereotypical lesbian feminist as:

flannel shirt androgyne
closeminded, antisex puritan
humorless moralist
racist and classist ignoramus
essentialist utopian

The lesbian feminist movement certainly had its excesses—what movement hasn't?—but this stereotype is far from my experience. And yet it rings familiar: I recognize in it the Western, anti-Communist stereotype of the Soviet iron lady parodied by—who else?—Greta Garbo in *Ninotchka*. And, like (stereotypic) lesbians in the 1990s, Garbo-as-Ninotchka (inspired by the oh-so-gay Walter Pidgeon) morphs into the material girl who just wants to have fun. How much else, I wonder, of contemporary condemnations of 1970s lesbian feminism—its vanguardism, centrism, puritanism, ideological rigidity—can be traced back to anti-Communist, anti-Marxist stereotypes? These stereotypes and condemnations in effect displace the notion of lesbianism as a political stance/identity/label and replace it with a currently more chic notion of lesbianism as sexual behavior (or, increasingly, gender performance). This is occurring in part through a meaningful exchange of theories and ideas, but in (large) part through misrepresentation, parody, and trashing.

III

I have laid out an idiosyncratic minihistory of lesbian feminist origins. I now want to address the impact of this history on my understanding of lesbian criticism and of myself as a lesbian feminist critic. As the editor of this volume pointed out to me, something appears to have happened to the feminist between the appearance of my essays "'What Has Never Been': An Overview of Lesbian Feminist Criticism" in 1981, and "'Lesbians Like This and That': Some Notes on Lesbian Criticism for the Nineties" in 1992.[11] How did lesbian feminist criticism become lesbian criticism, and what have been the gains and losses of this transition?

In pondering this question, I have concluded that in 1981 I still felt the need to assert the connection between lesbian and feminist, while by 1992 I had come to take it for granted. The most striking realization I have had in writing the present chapter is that three short years later I can no longer make that assumption. Although I have never separated lesbian and feminist in my work, other critics certainly do in theirs. Consequently, I may need once again to assert the lesbian feminist connection. Or others may do so for me—and pejoratively.[12] As far as my subjectivity or critical stance is concerned, however, nothing happened to the feminist except that she became everybody's favorite whipping girl. In other words, although I have written as much as anyone in the profession about homophobia in academic feminism, I still situate myself thoroughly "inside" feminism, not outside or against it.

The question that seems to be in the forefront of critical theory today is, what theory speaks for lesbians? For nearly two decades, we took it for granted that feminism was that theory. Lesbian criticism of any and all varieties was constructed by flesh and bone lesbians starting in the early 1970s. For us, feminism was not a distinct discourse that spoke "for" lesbians but an epistemology used by lesbians to speak for ourselves. Indeed, I do not see feminism as a set of paradigms and beliefs that "preexists"—conceptually or historically—lesbianism. The second wave of feminism may predate the lesbian movement, but not by much.

Feminist and lesbian theory and critical practice arose at roughly the same moment in history, as a response to the same set of social and intellectual conditions and in many of the same institutions. Feminist theory and politics has been as thoroughly shaped by lesbians as lesbian ideology and activism has been shaped by feminism. And I believe it can be shown that, historically, lesbianism and feminism have been coterminous if not identical social phenomena. Let's not forget that in the popular (sexist and heterosexist) mentality, feminism and lesbianism are pretty much the same affront to law and morality.

Perhaps this is why it can be so difficult to distinguish between feminists and lesbians, to isolate a specific lesbian existence historically. For example, to what extent did passing women pass in order to obtain the social rights and freedom of men (a feminist motivation) and to what extent in order to be free to love as they wished (a lesbian motivation)? Should the distinction be collapsed even further: isn't the "right" to love women a masculine prerogative, and hence both a feminist and lesbian demand? From Havelock Ellis to Natalie Barney to the Daughters of Bilitis, strong links between lesbianism and feminism were articulated long before the 1970s.[13]

Lesbian existence and critical practice is "different from" feminist, to be sure, but I question to what extent it is "other than" feminist. Rather than thinking of lesbianism as "inside" or "outside" feminism, I think of both as occupying the same conceptual "space"—only with different inflections and stances. The spaces opened by lesbian criticism (like lesbian activism) are those that lesbians have claimed throughout history: woman to woman eroticism; intense, primary love and bonding; female independence; gender bending (whether inversion or elimination); separate female communities.[14] I see considerable overlap with nonlesbian feminism here. Perhaps lesbian space is simply female-separatist space; lesbian space is that space where men are not. Any female-only environment is experientially or symbolically associated with lesbianism: convents, girls' schools and women's colleges, women's liberation and women's studies, women's prisons, and so on. When one's analysis is rooted in gender or a theory of patriarchy, it makes sense that lesbianism should flourish or be assumed to flourish within these all-female environments. Hence, the close association of the critical or theoretical spaces of lesbianism and feminism.

These words—inside and outside, space and territory (like margins and centers, borders and borderlands)—also may remind us of how popular geographical metaphors have grown in recent years. Geographical metaphors are seductive, to be sure, but ultimately problematic. What does it mean to suggest, as this volume does, that lesbianism "troubles the borders" of feminism and feminism "troubles the borders" of lesbianism? Although I have done as much troubling of these borders as anyone, I find it difficult to conceptualize feminism and lesbianism as separate "territories." What kind of territories would these be? Would it be accurate instead to say that lesbian feminism is the borderland, the overlapping, between lesbianism and feminism, rather than a strict border? Spatial metaphors such as territories and borders imply (once again) that there are monolithic "spaces" called feminism and lesbianism. But lesbianism and feminism are not actual spaces, they are epistemologies, methodologies, ways of being and experiencing reality. Moreover, living as I do in a true borderland—and observing daily the facticity of concrete borders—I have serious questions about the advisability of using geographical metaphors at all.

Despite my firm commitment to the mutual "territory" of lesbianism and feminism, throughout my career I have insisted that there is a distinct lesbian approach to reading and interpreting texts. I raised that question first in relation to feminist criticism—that is, how does a lesbian read in contrast to how a generic (heterosexual) woman reads? The more urgent question for me today is how to maintain the specificity of lesbian textuality, culture, identity, community—in short, existence—within the claim of a generic gayness or queerness. So the relation of lesbian to feminist (or woman) seems even more urgent to me today than it did in the 1970s when I began this work. I strongly want an individuated lesbian studies, but the challenge to me in the mid-1990s is to individuate it from gay and queer studies, not feminist studies.

It should be obvious to anyone in the field that, today, old-fashioned feminism must compete with poststructuralist feminism and queer theory as explanations of lesbianism. Nonetheless, I continue to believe that feminism gives the richest and most complex set of meanings to lesbian experience. The only realistic alternative—queer theory—can actually be argued to obliterate lesbianism as a specific identity, subject position, or signifier. Within "queer," whatever "lesbian" refers to is immediately deconstructed. Rather like electrons in the Heisenberg uncertainty principle, once you "name" a lesbian she disappears. This may be critically fashionable, but can it permit a distinct lesbian experience, identity, or critical practice?

IV

I want to conclude this meditation by confessing my love for a particular kind of word game: the duo-(or ana)crostic. A complex form of crossword puzzle, the duo-crostic requires solving two puzzles at once by working out the solution from two different ends. As you fill in the blanks of one puzzle, you transfer its letters to the second, thereby revealing its text. And then, working back, the letters you add to the second puzzle are transferred to the first. You can't solve one without the other. Lesbian feminism, to me, is like a duo-crostic: a "crossing" between two discourses that is both necessary and enriching. Filling in a blank space in one puzzle (lesbianism) reveals the solution to the other puzzle (feminism), and vice versa. To be sure, the felt facticity of our material being cannot be represented as a neat solution or determinate piece of text: every analogy has its limitations. But lesbianism contains valuable clues that reveal the hidden texts of feminism, and feminism provides a key to deciphering the meaning of lesbianism. And that is why I confess to being still a lesbian feminist.

NOTES

1. Elspeth Probyn, *Sexing the Self: Gendered Positions in Cultural Studies* (London: Routledge, 1993) 5; Teresa de Lauretis, *Alice Doesn't: Feminism, Semiotics, Cinema* (Bloomington: Indiana University Press, 1984) 159. I have addressed these issues myself in "In Academia, and Out," in *Changing Subjects: The Making of Feminist Literary Criticism*, ed. Gayle Greene and Coppelia Kahn (London: Routledge, 1993) 112–20.

2. I don't know who should be credited with this formulation, but I first encountered it in Linda Alcoff, "Cultural Feminism versus Post-Structuralism: The Identity Crisis in Feminist Theory," *Signs* 13.3 (Spring 1988): 405–36.

3. See Biddy Martin, "Lesbian Identity and Autobiographical Difference(s)," in *Life/Lines: Theorizing Women's Autobiography*, ed. Bella Brozki and Celeste Schenck (Ithaca: Cornell University Press, 1988) 90; Judith Halberstam, "Forum: The Question of Lesbian Separatism," *Lesbian Review of Books* 1.2 (Winter 1994–95): 5.

4. The quote echoes the McCarthy anti-Communist witchhunts of the 1950s.

5. Alice Echols, *Daring to Be Bad: Radical Feminism in America 1967–1975* (Minneapolis: University of Minnesota Press, 1989) 238.

6. Sidney Abbott and Barbara Love, *Sappho Was a Right-On Woman* (New York: Day Books, 1978) 117; Anne Koedt, "Lesbianism and Feminism," in *Radical Feminism*, ed. Anne Koedt, Ellen Levine, and Anita Rapone (New York: Quadrangle, 1973) 246.

7. Ti-Grace Atkinson, *Amazon Odyssey* (New York: Links, 1974) 83, 134.

8. Charlotte Bunch, *Passionate Politics: Feminist Theory in Action* (New York: St. Martin's, 1987) 161–67.

9. Andrew Parker, "Forum," *Radical Teacher* 45 (Winter 1994): 55.

10. See, for example, some of the essays in *Sisters, Sexperts, Queers: Beyond the Lesbian Nation*, ed. Arlene Stein (New York: Plume, 1993).

11. Bonnie Zimmerman, "'What Has Never Been': An Overview of Lesbian

Feminist Criticism," in *The New Feminist Criticism*, ed. Elaine Showalter (New York: Pantheon, 1985) 200–24, and "'Lesbians Like This and That': Some Notes on Lesbian Criticism for the Nineties," in *New Lesbian Criticism*, ed. Sally Munt (New York: Columbia University Press, 1992) 1–15.

12. For example, a review in the *Advocate* (July 26, 1994) of Maureen Brady's *Folly* identifies my Afterword as a "lesbian-feminist" reading. No mention is made of the fact that I spend more time placing *Folly* in the traditions of literary realism and labor fiction than that of lesbian novels. I can only assume that my name is so closely associated with lesbian feminism that my actual words are irrelevant.

13. See, for example, Havelock Ellis, *Studies in the Psychology of Sex, Part Four: Sexual Inversion* (New York: Random House, 1936) 261–63; Karla Jay, *The Amazon and the Page: Natalie Clifford Barney and Renee Vivien* (Bloomington: Indiana University Press, 1988) esp. p. 2; Del Martin and Phyllis Lyon, *Lesbian/ Woman* (New York: Bantam, 1972), esp. chap. 9.

14. These conceptual spaces enable writers to imagine lesbianism in the absence of hard fact. See, for example, Paula Gunn Allen, "*Hwame, Koshkalaka,* and the Rest: Lesbians in American Indian Cultures," *The Sacred Hoop* (Boston: Beacon, 1986) 245–61; Vivien Ng, "Looking for 'Lesbians' in Chinese History," in *The New Lesbian Studies: Toward the 21st Century*, ed. Bonnie Zimmerman and Toni McNaron (New York: Feminist Press, 1996).

"Don't Call Me *Girl*"

Lesbian Theory, Feminist Theory, and Transsexual Identities

KATHLEEN CHAPMAN AND MICHAEL DU PLESSIS

I

Kate Millett begins her 1974 autobiography *Flying* almost emblematically by delineating an enunciative space for herself between two poles that seem to frame women's oppression. On the bus to her temporary address in London, she notes the display window of "the place that advertises contraception, medical supplies, dusty pamphlets on fertility, ugly women in perverse pose titled *Butch Love*" (3). In the very next paragraph she sees billboards for Danny La Rue, the British drag entertainer, "[playing] the corner at the Palace, wigs and gowns. . . ." Of *Butch Love* and its "perverse pose" Millett remarks succinctly that it is "written for guys," and she deems La Rue's drag to be nothing other than "acceptable British family entertainment." Both the promotion of lesbians as gender nonconformists ("butch," "perverse") and the advertising image of the male-to-female transvestite ("wigs and gowns") stand for Millett as buttresses of the patriarchal-national edifice, as "acceptable British family entertainment," "written for [and by] guys." Gender nonconformity, at least in this instance for Millett, is no transgression at all, but business—men's business, family business—as usual.

Minor as this moment is for the rest of Millett's autobiography, we choose to foreground it because it appears to characterize the cross-purposes that often exist between lesbians, feminists, lesbian-feminists, and the array of what Kate Bornstein calls the "transgressively gendered," those who do not depend for their identities "on the existence of [a] bi-polar gender system" (*Gender Outlaw* 13). We include transsexuals (female-to-male and male-to-female), butch women, femme men, she-males, he-shes,[1] drag kings and queens, transvestites, cross-dressers, passing women, some bisexuals, transgenders of all kinds.

While transgressively gendered people often claim to have a stake in the dismantling of gender oppression via their refusal to accept socially dictated gender roles based on biological sex, a long tradition of feminist and lesbian-feminist analysis and argument asserts that transgenders are actually staking a claim in gender oppression itself and that the transgressively gendered do no more than provide "family entertainment" for patriarchy. Thus, in a fairly representative move, Annie Woodhouse comes to the following conclusion at the end of *Fantastic Women,* her investigation into what the subtitle of her book describes as *Sex, Gender and Transvestism.*[2] "*Undoubtedly,*" she writes, "transvestism replicates gender divisions; it relies on images of women which have been used to objectify and oppress them" (145; our emphasis). She adds that "the transvestite" stages such objectifying and oppressive fantasies of women "for his own pleasure," and can (or will) "always" go back to "the primary status of masculinity." Thus transvestism as such "upholds the supremacy of masculinity." Woodhouse makes "transvestism" a solely male activity. Her analysis reasserts the "proper" gender of the "fantastic women" as male; her work presumes that almost *all* transgendered male-to-females are married and that their wives are the true "victims" of this wolf-in-sheep's-clothing ploy of patriarchy.

In response to such widespread attacks on transgenders in the name of feminism, many gender nonconformists propose that a feminism which asserts the primacy of women's identifications with other women seems to be nothing more than a tautology of gender identities already established in a bipolar system that features only two sexes and two genders. One might think of the formula of the "woman-identified woman" here, with its concomitant definition of the lesbian as "the rage of all women condensed to the point of explosion,"[3] as well as Adrienne Rich's well-known lesbian continuum, which proposes, "Woman identification is a source of energy, a potential springhead of female power . . ." ("Compulsory Heterosexuality and Lesbian Existence" 63).

What concerns us here is that for several feminists and lesbian-feminists, such a bipolar system has been secured through the use of transgender issues, concerns, subjectivities, and representations as markers of the limits against which feminist and lesbian selves and communities are defined. The Michigan Womyn's Music Festival, for example, has become a central site of struggle over who can claim to be a "woman," a "lesbian," and who cannot. It stands as one particular instance of how women's communities have attempted to cohere by drawing boundaries based on the strictures of sexual and gender bipolarity and how those restraints ultimately serve to exclude those who fall outside their naturalized definitions. Writing about the festival's policies of exclusion in *Call Me Lesbian,* Julia Penelope implies that such boundary-formation keeps the male world of dominance at bay: "Standing naked 'downtown' at the Michigan Womyn's Music Festival, I've thought of myself as 'inside' and of the patriarchal world as 'out there' somewhere beyond the borders of the womyn-owned land" (55). While the ideal of a safe space is appealing, the enforcement of a policy that keeps the "inside" of a women-only space separate from the "out there" of patriarchal society depends upon, or even requires, a debate over whether or not to include male-to-female transsexuals.[4]

Emergent transgender studies and politics challenge such bipolarity and extend feminist struggles to dismantle the gender roles prescribed by a sexist society. Transgender-supportive work suggests different and, to our minds, more politically nuanced approaches to the problems of gender, since it views the reliance of most accounts of gender on a dualistic model of sex and gender as contributing to the persistence of conventional gender roles. For example, anthropologist Gilbert Herdt questions the comfortable tendency of "many in the Western tradition, including scholars in the field of sex and gender, [to] assume without reflection, the 'naturalism' of sexual dimorphism" (*Third Sex, Third Gender* 11). This "naturalism" is then reflected, according to Herdt, in the functioning of sexual dimorphism, or bipolarity, as an ideology that is "rigorously dichotomized into the 'natural,' i.e., moral entities of male and female . . . and [that] provides for persons who are . . . *one or the other*" (13).[5] In Herdt's analysis, all persons who stray outside these naturalized categories of male and female, man and woman, are stigmatized by this system.

Like Herdt, social anthropologist Anne Bolin states that transgenders "challenge the dominant . . . gender paradigm with its emphasis on reproduction and the biological sexual body as the sine qua non of gender identity and role" ("Transcending and Transgendering" 447). By refusing to identify as "one or the other" and by splitting their gender identities from the sex determinations assigned to them at birth, gender nonconformists both reject the confines of a gender system which cannot account for their existences and simultaneously outline the possibilities of expanding ways of thinking gender and sex. While some feminists and lesbian-feminists, as we have seen, maintain a gender dualism, Bolin describes the "transgender community" as a political movement that contests this dualism:

As a political movement, the transgender community views gender and sex systems as relativistic structures imposed by society and by the privileged controllers of individual bodies, the medical profession. The transgenderist is disquieting to the established gender system and unsettles the boundaries of bipolarity and opposition in the gender schema by suggesting a continuum of masculinity and femininity, renouncing gender as aligned with genitals, body, social status and/or role. (447)

Here Bolin champions the blurring of the pseudobiologically inscribed lines between male and female as a move toward creating new genders, new identities, and thus new politics.

Bolin and Herdt may share with most feminists the goal of challenging gender roles as they continue in a sexist society, but a long and well-ensconced line of feminist and lesbian-feminist writers disagree with Bolin and Herdt's optimistic celebration of gender transgression as politically groundbreaking. In fact, these writers tend to spell out a more or less violently antitransgender/transsexual stance, depending upon how strongly they believe that gender nonconformists are merely products of sexual dimorphism in action and thus entrench the very roles they set out to undermine.

Attacks on transgenders can be formalized as three distinct, frequently overlapping clusters of analogies, images, fantasies, and arguments. We will try to point out those clusters and their surprising persistence in writings as apparently antithetical as those of radical feminists, notably Janice Raymond, Mary Daly, and Sheila Jeffreys, and some influential queer theorists, such as Marjorie Garber and Judith Butler. In tracing how these discourses exploit transgenders to establish a tacit consensus about "appropriate" gender, we do not intend to assign blame, but hope to establish a dialogue instead of cross-talk, between feminist-identified genetic women and gender communities.[6] Most important, we are dedicated to giving a voice to gender nonconformists who too often are spoken about or for, and who are rarely permitted to participate equally in the discussion of how to end gender oppression, or whose experiences and analyses of gender oppression are even dismissed as coterminous with gender oppression itself.

In the final section of our chapter, we will read an example of how the case of Brandon Ray Teena, a twenty-one-year-old female-to-male transgender who was raped and murdered on December 31, 1993, has been represented in the media. We see this case as a paradigm for the ways in which a dimorphic sex/gender system cannot or will not account for transgender identity and self-definition. Since the voice of Brandon Teena is entirely lost, we have used a quotation from a poem dedicated to him by Mary Burger for our title, which names for us some of the poignancies and urgencies of gender redefinition and self-identification. The final lines of the poem, "Love Song of Teena Ray Brandon," read: "Call me Billy. / Brandon. / Ray. / Don't call me *girl.*" For us the line "Don't call me *girl*" asserts a transgender rejection of ascribed gender as well as a feminist refusal of the infantilization and powerlessness of women. Most important, the line claims the right to self-definition in a way that is simultaneously feminist and transgender.

II

While there are many different feminisms, the one particular form that has consistently addressed transsexuality has, unfortunately, focused on making the proper sphere of feminism its opposition to all transsexuals. This has led to an identification of transsexuals with masculinity as the antithesis of both feminism and lesbianism, an identification which sometimes has comic consequences—Jeffreys, for example, who consistently rejects transgender and transsexual self-definition and thus considers male-to-females as "men," has to understand female-to-males as "men" as well, especially when female-to-males identify as gay men, a particular anathema to Jeffreys. All transgender roads lead back to maleness or male identification, as it were, and all transgenders are therefore, one way or another, by their very nature as men, banished from feminism and lesbianism (*The Lesbian Heresy* 128–30).

While a variety of lesbian communities have reembraced femme-butch identities, often as a rejection of a normative feminism, such embrace seems to stop short of transsexual or overt transgender self-definition.[7] In their uncovering of the essential "womanliness" of the butch, recent femme-butch celebrations have not gone all that far beyond Isabel Miller's 1969 lesbian-feminist classic, *Patience and Sarah:* "Time was enough later to teach her that it's better to be a real woman than an imitation man, and that when someone chooses a woman to go away with it's because a woman is what's preferred" (23), muses Patience of the cross-dressing Sarah.[8] In contrast, Gayle Rubin in her recent essay "Of Catamites and Kings: Reflections on Butch, Gender, and Boundaries," calls for a renegotiation of the category of "gender" within theories and politics of "sexuality": ". . . I have wanted to diversify conceptions of butchness, to promote a more nuanced conceptualization of gender variation among lesbians and bisexual women, and to forestall prejudice against individuals who use other modes of managing gender" (476).[9]

In choosing the ensemble of writings that unfortunately represents the most frequently articulated feminist response to transsexuality as the focus of our critique, we are aware that we limit ourselves to a very narrow canon of texts produced exclusively by white women, for the most part of a particular ideological persuasion. Nevertheless, the influence of this canon persists. The formulation of transgender/transsexual identity given in Raymond's *Transsexual Empire,* Daly's *Gyn/Ecology,* and work by Jeffreys finds its echoes in writings as apparently ideologically removed from radical feminism as Marjorie Garber's *Vested Interests* and Judith Butler's *Bodies That Matter.* Daly's *Gyn/Ecology* (1978) spells out *The Metaethics of Radical Feminism,* as its subtitle indicates; for our purposes, it is a central text because it shows the role that transsexuals play in a self-identified radical feminist text.

Daly represents the borders between men and women as absolute; male-to-female transsexuals, therefore, must be intruders on the space of women's identity. Moreover, that space is all too frequently figured as "pure" through an invocation of race. To shore up her understanding of women's femaleness as essential, Daly has to reinforce gender boundaries by appealing to supposedly racial divisions. "Like whites playing 'black face,' [the drag queen] incorporates the oppressed role without being incorporated in it" (67). When she moves to transsexuality in the next sentence, her racial analogy breaks down, but she maintains it tacitly by appealing to the borderline metaphor: "In the phenomenon of transsexualism, the incorporation/confusion is deeper" (67). (But "deeper" than what?) Later, Daly speculates that it is "interesting to compare" female clitoridectomy in African countries, especially Kenya, with sex reassignment surgery for "male-to-constructed-female transsexuals" in the West (167). In the last example, it is as if race alone is not enough to underwrite the boundary between the sexes that Daly wants to maintain, so she has to appeal to an imperialist frame to demonize male-to-female transsexuals and African countries in the same movement.[10]

Raymond's *Transsexual Empire* (1978; reissued 1994) likewise establishes the analogy with race as a pre-eminent criticism of transsexuality via a truly confused running together of transsexual identity, the medicalization of that identity and a spurious "ironic" comparison with race: "It is significant that there is no specialized or therapeutic vocabulary of *black dissatisfaction, black discomfort,* or *black dysphoria* that has been institutionalized in black identity clinics" (9). In her new introduction to the text, Raymond quotes from a *New York Times* review of her book by Thomas Szasz with no little satisfaction, and what Raymond via Szasz does is simply to multiply a series of false analogies to transsexuality. She asks if an old person wishing to be young is "transchronological," if a poor person wanting to be rich is "transeconomical," and reiterates, "Does a Black person who wants to be white suffer from the 'disease' of being a 'transracial'?" (xv). Again, despite Raymond's cognizance of the current resistance by transgender communities to notions of "dysphoria" and "disease," she persists in the racial analogy: "This very comparison is weak since there is no demand for transracial medical intervention precisely *because* most Blacks recognize that it is their society, not their skin, that needs changing" (xvi).

If, as Raymond acknowledges, the "transracial" "comparison" is so weak, why dwell on it? Why return to it? Why even invent it and introduce it? Because race is made to function expediently here as a marker of essence—the issue is not so much *that* Raymond is a gender essentialist as that her essentialism must avail itself of race and racial difference. Note that Raymond does conceive of "skin" as a synecdoche of race that is comparable to genitals as synecdoche of sex/gender in a sex-gender system, an extremely facile view of the history of how populations have been racialized.[11]

Even an ostensibly "sympathetic" feminist ethnographer of gender, Judith Shapiro, turns to the racial analogy: "Though the analogy cannot be pushed too far, addressing issues through sex change surgery is a bit like turning to dermatologists to solve the race problem" ("Transsexualism" 262). Shapiro's need to bolster her analysis with the racial reference is especially troubling given her "ethnographic" tour of cultures in which third or fourth genders feature. It is also significant that Raymond herself would cite Shapiro's reliance on the racial analogy in her updated introduction. Transsexuality can then function as a stand-in for a serious analysis of racism.

Transgender activist Marisa Swangha issues what we see as a definitive response to what she calls "WHITE FEMINIST STATEMENT," namely, "A man wanting to be a woman is like a white person wanting to be black."

> It implies that *all* transsexuals are white, that all transsexuals are MTF and that being a woman is like being Black. But most of all it negates the millions of lives of transsexuals/transgendered peoples of First Nations, Afrikan and Asian descent, who are the worlds [sic] MAJORITY of transsexuals. An Afrikan/Asian/Native "man wanting to be" an Afrikan/Asian/Native woman is not "like a white person wanting to be black," it is like a "man" of a certain color wanting to be a woman of the same color as "he" already is. GENDER is not like RACE. ("A Man Wanting to Be a Woman" 20)

"Race" can also overlap with a discourse in which the bodies of genetic women signify "history" and "nature" at once. "To deny that female history is, *in part,* based on female biology is like denying that important aspects of black history are based on skin color. As with biological skin color, female biology doesn't confer an essential femininity; rather it confers a historical reality about what it means to be born with XX chromosomes," writes Raymond in her 1994 introduction (xx). Note, despite her disavowal, that for Raymond "skin color" does "confer" history rather than the other way around. Indeed, even sex in Raymond's analysis is not history proper, but history made "nature," and it is a highly ideologically charged "nature" that she proposes: "... the history of menstruation, the history of pregnancy or the capacity to become pregnant, the history of childbirth and abortion, the history of certain bodily cycles and life changes, and the history of female subordination in a male-dominant society." In other words, she views women's reality in standard normatively heterosexual terms which view women as primarily shaped by their capacity to reproduce, to bear children, to mother, and the limitations that such biological functions impose in society as it now exists. Raymond states emphatically that biology is history and that transsexuals cannot have this history. For her, lived experience of the genetically female body makes women's history. "It is that history that is basic to female reality, and, yes, history is based to a certain extent on female biology."

Just as Raymond makes women's "history" inseparable from their—ahistorically understood—bodies, so Elizabeth Grosz (a writer who has sometimes allied herself with "queer theory")[12] conjures up an "irreducible specificity" that shapes women's life histories via their reproductively linked bodily fluids and the lived reality of dealing with them, which eternally separates biological women from biological men (*Volatile Bodies* 207). Therefore, she writes, "[m]en, *contrary to the fantasy of the transsexual,* can never, even with surgical intervention, feel or experience what it is like to be, to live, as women ..." (207; emphasis ours). She reaffirms that the genetically specific body, albeit in its cultural mediations, is the pseudohistorical limit of gendered experience. The transsexual, once again unthinkingly presented as exclusively male-to-female, can know no history—a synthetic, amnesic creature, as Daly has it, "an example of male surgical siring which invades the female world with substitutes" (*Gyn/Ecology* 71).[13]

The transsexual-as-simulacrum is a third discursive formation that has shaped feminist versions of transsexuality. What one might call the mimetic fallacy of transsexuality provides an odd common ground for feminists and queer theorists alike, despite a superficial difference in their assessment of the value of transsexuality. One of Daly's associative chains is characteristic: "hollow holograms" of women in patriarchy lead to "transsexualism . . . and cloning" (53). Transgenders and transsexuals, who are "fantastic women" in Woodhouse's phrase, lack realness. Even in an apparently benign version of the mimetic fallacy, transsexuals can be valued only for what "they" tell "us" about "our" gender: Shapiro puts it succinctly: ". . . *they* make *us* realize that we are all passing" ("Transsexualism" 257; our emphasis). She is not alone in this particular appropriation of transsexuals, as similar accounts show up in work by Butler, Garber, and Judith Halberstam, albeit inflected by poststructuralist theory, notably Jacques Lacan and Michel Foucault.[14]

Garber makes transvestism "a category crisis elsewhere" (*Vested Interests* 11), an elsewhere that is increasingly removed from an engagement with transgender/transsexual subjectivity: ". . . *transvestism is a space of possibility structuring and confounding culture:* the disruptive element that intervenes, not just a category crisis of male and female, but the crisis of category itself." As such, transvestism can only be a signifier with a signified someplace other than itself, and while transsexuality or transvestism is obviously not closed off from other social phenomena, Garber shows little interest in what we might call, to echo Grosz, the irreducible specificity of transgender existence. Thinking of transvestism as a metaphor of metaphor leads Garber to trivialize transgender politics, which she presents as "[unity] around issues like the right to shop—access to dresses and nightgowns in large sizes and helpful, courteous sales personnel . . ." (4). (To spell out Garber's presuppositions: all transgenders are male-to-female; all "men" need large dresses; all transgendered "men" need is large dresses . . .)

At the end of *Bodies That Matter*, Butler reiterates a similar mimetic interpretation of transgendered practices, understood as gay men doing "female impersonation" with perhaps the occasional lesbian doing "male impersonation." She states that "what drag exposes . . . is the 'normal' constitution of gender presentation" and that "a different domain of the 'unperformable'" underlies such a "normal" presentation of gender (235–36). That domain turns out to be not gender at all but sexuality, for Butler suggests a kind of relay in which sexuality plays as gender: "Indeed, it may well be that what constitutes the *sexually* unperformable is performed instead as *gender* identification" (236). Sexuality becomes, in Butler's reading, the true referent of gender, while "normal" gender (that is, "real" women and men) stays in place as the referent that drag or any other transgendered activity mimes or represents.[15]

Butler tries to distinguish herself from what she calls the "highly deterministic" (238) theory of gender offered by Catharine MacKinnon, for whom any permutation of gender can be reduced, in the last instance, to a representation of "men" and "women." Yet Butler makes it clear that she, not unlike MacKinnon, believes that there are only two genders: "The critical promise of drag does not have to do with the proliferation of genders, as if a sheer increase in numbers would do the job, but rather with the exposure or the failure of heterosexual regimes ever fully to legislate or contain their own ideals" (237). Drag, standing in for transgenderism, works as "an allegory . . . through the hyperbolic," Butler states, making it clear that drag is *only* a representation of gender norms. Any attempt to contest sexual dimorphism or gender dualism goes the route of fetishism (238).

"Queer theory" is perhaps a testimony, then, that the more a theory of sex changes the more it stays the same. Judith Halberstam even pushes the mimetic version of transsexuals to a complete erasure of *any* transsexual reality: "There are no transsexuals. We are all transsexuals," she tells us ("F2M" 228), in a sweeping statement that sweeps transsexuality as specific social struggle under the carpet.

III

As an example of how an openly lesbian writer reflects the tradition we have described, we turn to an article about Brandon Teena by Donna Minkowitz in the *Village Voice*, "Love Hurts." Minkowitz's article is one of the most comprehensive, widely available accounts of Brandon Teena's story, and is extremely illuminating in the material it offers, yet an antitransgender bias skews its interpretation of that material. We will try to read the evidence which the article presents against the grain of its interpretation.

Brandon Teena, né Teena Brandon, was a twenty-one-year-old female-to-male transgender living in a small town outside Lincoln, Nebraska, who dressed as a man and named himself as a man by transposing his first and last names. He courted and had fulfilling sexual relationships with a number of young women in the town. When he was arrested and charged with eighteen minor crimes, ranging from auto theft to forgery, the local newspaper exposed his preoperative sexual categorization as anatomically female. He was subsequently multiply raped and severely beaten by two local men; he reported the assault to the local police, who did nothing. A little less than a week later, the same two men murdered Brandon and his two housemates. Brandon Teena's story was sensationalized by the media from the *New York Times* to *A Current Affair,* which predictably dubbed the case "a female *Crying*

Game" (*Village Voice*, April 19, 1994, 26).[16] As the latter appellation indicates, Brandon Teena's gender and sexual identity, or apparent lack thereof in the view of a heterosexist press, received a great deal more attention than the violence perpetrated against him.

Minkowitz shows little comprehension of Brandon Teena's struggle for self-definition or his ultimate violation as she follows a strategy of blaming the victim. She pathologizes Brandon Teena, whose death she attributes to a deception and violence that she locates within Brandon's identity and which his death merely externalizes: "Brandon had to go to Humboldt because someone who loved her in Lincoln was too infuriated because she had stolen their love or taken the money they needed to live. The frustration she had felt for so long had finally frustrated others and the fury she could not express was ultimately expressed on her. By men" (30).

As we see from the quotation, Minkowitz refers to Brandon throughout as "she," a pronoun choice that is far from innocent. The mismatch between Minkowitz's use of a female pronoun for Brandon and his girlfriends' persistent references to Brandon as "he" even after being informed of his anatomical sex occurs time and time again throughout the article: "Even after Brandon's true gender became known—when she'd been jailed on check forging charges in late December—Lana [his last girlfriend] stood by her, not an easy thing to do in a town where gossip is the major form of recreation. Later, Lana would dare to tell the press that Brandon had been 'a great kisser' and that 'he was my sweetheart. He still is'" (24). (Despite what Minkowitz says, Brandon's "true gender" was male; his genitals were female.) Repeating her assumption that Brandon's "gender" was female, Minkowitz writes: "Gina figured out about Brandon's gender a month into their relationship, and decided to continue dating Brandon, she says, 'Because of the way he treated me. I'd never had that in a relationship with a man. And he kept saying he was going to get the operation" (26). Tellingly, Minkowitz reduces the girlfriends' presentation of Brandon Teena as a man to internalized "homophobia" (26), as panicked reactions to the possibility that they might be involved in lesbian relationships (26, 27). Such a reading is belied by the willingness of the girlfriends to speak to the media and their refusal to present themselves as deceived by Brandon Teena.

Drawing on the well-established tradition of presenting the transsexual as a deceiving imposter, Minkowitz presents Brandon's struggle to achieve his gender identity as fragmented and pathological: "[She] told many different stories about her own physical sex, sexual orientation and gender identity" (25); this is Minkowitz's implied response to

Sheriff Laux's comments and question to Brandon Teena's sister: "You can call it 'it' as far as I'm concerned. . . . What kind of sister did you have?" Brandon had at various times presented himself as a gay woman, a man who would cruise with gay men, a hermaphrodite, a preoperative transsexual and a nonoperative transsexual (25–26). What we can read through Minkowitz's misrepresentation is a fairly consistent and coherent search for gender identity in a very hostile environment. Caught within the confines of an antitransgender epistemology, Minkowitz's analysis shows us the limits of "homophobia" as conceptual device for a critique of sexual dimorphism. The spiral of homophobia that she presumes to uncover in her reading of Brandon Teena as a figure in an epistemology of the closet reduces Brandon, his girlfriends, and the rapists/murderers to victims of a *Crying Game* of misrecognition.[17]

Moreover, Minkowitz's comments are sustained by a comfortable, indeed somewhat smug, middle-class lesbian identity. Thus her attribution of homophobia, internalized as well as externalized, to the trailer park milieu of Falls City, Nebraska, relies on the presupposition that given different class choices, Brandon Teena would have been Teena Brandon, out and well-adjusted lesbian. Such a presupposition leads Minkowitz to more insensitive comments: "How could someone be so sexy and alluring when she never let another human being touch, or even see the places on her body where she could be given pleasure? A related question is why Brandon, when she escaped her hometown, didn't go somewhere like San Francisco or even Denver, the gay mecca of choice for corn belters" (28). Minkowitz appears thoroughly oblivious to the economic immobility that forced Brandon Teena to the petty crimes for which he was arrested.

In response to a letter that protests Minkowitz's version of Brandon Teena's story, Minkowitz writes, "All women are socialized to hate themselves for being female. I think anyone who wants sex reassignment surgery should be supported in that choice, but I don't believe in either 'real' men and women or 'true' transsexuals. Gender is an injurious construct, not a biological (or spiritual) reality" (*Village Voice*, April 26, 1994, letters page). In the usual flippant style of the *Village Voice*, the heading for both letter and response is "If the Dress Fits . . ." thereby underscoring once again the fallacy that Brandon was a woman. While Minkowitz may recognize that gender is an "injurious construct," she fails to recognize that what she presents as gender is, in fact, sexual dimorphism, according to the logic of which Brandon must be a "real" woman, a secret lesbian, not a "true" transgender.

A different, more astute reading of Brandon Teena's story appears in an article in *FTM Newsletter*, an independent publication by and for the gender community. The writer, Jordy Jones, argues: "Brandon Teena was not killed because *she* was a Lesbian, *he* was killed because *he* was transgendered. This is neither more or less horrific than if he had been killed for lesbianism, but it is different. . . . His death was directly related to other people refusing to let him define himself for himself, and go his path in peace" (3). Jones concludes "I'm looking to the queer community to have respect for the memory of Brandon Teena, and allow him what the thugs in Nebraska would not: his right to self-define." Here Jones underlines the political stakes of a politics of self-definition in understanding the story of Brandon Teena.

Jones's focus on the right to self-definition and our emphasis on one instance of transgender identity do not mean that a transgender politics is, as Raymond would have it, a *"style rather than a politics of resistance,* in which an expressive individualism has taken the place of collective political challenges to power" (*The Transsexual Empire* xxiv). Rather, transgender self-definition is about gender definition in public, collective, and coalitional forms. Because of its embodied resistance to prescribed gender roles, transgender and transsexual politics can join transgressively gendered people, lesbians, and feminists in a communal challenge to the effects of sexual dimorphism. Together, as transsexuals, transgenders, feminists, lesbians, queers, we can counter the violence—both physical and epistemological—of heterosexism.

NOTES

1. Leslie Feinberg uses the term *he-she* in *Stone Butch Blues* (Ithaca: Firebrand, 1993) 7.

2. Woodhouse also describes her book as "the first feminist analysis of transvestites in Britain today [1989]" (*Fantastic Women* xi).

3. Radicalesbians, "The Woman-Identified Woman," a manifesto first distributed on May 1, 1970, opening night of the second Congress to Unite Women; reprinted in Alice Echols, *Daring to Be Bad.*

4. For a record of the expulsion of male-to-female transsexual lesbians from the Eighteenth Annual Michigan Womyn's Festival, see "Transsexual Womyn Expelled from Michigan Womyn's Music Festival," *Gendertrash* 2.1 (Fall 1993): 17-20. In the same issue (pp. 21-23) Janis Walworth wrote that 73 percent of the women interviewed in a survey conducted at the festival thought that male-to-female transsexuals should be welcome at the gathering, as opposed to 22.6 percent who believed that they should be excluded. Eighty percent of the respondents were against the inclusion of female-to-male transsexuals. Despite the seeming acceptance of male-to-female transsexuals among self-identified womyn, most feminist writings do not reflect this open-mindedness. On the significance of definition to lesbian identities and communities, see Vera

Whisman, "Identity Crises: Who Is a Lesbian, Anyway?" Whisman writes, "Every definition [of lesbian identity] has placed some lesbians in the blessed inner circle and some outside it," 53.

5. Here (*Third Sex, Third Gender* 13), Herdt cites the work of sociologist Harold Garfinkel, who critiques the "essentialism" of Western notions of sexual dimorphism.

6. Following the example of writers in the gender community, we use the term *genetic* to designate those persons whose gender presentation is in accordance with their medically established genetic sex. We do not do this because we have some firm belief in science (particularly in something as questionable and historically suspect as genetics), but because it is a term which is often invoked to differentiate "born" women from transsexual women. Additionally, we use the terms *gender, gender-defined, gender-described,* and *gender community* to refer to persons and groups who construct their genders in opposition to the sex assigned to them at birth. See "TS Words and Phrases," *Gendertrash* 1.1 (1993): 19.

7. While not disassociating themselves from feminism as such, many of the contributors to *The Persistent Desire: A Femme-Butch Reader* relate their self-identification as either femme or butch to a rejection of normative feminist codes. See, among others, Jeanne Cordova, "Butches, Lies and Feminism," Amber Hollibaugh and Cherríe Moraga, "What We're Rollin' around in Bed With: Sexual Silences in Feminism: A Conversation toward Ending Them," Joan Nestle, "The Femme Question," all in Joan Nestle, ed., *The Persistent Desire.*

8. We are indebted to important work by Nan Alamilla Boyd, "Bodily Bonds and Gendered Play: Historicizing Butch/Fem, S/M, and Transgender 'Lesbians.'"

9. Rubin has been the sustained focus of a recent attack by Sheila Jeffreys (*The Lesbian Heresy* 128–30), who sees Rubin's support for FTMs as evidence that Rubin is not a feminist at all.

10. Much has been written on the subject of Daly and race, for example, Audre Lorde, "An Open Letter to Mary Daly," and Ely Bulkin, "Racism and Writing: Some Implications for White Lesbian Critics." The peculiar metonymic link that Daly forges between race and transsexuality has drawn less comment.

11. See Michael Omi and Howard Winant, *Racial Formation in the United States.*

12. Elizabeth Grosz, "Lesbian Fetishism?" appeared in the self-styled "Queer Theory" issue of *differences* 3.2 (1991): 39–54.

13. See Susan Stryker, "My Words To Victor Frankenstein above the Village of Chamounix: Performing Transgender Rage." See also Sandy Stone, "The *Empire* Strikes Back: A Posttranssexual Manifesto."

14. Despite its concern with the construction of the phallus in the symbolic order, Lacan is no less binaristic about gender than radical feminism, although Lacan's ostensible gender politics are obviously very different from, for example, Mary Daly's. When it comes to transsexuality, however, there is little difference: for an instance of how a Lacanian "theory" of transsexuality can end up being much like the ones we have discussed above, see Catherine Millot, *Horsexe.*

15. See Ki Namaste, "'Tragic Misreadings': Queer Theory's Erasure of Transgender Subjectivity."

16. The reference is to Neil Jordan's 1992 film *The Crying Game,* which turns on the "revelation" of a male-to-female transsexual's genetic sex.

17. Carole-Anne Tyler also makes "misrecognition" central to her account of transgenderism; see Tyler, "Boys Will Be Girls: The Politics of Gay Male Drag."

WORKS CITED

Bolin, Anne. "Transcending and Transgendering: Male-to-Female Transsexuals, Dichotomy and Diversity." In *Third Sex, Third Gender: Beyond Sexual Dimorphism in Culture and History.* Ed. Gilbert Herdt. New York: Zone Books, 1994, 447–86.
Bornstein, Kate. *Gender Outlaw: On Men, Women and the Rest of Us.* New York: Routledge, 1994.
Boyd, Nan Alamilla. "Bodily Bonds and Gendered Play: Historicizing Butch/ Fem, S/M, and Transgender 'Lesbians.'" Paper presented at the American Studies Association conference entitled "Borders and Bonds: Society and Customs in a World of Regions." Nashville, October 28, 1994.
Bulkin, Ely. "Racism and Writing: Some Implications for White Lesbian Critics." *Sinister Wisdom* 13 (1980): 3–22.
Burger, Mary. "Love Song of Teena Ray Brandon." Manuscript.
Butler, Judith. *Bodies That Matter: On the Discursive Limits of "Sex."* New York: Routledge, 1993.
Cordova, Jeanne. "Butches, Lies, and Feminism." In Nestle, ed. *Persistent Desire* 272–92.
Daly, Mary. *Gyn/Ecology: The Metaethics of Radical Feminism.* Boston: Beacon, 1978.
Echols, Alice. *Daring to Be Bad: Radical Feminism in America 1967–1975.* Minneapolis: University of Minnesota Press, 1989.
Feinberg, Leslie. *Stone Butch Blues.* Ithaca: Firebrand, 1993.
Garber, Marjorie. *Vested Interests: Cross-Dressing and Cultural Anxiety.* New York: Routledge, 1992.
Grosz, Elizabeth. "Lesbian Fetishism?" *differences* 3.2 (1991): 39–54.
———. *Volatile Bodies: Toward a Corporeal Feminism.* Bloomington: Indiana University Press, 1994.
Halberstam, Judith. "F2M: The Making of Female Masculinity." In Laura Doan, ed., *The Lesbian Postmodern.* New York: Columbia University Press, 1994, 210–28.
Herdt, Gilbert. Introduction. *Third Sex, Third Gender: Beyond Sexual Dimorphism in Culture and History.* Ed. Gilbert Herdt. New York: Zone Books, 1994, 21–81.
Hollibaugh, Amber, and Cherríe Moraga. "What We're Rollin' around in Bed With: Sexual Silences in Feminism: A Conversation toward Ending Them." In Nestle, ed. *Persistent Desire* 254–67.
Jeffreys, Sheila. *The Lesbian Heresy: A Feminist Perspective on the Lesbian Sexual Revolution.* Melbourne: Spinifex, 1993.
Lorde, Audre. "An Open Letter to Mary Daly." *Sister Outsider.* New York: Norton, 1984, 66–71.
Miller, Isabel. *Patience and Sarah.* 1969; reprint, New York: Fawcett, 1972.
Millett, Kate. *Flying.* New York: Knopf, 1974.

Millot, Catherine. *Horsexe: Essay On Transsexuality.* Trans. Kenneth Hylton. New York: Autonomedia, 1990.

Minkowitz, Donna. "If the Dress Fits . . ." Letters page. *Village Voice,* April 26, 1994, 11.

———. "Love Hurts." *Village Voice,* April 19, 1994, 24–30.

Namaste, Ki. "'Tragic Misreading': Queer Theory's Erasure of Transgender Subjectivity." In Brett Beemyn and Mickey Eliason, eds., *Queer Studies: A Multicultural Reader.* New York: New York University Press, forthcoming.

Nestle, Joan. "The Femme Question." In Nestle, ed. *Persistent Desire* 138–46.

———, ed. *The Persistent Desire: A Femme-Butch Reader.* Boston: Alyson, 1992.

Omi, Michael, and Howard Winant. *Racial Formation in the United States: From the 1960s to the 1980s.* New York: Routledge, 1986.

Penelope, Julia. *Call Me Lesbian: Lesbian Lives, Lesbian Theory.* Freedom: Crossing Press, 1992.

Raymond, Janice. *The Transsexual Empire: The Making of the She-Male.* 1978. Reissued with a new introduction on transgender, New York: Athene, Teachers College Press, 1994.

Rich, Adrienne. "Compulsory Heterosexuality and Lesbian Existence." *Blood, Bread, and Poetry: Selected Prose 1979–1985.* New York: Norton, 1986, 23–75.

Rubin, Gayle. "Of Catamites and Kings: Reflections on Butch, Gender, and Boundaries." In Nestle, ed. *Persistent Desire* 466–82.

Shapiro, Judith. "Transsexualism: Reflections on the Persistence of Gender and the Mutability of Sex." In Julia Epstein and Kristina Straub, eds. *Body Guards: The Cultural Politics of Gender Ambiguity.* New York: Routledge, 1991, 248–79.

Stone, Sandy. "The *Empire* Strikes Back: A Posttranssexual Manifesto." In Epstein and Straub, eds., *Body Guards* 280–304.

Stryker, Susan. "My Words To Victor Frankenstein above the Village of Chamounix: Performing Transgender Rage." *GLQ* 1.3 (Fall 1994).

"Survey at Michigan." *Gendertrash* 2.1 (Fall 1993): 21–23.

Swangha, Marisa. "A Man Wanting to Be a Woman Is Like a White Person Wanting to Be Black." *Gendertrash* 3 (1995): 20 and 24.

"TS Words and Phrases." *Gendertrash* 1.1 (1993): 19.

Tyler, Carole-Anne. "Boys Will Be Girls: The Politics of Gay Male Drag." In Diana Fuss, ed. *Inside/Out: Lesbian Theories, Gay Theories.* New York: Routledge, 1991, 32–71.

Walworth, Janis. "Transsexual Womyn Expelled from Michigan Womyn's Festival." *Gendertrash* 2.1 (Fall 1993): 17–20.

Whisman, Vera. "Identity Crisis: Who Is a Lesbian Anyway?" In *Sisters, Sexperts, Queers: Beyond the Lesbian Nation.* Ed. Arlene Stein. New York: Plume, 1993, 47–60.

Woodhouse, Annie. *Fantastic Women: Sex, Gender and Transvestism.* New Brunswick: Rutgers University Press, 1989.

TRANSGENDER RESOURCES

Boys Own. 376 Upper Brook Street, Victoria Park, Manchester M13 OEP, England.

Boys Will Be Boys. P.O. Box 1349, Strawberry Hills, Sydney 2012, Australia.

Chrysalis Quarterly. A.E.G.I.S., P.O. Box 33724, Decatur, GA 30033. $30 per year.

Cross-Talk. P.O. Box 944, Woodland Hills, CA 91355. $21 per year.

EDENews. P.O. Box 22742, Ft. Lauderdale, FL 33335-2742.

En*Gender. Recast Educational & Informational Network, P.O. Box 224001, Dallas, TX 5222-4001. $10 per year.

FOCUS. P.O. Box 215354, Sacramento, CA 95821.

FTM Newsletter. 5337 College Ave. #142, Oakland, CA 94618. $10 per year minimum suggested donation.

GenderFlex. 3430 Balmoral Drive #10, Sacramento, CA 95821.

Gender Identity Center (G.I.C.) Newsletter. 3715 W. 32nd Ave., Denver, CO 80211.

Gendertrash (From Hell). Box #500-62, 552 Church Street, Toronto, Ont., M4Y 2E3, Canada. $2.50 an issue.

Girlfriend. P.O. Box 191781, San Francisco, CA 94119-1781. $4 an issue.

INSIGHT. P.O. Box 33311, Decatur, GA 30033. $22 per year.

Journal of Gender Studies. 405 Western Street, Suite 345, South Portland, ME 04106. $16 for two issues.

Sullivan, Lou. *Information for the Female to Male Cross Dresser and Transsexual.* Seattle: Ingersoll Gender Center, 1990.

TNT: Transsexual News Telegraph. 584 Castro Street, Suite 288, San Francisco, CA 94114-2588. $15 subscription.

Transitions. Ingersoll Gender Center, 1812 East Madison #106, Seattle, WA 98122-2843.

The Transsexual Voice. P.O. Box 16314, Atlanta, GA 30321. $18 per year for six issues.

TransSisters: The Journal of Transsexual Feminism. 4004 Troost Avenue, Kansas City, Missouri 64110. $12 for four issues.

The TV/TS Tapestry Journal. I.F.G.E., P.O. Box 367, Wayland, MA 01778. $40 per year; subscription includes voting membership in the International Foundation for Gender Education.

ALL OF THE AUDIENCE IS COMING HERE TO STAY
EACH OF US AN ACTRESS, EACH OF US A PLAY.
I'VE BEEN WAITING SO LONG FOR ANOTHER SONG
I'VE BEEN THINKING SO LONG I WAS THE ONLY ONE
WE'VE BEEN HOPING SO LONG FOR ANOTHER WORLD.

—MEG CHRISTIAN, "HELLO HOORAY," *I KNOW YOU KNOW* (1974)

AS WE ADDRESS THE INSTITUTION [OF HETEROSEXUALITY] ITSELF . . . WE BEGIN TO
PERCEIVE A HISTORY OF FEMALE RESISTANCE WHICH HAS NEVER FULLY UNDERSTOOD
ITSELF BECAUSE IT HAS BEEN SO FRAGMENTED, MISCALLED, ERASED.

—ADRIENNE RICH, "COMPULSORY HETEROSEXUALITY AND LESBIAN EXISTENCE" (1980)

Notes for a Musical History of Lesbian Consciousness

KARIN QUIMBY

It remains indisputable that feminism, from the start of the contemporary Women's Liberation Movement over twenty years ago, both practically and theoretically *needs* lesbians. That the modern feminist movement could not (and does not) exist without lesbians to run its clinics, march in its protests, fight its legal battles, produce its scholarship, and in every other material and psychic way support the spread and strength of women's rights has been pointed out frequently. As well, Teresa de Lauretis has recently argued that psychoanalytic feminism needs the figure of female homosexuality in the form of the "homosexual-maternal imaginary" in order to conceive (fantasmatically) the very *"possibility* of [female] subject and desire."[1] It was once clear, too, although increasingly less so, that lesbians *need* feminism. A new generation of lesbians appears, to the concern of many, to be aligned not with the feminist cause of abolishing male supremacy but either with a politics that combines lesbian, bisexual, transgendered, and gay male concerns or with what some consider assimilationist lifestyles, pictured by one activist as "a politically nonthreatening monogamous female couple, with a child, a dog, a house, and a Honda."[2] For many lesbians who came out together with the feminist movement, these shifting alliances are alarming.

In the following discussion of women's music, I investigate the kinds of lesbian consciousness and identities that were produced through the concurrent emergence of feminism and lesbian politics and that literally were (and continue to be) staged at women's music concerts and festivals. Rather than simply registering horror at the way feminism seems to be losing popularity with lesbians or sliding longingly into nostalgic reconstructions of the good old days of lesbian feminism, we should continue to interrogate the discursive and material fields of lesbian feminism even (and especially) as we move into a world more defined by queer politics. Women's music provides a particular moment and cultural representation of lesbian feminism to which we can now historically refer as a defining moment in lesbian consciousness. The popular memory of lesbians who came out with women's music serves today as an especially important way not only to carry out the political task of resisting cultural amnesia but also to reassess and interpret the historical beginnings of lesbian feminist culture.

As part of this project I interviewed twelve women (an admittedly small sample) from the West Coast who came out with women's music in the 1970s. Many of them recalled the euphoria of attending women's music concerts and festivals where they discovered for the first time a community of women and lesbians who shared common feminist goals. They also mourned the loss of this communal feeling and time. These lesbians' memories of that cultural moment reveal a dual consciousness informed by the dream of sisterhood and concurrent acknowledgment of women's profound differences from one another that prevented the realization of this ideal. For most of the women interviewed, nostalgic recollections of this 1970s movement and moment were consciously paradoxical. One woman put it this way: "There's this double feeling, like being inspired and also grieving at the same time." Today she and others who came out with women's music remember that time of enormous possibility, but also grieve the lesbian nation that never materialized.

Recent lesbian theory and history continues the difficult work of rescuing lesbian stories from the consistent erasure they have suffered in heterosexist literary and historical studies. It is not surprising that the metaphorical and theoretical terms of this rescue have landed very solidly on the unseen, the undead, or the unknown. Lesbian culture and consciousness, it seems, was and is shaped as much by what is not said, named, or seen as by what is. For instance, Terry Castle suggests that the paradox of lesbian existence is located in the repeated ghostly appearances of the lesbian in literature dating from the eighteenth century.[3] As well, the theoretical and popular return of the lesbian vampire in such works as Jewelle Gomez's *Gilda Stories* and Sue-Ellen Case's "Tracking the Vampire"[4] further suggests the ways in which lesbians have come to understand and represent the paradoxical nature of their (non)existence.

188 | KARIN QUIMBY

Eve Kosofsky Sedgwick's analysis of how ignorances and opacities structure knowledge of homosexuality develops a further means for lesbians to discuss how "a particular ignorance is a product of, implies, and itself structures and enforces a particular knowledge."[5] Women's music serves as a historical event through which we can explore the continuing paradoxical way lesbianism has been defined in this century and hence how lesbian consciousness has been shaped. The trope of lesbian absence, ignorance, or invisibility is represented particularly in the very elision of *lesbian* from the term *women's music,* and in the common absence of overt lesbian lyrics from songs by, for, and about lesbians. The general conflation of lesbianism and feminism in the 1970s exemplifies especially the ways that requisitions of secrecy and ignorance structured lesbian definition at that time. Yet the cultural practice of separatist women's music festivals might be understood also as representing a contemporary and *empowering* rendition of the vanishing lesbian—because this time she is *choosing* to disappear into the woods, once a year, no men allowed.[6]

Women's music festivals continue to provide lesbians a place to fantasize and live, if only for a few days, in another kind of reality which for most is so radically different from everyday existence in a heterosexual world that it surely continues to shape their lesbian consciousness and desire. There are many stories and experiences of women's music festivals—painful, conflicting, as well as euphoric—and the discussion here can address only a fraction of this history. While many women find women's music festivals to be essential if temporary retreats from patriarchal culture, the sense of safety and sisterhood is not shared by all festival goers. Within the festival communities, women of color in particular have increasingly formed separate spaces in order to address their particular concerns and needs.[7] Although the early rhetoric of the (mostly white) performers at these festivals addressed racism often, material strategies to attend to the needs of women of color within the borders of the festivals have been developed only more recently.

We might consider whether or not the future of lesbian feminism exists at least in part in our individual and collective demands for separate space or whether these spaces are too exclusionary and limiting, as many women of color and now transgender women have charged. There can be no question that strategically separating ourselves from the patriarchy is an empowering and important act for many women. As Marilyn Frye asserts, "When women separate (withdraw, break out, regroup, transcend, shove aside, step outside, mitigate, say *no*), we are simultaneously controlling access and defining. We are doubly insubordinate, since neither of these is permitted."[8] What remains in question, however, is whether separatist women's music festivals can maintain the dream of a lesbian feminist sisterhood while growing and changing with the new demands of a more varied lesbian and feminist population. The question posed is one that women's music icon Cris Williamson's most famous album implicitly asked, and that is whether lesbian feminists can be both "the changer and the changed." The history of lesbian feminism as represented through the practice of separatist women's music festivals provides unique insights into how we might proceed, and indeed survive, as lesbians and feminists as we enter the next century.

STRATEGIES OF SPACE

The contemporary women's movement, which began toward the end of the 1960s in the United States, set out to radically change the gendered distribution of economic and social power.[9] One of the material strategies that emerged in the middle part of the 1970s to achieve these ends was the phenomenon of what was and is called "women's music," a (sub)genre of music frequently defined as music "by, for, and about women." The production of this music not only forwarded the women's movement with lyrics that reflected and celebrated women's political, emotional, and sexual connection to each other; it also constructed a space in which women could gather for the safe celebration of these ideas. Women's concerts, recording studios, and music festivals all marked a new way of defining women's space. In lesbian culture, attempts to secure public space have always been a central concern, and the various ways in which lesbians have defined this space (bars, salons, coffeehouses, music festivals/concerts, womyn's land, women's vacation cruises) point out the shifting material and spatial responses to living in a homophobic world.

In an oral history study of lesbians in Buffalo (1940–1960), Madeline Davis and Elizabeth Kennedy found that securing lesbian public space was driven strongly by "a need to provide a setting for the formation of intimate relationships."[10] They conclude that "it is the nature of this community that it created public space for lesbians and gay men, while at the same time it organized sexuality and emotional relationships."[11] In the early 1970s, feminists too realized the value of separate space, and formed consciousness-raising groups. Gloria Steinem explains in a 1972 article in *Ms.*: "We had no street corners, no bars, no offices, no territory that was recognized as ours. Rap groups were an effort to create that free place: an occasional chance for total honesty and support from our sisters."[12] Of course, lesbians had long been engaged in creating these separate spaces, if not to discuss politics outright then to experience "occasional" moments of relative freedom from heterosexual oppression and to locate sexual partners. Women's music festivals drew on both these histories or needs for separate space by effectively combining feminist politics and lesbian requirements for places to organize sexuality. The definition of public space through women's music thus redefined lesbian relationships to the closet significantly by relocating gatherings of lesbians outside of the bars. These festivals were primarily formed and attended by white middle-class lesbians, many of whom had never found the scarce lesbian bar. For these women the audiences created by women's music provided their first realization that there were even other lesbians in existence.[13]

The trouble, however, that concurrently emerged with this new public lesbian space was the simultaneous and paradoxical erasure or denial of lesbian sex or sexuality through definitions of feminism and women's music. The irony of this elision is no more apparent than, for instance, in the way lesbian feminist musician Diedra McCalla defined women's music solely as a feminist network, failing to acknowledge the strong lesbian presence in this culture. Alix Dobkin, a radical lesbian feminist singer-songwriter, concurs, adding that women's music is not so much a sound but has to do with consciousness, a word most often associated with the "larger" women's movement.[14] Thus definitions of women's music by lesbian musicians themselves fail to acknowledge the material result of this cultural phenomenon which was clearly to form a distinct lesbian audience and community.[15] These interpretations exemplify the slippage between lesbianism and feminism that relies on subsuming lesbianism within the definition of feminism. The practice of lesbian community, which deeply informed lesbian consciousness at that time, was thereby shaped by a recurring definitional obscurity.

Other defining terms of women's music can be found in the original creation of the music scene as well as in the eventual beginnings of Olivia Records, the first women's national recording company, founded in 1973. In an interview, Meg Christian, one of the central founders of women's music, discusses how she became involved in this musical project. Christian began her women's music career in an only slightly less ironic space than the closet—the basement of a house in Washington, D.C.—which served as the Women's Center in 1972: "sometimes ten women would come, sometimes a hundred, and we'd pass the hat. And that's really how I started [playing music] constantly, and thinking how valuable it was for women to have a space to come together that was safe, and that everybody there had this basic connection and this basic bond of experience."[16] The undefined "basic bond of experience" that drew these women together certainly means being women in a patriarchal world, yet the women musicians as well as the audience were mostly lesbian. Thus even the initial practice of this new lesbian community was defined entirely by feminist principles.

These principles involved providing women with economic and artistic independence, and are defined in the four original goals of Olivia Records: "to make women's music available to the public; to provide women with access to the recording industry and to retain control over their music; to provide training for women in all aspects of the music industry; and to provide jobs for large numbers of women with reasonable salaries and in unoppressive situations."[17] The overt feminist objectives of the business show how although all the women were lesbians they did not have any explicit "lesbian" goals for their project.

That the phenomenon of women's music was almost entirely formed and attended by lesbians in the name of feminism should not be disparaged, but rather recognized as a recent example of a long history of lesbian consciousness and subjectivity defined by the paradox of presence/knowledge and absence/ignorance. That is to say, at a moment in which lesbians emerged en masse out of closets and bars into public culture (business and politics), they remained largely invisible, reenacting the metaphoric role of the apparitional lesbian as Terry Castle describes it: "The lesbian remains a kind of 'ghost effect' in the cinema world of modern life: elusive, vaporous, difficult to spot—even when she is there, in plain view, mortal and magnificent, at the center of the screen"—or, we might add, on the festival stage.[18]

DEFINING IGNORANCES: I KNOW YOU KNOW

The first album produced by Olivia Records was tellingly named *I Know You Know* (1974) and featured Meg Christian singing, among other songs, the now classic musical chronicle of lesbian life, "Ode to a Gym Teacher," which put into lyric form, for the first time, the common lesbian experience of falling in love with a gym teacher.[19] The overt lesbian content of this song, together with songs about women's empowerment and songs about mothers, blends lesbian and feminist lives and issues together in this album. The album title is a rhetorical configuration which plays off of the conflicting demands of knowledge and secrecy that commonly inform the epistemology of lesbian existence.[20] The decision to name this first album thus acknowledges the tension between lesbian and feminist definition that was challenging the coherency of the movement at that time.[21]

Although many have criticized the conflation of lesbianism and feminism, saying that it denies the very possibility and specificity of lesbian SEXuality, we might also consider that feminism made visible, articulate, and even possible many nuanced forms of lesbian desire. Currently, when the only way sex positive critics seem to be able to distinguish lesbian desire is through explicit representations of lesbian sex, we tend to forget the *many* ways lesbians do desire other women. One could argue, for instance, that Cris Williamson's album *The Changer and the Changed* (1975), which was the second album Olivia Records cut and which became one of the all-time best-selling records on an independent label, promotes the kinds of ignorances (namely the absence of overtly sexual lesbian lyrics) which structure knowledge of lesbianism through ellipses and codes.

But the kinds of ignorances which define knowledge of lesbianism, as demonstrated in Williamson's album, represent at the same time multilayered levels of affectional preference and care for women that quite rightly define, for many lesbians, the vicissitudes of their lesbian desire. Williamson's songs encompass and represent the levels of pain and pleasure that go along with loving women, with being a lesbian. These variations of lesbian desire and existence are represented in the lyrics to the songs that comprise the album. One song, "Having Been Touched (Tender Lady)," has lyrics which read in part: "The tender lady had sadness in her eyes / She sees the fallen hopes, the loneliness and lies / . . . Won't you draw her close to you / And comfort her for me," suggesting the ethics of caring and support that were encouraged at this time in lesbian feminist communities and between lesbian friends and lovers.

Another of Williamson's songs on this album, "Sweet Woman," was written in response to the first National Women's Music Festival which she attended, and suggests not only the powerful impact this gathering of women had on her but also its continuing, undefinable hold on her and a longed-for incorporation of this powerful experience figured in the erotic embrace of a woman: "Oh the warmth, surrounding me, / It just won't let me be / Just won't let me be. / A little passage of time till I hold you and you'll be mine / sweet woman, risin' so fine." In many ways, Williamson's songs represent the definition of lesbianism that was issued in the 1970 Radicalesbians position paper "The Woman-Identified-Woman." Charlotte Bunch says that this statement "expanded the definition of lesbianism by developing the idea of women-identification as an act of self-affirmation and love for all women."[22] This early radical attempt to redefine lesbianism as political (in order to move away from an understanding of lesbianism as a purely sexual practice) was also a response to homophobia in the emerging feminist movement. The implication that all women could consider themselves woman-identified was both a strategic concession to homophobic forces that could not accept the label of "lesbian" and a potent redefinition of lesbian identity that irrevocably linked it to the practice of feminism.

This elision of the word *lesbian* at the very moment of its emergence into public discourse ushered in another version of the apparitional lesbian that was played out in cultural venues such as women's music festivals and in lyrics such as those by Cris Williamson. Lesbian feminism, as it was defined then, according to Charlotte Bunch, was a political analysis of "a crucial aspect of male supremacy—heterosexism." She further asserts that "the development of this political perspective was one of the most important results of lesbian separatism."[23] The focus on abolishing male supremacy seems now to have been displaced in contemporary queer politics not only by the combination of male and female concerns but also by the theoretical challenge to the very validity of gender categories. Although a radical deconstruction of gender and sexuality certainly has the potential to ultimately (and hopefully) destroy male and heterosexual supremacy, in mass culture women and lesbians still face specific oppression as women, and thus we must continue to develop analysis and strategies to fight *this* oppression.

At a time when gender categories were not questioned in the ways they are today, one such strategy that was advanced by women's music concerts and festivals was what might be called "strategic separatism." At these festivals women separated from men in order to build a woman- or lesbian-centered culture that explored and tested (often with great contradiction) what an alternative, antipatriarchal society might offer to women. Yet many lesbians paradoxically rejected the theory of separatism while practicing it not only at festivals but also in their everyday lives. Alix Dobkin points out in a 1979 interview: "Most lesbians I know are in fact separatists in every way that they can be, without actually saying that . . . they never see men; they live all their lives with women; they avoid men as much as possible, and yet they will object to the word, the term."[24] Attendance at women's music festivals (which many lesbians would not define as a radical separatist act but as a good time) is another way that a refusal to name what we practice structures what we know and how we live our lives as lesbians.

THE PERSONAL IS NOSTALGIC IS POLITICAL

As the practice of telling and retelling coming-out stories shows, the ways we remember the past significantly help us redefine our present. For subcultures and politically oppressed groups, restaging the past can be an act of recuperation and resistance. Given the paucity of any official lesbian history, the investigation of popular memory remains a crucial way to assess lesbian consciousness.[25] Popular memory functions as one way to reconstruct past events, not so much to distinguish a certain truth as to show how that past gets interpreted and informs present-day lesbian culture and consciousness. Lynn Spigel suggests that popular memory "strip[s] away closure from the past by restaging events from another time—redoing them in ways that satisfy contemporary needs and desires. Popular memory, in other words, is bound up with its use value in the present."[26] Women's music today provides access to shared memories—it provides, for many lesbians who came out in the 1970s, and even for some who came out in the eighties and nineties, a "common sense" of a lesbian past.

The replaying of some of the classic songs from the golden age of women's music at present-day lesbian gatherings such as commitment ceremonies, funerals, and parties, suggests the enduring currency of that moment of women's music. This music today invokes a certain nostalgic lesbian feminist fantasy of sisterhood (of a white, middle-class kind, at least). The fantasy of a homogeneous lesbian nation is much harder to sustain today with the increased awareness of women's vast differences from one another, and hence this music now allows us to nostalgically recall a past time of collective lesbian feminism. The replaying of this music satisfies a contemporary need for some to remember and relive that idealized moment in lesbian history from which many still draw strength.

Cris Williamson's song "Waterfall" has been described repeatedly as "the lesbian anthem," even while the lyrics themselves reveal no specific lesbian meaning and only through connotative reading practices can the chorus "Filling up and spilling over, like an endless waterfall" be interpreted, as it often is, as signifying the multiple orgasms possible in lesbian lovemaking. The defining and legitimating effects this music had on many lesbians who came out at that time are overwhelming; the ability to invoke a sense of a common past through the medium of music is a new and empowered affirmation of lesbian history. For many lesbians, women's music first created a distinct lesbian culture, a distinctness that some fear is being lost not only as it becomes impossible to define a single lesbian community because of the recognition of important differences between lesbians, but as more and more lesbians assimilate into the mainstream and become relatively indistinguishable from heterosexuals. In many ways the collective experience invoked by women's music is not being reproduced today with cross-over artists like Melissa Etheridge and k. d. lang because they appeal to heterosexual audiences to the degree that lesbians are assimilated into the mainstream, rather than challenging the dominant culture with political, lesbian music. Because lesbian existence remains, for some, very different from heterosexual existence, it seems especially important to insist on defining the specificity of lesbian cultures as we become more visible.

While some may applaud the apparent increase in lesbian visibility, Holly Near reminds us how patriarchal culture continues to "fragment, miscall, and erase"[27] significant cultural phenomena such as women's music:

> There was something happening in the 70's for women that will, if we let them, be completely ignored and left out of history by mainstream male-dominated historians. You hear most of the male representatives of culture say that the 60's was really when things were happening and that the 70's and 80's were dead. But I think that's because women rose to a sense of self value and appreciation in the 70's and developed a cultural phenomenon that men weren't in the middle of, so they don't think it happened. If they didn't lead it, direct it, own it, profit by it, control it, they think it didn't exist.[28]

If a cultural phenomenon such as women's music has been strategically erased from mainstream history, one must wonder what will be remembered about our claim of a new lesbian visibility represented by a few "lesbian" photos in *Vanity Fair* or a lesbian country-western singer?

Through popular lesbian memory we not only can piece together and narrativize the significant personal and political events of our pasts but also can replay those times in ways that will continue to shape us today. For oppressed groups, popular memory is a tool of resistance. The Olivia Records documentary *The Changer: A Record of Our Times* (1991), together with individual accounts of that time in lesbian history, reveals the heightened sense of possibility that comes with the emergence of a new cultural phenomenon. Women who came out at that time remember how a new generation of lesbians was on the road to freedom, and their recollections invoke the euphoria of a new world in process. One woman I interviewed recalls that the emergence of women's music in the 1970s was about having

> total freedom as a lesbian . . . the image is of me driving in my V.W. van packed with lesbians, and what we would do is every summer we would go on these lesbian pilgrimages to the Michigan Womyn's Music Festival. And we would go from town to town and literally pick up lesbians, stay in lesbian households, and thought nothing of it. . . .

> At that time I had no pain at all associated with being a lesbian, whereas now, a decade later, I have some pain associated with the oppression I feel as a lesbian. But in those days it was just bliss . . . it really was a very special moment. . . . At that time I thought the Womyn's Music Festivals were the beginning of a lesbian culture that we were creating. . . . I think it has actually backslid.

This woman contextualizes the excitement of the past lesbian feminist moment by comparing it with her present reality in which she experiences an absence of a similar idealism. She does not, significantly, recall the concurrent battles that were being waged by women of color and others who felt separated and excluded from this particular fantasy of the lesbian nation. The image of the yearly religious return to the "lesbian nation," where 6,000 to 8,000 women still gather annually, suggests the kind of practice or event that deeply shapes an individual and generation (not, incidentally, unlike Woodstock, which, although only a single musical event, is understood as representing and defining an entire heterosexual generation).

One of the most important conflicts that women's music concerts and festivals faced was the unequal representation of women of color in their organization, performances, and attendance. These issues were addressed rhetorically, but material inequities persisted. Women's music concerts and festivals are noted as the first mass public gatherings that were committed to the feminist principle of providing accessibility to every woman through use of sign language interpreters, child care, wheelchair accessibility, safety from men, alcohol and chemical free zones, space for organization of lesbian and women's business, social and political groups. They also broadcast, through concert programs and announcements, the political positions and purposes of their performers.[29] A concert flyer (circa 1977) introducing a new womyn's musician, Teresa Trull, provides her space to introduce and politically situate herself:

> I want my music to speak to different phases of wimmin's lives . . . particularly lesbian wimmin. . . . As a lesbian-feminist, I feel that one of my major responsibilities is to try and break down the class and race barriers existing in our predominantly white and privileged movement. Music is a potential starting point for the meeting of wimmin's minds and souls—wimmin from all different cultures and backgrounds."[30]

Trull's statement, which echoes many others by women musicians, shows that race and class issues maintained a central position in lesbian feminist discourse from its beginnings.

Yet while these kinds of inclusive statements were made, there was much tension between women of color and the white-women-dominated music festivals and concerts. Sweet Honey in the Rock, an African American women's singing group, emerged concurrently with the Olivia Records collective in 1973. Its participation in a West Coast tour with the Olivia singers in 1977 illustrates the conflicting "feminist" agendas for white lesbians and women of color.[31] Both "groups," which began independently of each other in 1973, had a strong commitment to feminist principles and politics, but significantly diverged in emphasis regarding black women's concerns and lesbian feminist issues.

In 1977, Sweet Honey in the Rock was invited to go on a West Coast tour with Olivia Records singers Meg Christian and Cris Williamson, whom Bernice Johnson Reagon, the leader of the group, describes as "political lesbians."[32] For Sweet Honey this tour was a cultural shock. Reagon explains: "We went from Washington, D.C., where we sang for Black people, churches, schools, theaters, folk festivals, and political rallies, to the radical, separatist, White-women-dominated, lesbian cultural network in California."[33] There were immediate conflicts between the two groups, not the least of which was that Sweet Honey was "people identified," which meant that they included men in production and audiences. But they were working now in a community that excluded men. These differences clearly had race and culture origins and ignited biases that deeply challenged both groups.

Rhetorically, both the white lesbian feminist musicians and the African American group Sweet Honey paid attention to the intersecting issues of race and sexuality, but there remained a clear division of commitment and emphasis in each group. In one of Meg Christian's concert programs she states: "Recently I have felt an increasing responsibility to use my music and my concerts to make women more aware of political issues which are vital parts of our movement struggles—especially lesbianism, class, race, and the commonality of women's struggles everywhere."[34] Christian's rhetoric here may seem essentialist to us today (the "commonality of women's struggles everywhere") but at that time was an inclusive language that served to draw women into a collective movement. The dual urge to recognize women's differences while acknowledging their similarity defines most clearly the dynamic of the white lesbian feminist women's music cultural phenomenon, and indeed of the white-dominated feminist movement at that time.

Sweet Honey also attempted to bridge the differences between their group and the lesbian feminist movement. Their challenge to overcome homophobia is apparent in Reagon's memory of the time she wrote her first lesbian song after the 1977 tour. The chorus reads: "Every woman who ever loved a woman / You ought to stand up and call her name / Mama, sister, daughter, lover." Reagon admits that writing this song scared her to death and when she sang it to Sweet Honey "Evie started to cry—we were all scared. Would Sweet Honey survive in our base if we sang this song? Would Black people leave us before we got started? Would people think everybody in Sweet Honey was sleeping with women, or each other?"[35] The group decided to sing and record the song which plainly rehearses the strategy of subsuming lesbianism within feminism—in this case very specifically enacting what had been first defined in "The Woman-Identified-Woman" paper and what Adrienne Rich would, in a sense, later (re)name the "lesbian continuum." The "overt" lesbian lines read: "Woke up this morning feeling fine / rolled over, kissed a friend of mine."[36] It's hard to imagine that such disguised lyrics could cause such fear, but white lesbians of course were also writing lesbian lyrics equally camouflaged at that time, and although they addressed issues of race in their concert programs, few song lyrics did the same. Yet for both the white lesbians and the African American feminist women's group, feminism not only provided a point of ideological coherence (or the desire for one) but also acted as a paradoxical cover, one which simultaneously covered and uncovered lesbian existence and racial difference.

Nostalgic recollections of this 1970s movement and moment may be consciously paradoxical. That is, one might feel or desire a shared sense of sisterhood while simultaneously acknowledging its very impossibility and possible undesirability. The tension between the desire for collectivity and individuality is still played out in present-day women's music festivals. One woman recalls her experience at the 1993 West Coast Women's Music and Comedy Festival during which she was a stage crew worker. During one afternoon's sound check, the women on the crew were extremely tense with each other and with Cris Williamson, who was to perform that evening, revealing the personal and political conflict which is frequently present at these festivals, despite the desire for "sisterhood." When the sound engineer asked Cris to play a few bars on the piano, she began to play "Waterfall." The response from the women on the stage was immediate and powerful. The interviewee explains that

> all of a sudden there was just this snap and everybody stopped, and the same feeling in my heart that happens you know when I hear that [song]. . . . Everybody stopped and I knew other people were feeling it too . . . and I thought, this is the most incredible sound and I bet not

everybody would understand . . . it just goes beyond the song or the music or whatever, but everybody just stopped at that moment . . . it just kind of united the whole stage.

The popular or shared lesbian memory apparent at that moment when everybody stopped on the stage signals not only who is included in this community but also who is excluded—after all, "not everybody would understand." The undefinable nature of what is understood—exactly what it is that united the whole stage—also curiously reminds me of the way in which ignorances structure what we *know* as a community. The women on the stage might have felt that "not everybody would understand" but they could have easily turned to each other to say, "but I know you know."

Despite the constitution of community defined by the preceding example, the restaging of new and old music each year at women's music festivals insists on a constant redefinition of this community and provides a forum for younger women to define themselves in relationship to that particular moment in women's music which continues to resonate so strongly for some.[37] In a culture which claims few traditions, the combination of generations at women's music festivals provides the space to ideologically and materially attempt to cohere an ever changing movement. Demanding separate space from men provides, for most who attend, the most profound experience of altered consciousness. Securing this moment of separateness and safety from men, however, also foregrounds women's differences with each other and strongly urges festival participants to confront their own racism, apathy, homophobia, and misogyny.

CODA

Women's music presents a cultural and historical phenomenon that reveals and indeed stages the various discourses and debates which emerged with and continue to inform that collection of identities known as lesbian feminism. The lyrics and definition of women's music points out the difficulty of claiming a distinct lesbian identity or experience, yet through present-day memories of lesbians who were members of women's music audiences we might begin to perceive how a distinct lesbian culture was formed through feminism and this musical phenomenon. With a visible and auditory lesbian history to reference and remember, perhaps the ways we now define ourselves and our communities will be less structured by silence and ignorance of our history and of our very existence.

With the current emphasis on "queer" identities, on performativity, androgyny, the "queer straight," it becomes especially urgent to remember, as lesbians, our history of struggle, not in order necessarily to supplant the present celebration of increased visibility or acceptance with sobering memories of struggle—because the 1970s was also certainly a celebration—but in order to root lesbianism today within a vital, complex history of resistance in which lesbians contended with critical issues of race and class, sexism and homophobia, in a way that significantly ushered in current possibilities of politics, coalition, identity, and community. These debates were most visible on women's music stages and within women's music audiences of the 1970s. Judy Dulgaz, one of the founders of Olivia Records, reminds us of the original goals of the women's music movement: "What we were trying to do was reach as many women as possible with the concept of woman-identification, of relying upon yourself, of seeing yourself as primary and women as primary and considering other possibilities to heterosexuality, heterosexism and sexism."[38] The project of placing women first in a patriarchal culture remains today an important "strategic" separatist act. As we proceed into the next century, we should remember especially the practice of separatist politics that has defined the radical edges of lesbian feminist consciousness. And if we must disappear, as we continue to seem to do, let us make sure to disappear together, into the woods to confront pressing issues in our communities and to celebrate and sing. This separatist strategy, it seems to me, remains one of the most powerful legacies of our lesbian feminist past.

NOTES

1. Teresa de Lauretis, *The Practice of Love* 156–57.
2. Maria Maggenti, "Wandering through Herland," in *Sisters, Sexperts, Queers* 246.
3. Terry Castle, *The Apparitional Lesbian.*
4. Jewelle Gomez, *The Gilda Stories* and Sue-Ellen Case, "Tracking the Vampire."
5. Eve Kosofsky Sedgwick, *Epistemology of the Closet* 25.
6. The once clear requirement that no men may attend these separatist festivals has become increasingly problematic with the emergence of the transgender movement. The Michigan Womyn's Music Festival has instituted a "woman-born-woman only" policy that serves to keep transsexual women out. Minnie Bruce Pratt forcefully challenges this gender policing, laying bare the dangerous implications and bias in the festival's attempt to define a separate female space:

I find that to be admitted here I and the other women have to pass a biological test: Are you a pure, natural-born woman? Surely I can't be the only one who fears a sisterhood based on biological definitions, the kind that have been used in the larger world to justify everything from job discrimination . . . to hysterectomies. And I can't be the only one who grew up trained into the cult of pure white womanhood, and heard biological reasons given to explain actions against people of color. . . . If this gathering of women in the dusty fields beyond the gate is a community based on biological purity, then it offers me, a "real woman," no real safety. (*S/HE* 183)

7. In an ethnographic analysis of the National Women's Music Festival, Eder et al. report: "Unlike the White lesbians who felt part of a larger family, some lesbian women of color contended that unchallenged racist beliefs prevented them from feeling completely accepted at the festival. Although they may have felt more welcome as lesbians than in mainstream society, many did not feel accepted as women of color." Donna Eder, Suzanne Staggenborg, and Lori Sudderth, "The National Women's Music Festival" 501.

8. Marilyn Frye, *The Politics of Reality* 107. Although I see radical potential in the renewed practice of separatism, Robyn Wiegman makes an important critique of the growing consumerism of the lesbian community, whereby the lesbian production and purchase of "music, clothing, vacation cruises, festivals, art work, publishing . . . approximates in the 1990s a tamed separatism . . . [and is] evidence of political progress." Robyn Wiegman, "Introduction: Mapping the Lesbian Postmodern" 3. While separatism can mean the support of women-owned businesses, we should renew our attempt to move lesbian politics beyond a consumer market.

9. See Alice Echols's excellent history of the contemporary feminist movement for a full discussion of its beginnings; Echols, *Daring to Be Bad.*

10. Madeline Davis and Elizabeth Lapovsky Kennedy, "Oral History and the Study of Sexuality in the Lesbian Community" 9.

11. Ibid. 9.

12. Gloria Steinem, "Sisterhood" 49.

13. Two women I interviewed for this study revealed that before attending their first women's music concerts around 1975, they had no idea that there was a larger lesbian community out there. One woman said that she and her lover had been together for a few years, but "we didn't know anything about lesbian community and I think that the music is what brought lesbian community out and brought women together so we could see that we all existed. . . . I don't even think I knew the word lesbian until I had been one for a while." This woman's ability to define herself as lesbian rested, at least in part, on knowing if or how she and her lover connected to a larger community (personal interview, October 1993).

14. Alix Dobkin and Diedra McCalla, *Off Our Backs*, 1989, 20.

15. At these festivals it is clear through the workshops, crafts, and humor that most of the participants are lesbians. Eder et al.'s study of the National Women's Music Festival reports that organizers of this festival estimate that approximately 85 to 90 percent of the participants are lesbians (492).

16. Interview with Meg Christian, ca. 1979. Available at International Gay and Lesbian Archives, Los Angeles. Women's music file, no. 2.

17. Ruth Scovill, "Women's Music 1972–1977: A Documentation," thesis, California State University, Chico, 1983, 11.

18. Castle, *Apparitional Lesbian* 2.

19. The chorus to this song reads: "She was a big tough woman, the first to come along, / who taught me that to be female meant you still could be strong, / and though graduation meant that we had to part, / she'll always be a player on the ballfield of my heart."

20. Sedgwick argues that ignorance or secrecy operates just as strongly in homophobic discourse as knowledge to inscribe a person in distinct power relations. She writes: "silence is rendered as pointed and performative as speech . . . [which] highlights more broadly the fact that ignorance is as potent and as multiple a thing there is as knowledge" (*Epistemology* 4). By emphasizing how lesbian existence is defined through absence, silence, or invisibility, Sedgwick provides an important theoretical shift to Foucault's analysis of the history of sexuality.

21. See Alice Echols, "The Eruption of Difference" 203–41.

22. Charlotte Bunch, "Learning from Lesbian Separatism" 437.

23. Ibid. 436.

24. Interview with Alix Dobkin, ca. 1979. Available at the International Gay and Lesbian Archives, Los Angeles. Women's music file, no. 1.

25. In October 1993 I interviewed twelve women who all graciously shared with me their recollections of coming out with women's music on the West Coast. I wish to thank them not only for the interviews, but for the continuing inspiration I draw from their lives and words: Lynda Lefever, Molly Laula, Barbara Nemo, Elizabeth Barclay, Raisa Veronique, Susan Symonds, Jadi Gosnell, Jan Scott Fadden, Jennifer Freed, Karin Carrington, Bonnie Hope, and Karen Monson.

26 Lynn Spigel, "Communicating with the Dead" 180.

27. These warning words from Adrienne Rich are illustrated in the popular media's erasure of women's music:

> As we address the institution itself . . . we begin to perceive a history of female resistance which has never fully understood itself because it has been so fragmented, miscalled, erased. It will require a courageous grasp of the politics and economics, as well as the cultural propaganda, of heterosexuality to carry us beyond individual cases of diversified group situations into the complex kind of overview needed to undo the power men everywhere wield over women. ("Compulsory Heterosexuality and Lesbian Existence" 67–68)

28. *The Changer: A Record of Our Times.*

29. This philosophy of inclusion is being attacked today within the lesbian community as policing behavior that limits women's agency. Alisa Solomon argues against some lesbian feminist events which institute (in her opinion) extreme policies of inclusion such as prohibiting wearing perfume to accommodate women sensitive to scents, providing sugar-free beverages for diabetic women, and having accessible seating for all women, including very large women. She argues that these are practices that exceed consciousness raising and verge "on behavioral control" (in *Sisters, Sexperts, Queers* 211). This is easy to say if you are not one of the women being excluded from an event because of your size or your health.

30. Concert flyer, "Olivia Presents: A Concert with Meg Christian and Introducing Teresa Trull," ca. 1977.

31. Because of the brevity of this chapter I have not been able to mention

many other women musicians and groups who also emerged during this same period and became locally or nationally popular. Although much of women's music has folk origins, there were also very popular groups such as Be Be K'Roche, which combined Latin, soul, salsa, and jazz rhythms with rock. Differences in women's music were not only generic but also included the more radical lesbian separatism of such singers as Alix Dobkin, whose music and concerts are a notable exception to the kind of blurring of lesbian definition I have been discussing.

32. Bernice Johnson Reagon and Sweet Honey in the Rock, *We Who Believe in Freedom* 32.

33. Ibid.

34. "A Concert with Meg Christian and Introducing Teresa Trull," presented by Olivia Records, National Women's Recording Company, ca. 1977.

35. Reagon, *We Who Believe in Freedom* 33.

36. Sweet Honey in the Rock, "Every Woman."

37. For an excellent discussion of the effects on and exchanges between members of riot girrl bands and older womyn's music icons like Alix Dobkin, see Val C. Phoenix, "From Womyn to Grrrls."

38. Ibid. 41.

WORKS CITED

Bunch, Charlotte. "Learning from Lesbian Separatism." *Lavender Culture*. Ed. Karla Jay and Allen Young. 1978. New York: New York University Press, 1995, 433–44.

Case, Sue-Ellen. "Tracking the Vampire." *differences* 3 (1991): 1–20.

Castle, Terry. *The Apparitional Lesbian: Female Homosexuality and Modern Culture.* New York: Columbia University Press, 1993.

The Changer: A Record of the Times. Oakland: Olivia Records, 1991.

Christian, Meg. Personal interview. Ca. 1979. International Gay and Lesbian Archives, Los Angeles.

Davis, Madeline, and Elizabeth Lapovsky Kennedy. "Oral History and the Study of Sexuality in the Lesbian Community: Buffalo, New York, 1940–1960." *Feminist Studies* 12.1 (1986): 7–26.

de Lauretis, Teresa. *The Practice of Love: Lesbian Sexuality and Perverse Desire.* Bloomington: Indiana University Press, 1994.

Dobkin, Alix. Personal interview. Ca. 1979. International Gay and Lesbian Studies Archives, Los Angeles.

———, and Diedra McCalla. Interview. *Off Our Backs,* 1989, 20.

Echols, Alice. *Daring to Be Bad: Radical Feminism in America 1967–1975.* Minneapolis: University of Minnesota Press, 1989.

Eder, Donna, Suzanne Staggenborg, and Lori Sudderth. "The National Women's Music Festival: Collective Identity and Diversity in a Lesbian-Feminist Community." *Journal of Contemporary Ethnography* 23.4 (January 1995): 485–515.

Frye, Marilyn. *The Politics of Reality: Essays in Feminist Theory.* Trumansburg: Crossing Press, 1983.

Gomez, Jewelle. *The Gilda Stories.* Ithaca: Firebrand, 1991.

Maggenti, Maria. "Wandering Through Herland." In *Sisters, Sexperts, Queers: Beyond the Lesbian Nation.* Ed. Arlene Stein. New York: Plume, 1993.

Olivia Records. "A Concert with Meg Christian and Introducing Teresa Trull." Ca. 1977. International Gay and Lesbian Archives, Los Angeles.

Phoenix, Val C. "From Womyn to Grrrls: Finding Sisterhood in Girl Style Revolution." *Deneuve*, January–February 1994, 40–43.

Pratt, Minnie Bruce. *S/HE.* New York: Firebrand, 1995.

Reagon, Bernice Johnson, and Sweet Honey in the Rock. *We Who Believe in Freedom: Sweet Honey in the Rock . . . Still on the Journey.* New York: Doubleday, 1993.

Rich, Adrienne. *Blood, Bread, and Poetry: Selected Prose 1979–1985.* New York: Norton, 1986.

Scovill, Ruth. *Women's Music 1972–1977: A Documentation.* Thesis, California State University, Chico, 1983.

Sedgwick, Eve Kosofsky. *Epistemology of the Closet.* Berkeley: University of California Press, 1990.

Spigel, Lynn. "Communicating with the Dead: Elvis as Medium." *Camera Obscura* 23 (1990).

Steinem, Gloria. "Sisterhood." *Ms.,* Spring 1972, 47–49.

Sweet Honey in the Rock. "Every Woman." *Believe I'll Run On . . . See What the End's Gonna Be.* Redwood Records, 1978.

Wiegman, Robyn. "Introduction: Mapping the Lesbian Postmodern." In *The Lesbian Postmodern.* Ed. Laura Doan. New York: Columbia University Press, 1994, 1–20.

Toward a Butch-Feminist Retro-Future

SUE-ELLEN CASE

After throwing a major temper tantrum about the feminist tradition in my article "Toward a Butch-Femme Aesthetic," I now want to emphasize the fact that the tantrum was intended as a dramatic event that would, hopefully, by the force of its critique, initiate a dialogue to correct what seemed to me to be persistent omissions and oppressions in the history of feminist discourse around lesbian issues.[1] The scenario I sought to write was a butch seduction/bar fight with feminism, with no exit from the feminist arena on my mind. For, dysfunctional as the feminist family of critical notions proved to be, it was still "home" to my lesbian identity. And I mean specifically a "lesbian" identity. If the bar culture had given me "butch," feminism had given me "lesbian." Now maybe the reason I was entangled with feminism had to do with my pre-movement, oppressed habit of bringing out straight women—particularly straight middle-class women, who seemed to best grace my working-class arm. I kept trying to seduce feminism, then, as it toyed with representations of me. Classic behavior for a butch bottom.

Yet, while "butch" provided a way back into the bars, subcultural history, and signs, "feminism" had provided a way out of the bars, onto the streets, in coalitions with other women, and into theories of representation. Theoretical prowess—is that another name for academic upward mobility? Possibly. Barbara Christian and others have revealed the operations of class in such theory building. But, as those very authors have illustrated, it isn't in the theory that the class markers are embedded. After all, they theorize against theory, or theorize through autobiography and poetry. The class-specific signs, then, reside in the language of the theory. Part of an early feminist concern—that. The general proscription was not to duplicate the impersonal, unmarked language of the patriarchal tradition. Refined by some women of color and white-trash lesbians, the creative impulse within the movement was to abandon elitist, class-privileged language for experiments in the personal voice of the author. As in what was once called the arts, an embodiment of the abstracted position of the author was the practice. Author, as floating signifier, presumed access to the realm of timeless, genderless, subjective-less knowledge. In the case of the early feminist critique, the abstract, situated author, apart from "personal" or explicit historical and material attributes, practiced gender, class, and ethnic privilege. Slippage, then, signaled upward mobility. Dorothy Allison, author of *Trash*, quotes, in *Skin*, from a speech delivered by Bertha Harris that contrasts what she calls "lower class" writing with such signs of privilege:

> direct, unequivocating, grabby, impolite, always ready for a fight, and with a nose that can smell bullshit a mile away. The ecumenical, appeasing, side-stepping, middle-class mind never ever produces a great work of art, nor a great work of politics. (206)

Now, Allison reports that Harris delivered this homily in a manner that "scared" her. Harris "put her hands on her hips, glared out at us." Scared, seduced, and supported in one, Bertha's attitude and her admonition produced a therapeutic effect for Allison. She took them as a challenge to believe in herself—to overcome her class-based insecurities and lack of self-esteem. She then quotes how Harris threw down the gauntlet to stop shuddering and get busy:

> *Remember, the central female organ that makes us different and strong and artists is not the womb but the brain.* (207; italics hers)

Allison is citing a speech Harris delivered at the Sagaris feminist institute in 1975. Here is an essentialism of 1970s lesbian feminism—an appeal to the biological, delivered through that "unequivocating, grabby" style, aimed at the material practice of writing, and received within the class practices of she who would write. Harris's call to the body (the brain) is a rhetorical strategy, insisting upon a hands-on relation to the meat of mentality. To write, for Allison and Harris, is to work—appeals to the body reference manual labor—a far cry from the elitist notions of "ontology" or "presence" later ascribed to lesbian feminists. But those later charges presume the referents of writing to be philosophical systems. Their distance from the assumption of manual labor and class shame mark more the authors who deploy such charges than those they were set against.

In order to reframe the debates over critiques of lesbian and queer, I want to erect Harris, standing, feet apart, like a feminist butch colossus, overseeing the divide between the tradition of feminism and its *All about Eve* successor—the queer dyke. Allison's Harris, big, bad, gender- and class-specific, seductive and butch in her positioning of writing and the body, challenges the later charge of essentialism that has been funneled through the term *queer* in order to undo that pose of the feminist butch. The charge of essentialism, from those queer quarters, would bury that butch feminist and her likes beneath an image of lesbian feminists that look like button-wearing naive politicas. Queer dykes, flipping through fashion magazines while boarding at Northeastern private universities, proffer, instead, the semiotic copy of such material practices as a correction to the "essentialist" fallacy. If Allison sees in Harris a kind of *Night of the Living Dead*, starring brain-eating butch writers teaching at a 1970s feminist institute, the queer dyke sees herself seeing k. d. lang on the cover of *Vanity Fair*. How is it that Condé Nast(y) has become more poststructurally correct than Allison's *Skin?* The answer resides in the deployment of the term *queer.*

QUEER, NOT!

Early on, before its assimilation by postsomething or other's positioning of the discourses constructing sexuality, "queer" theorizing still emulated the sense of taking back the insult—inhabiting the "bad girl"—playing the monster—as 1970s lesbian feminism had taught some of us to do. Antiassimilationist in its intent, "queer" moved away from good-girl civil-rights petitioning. Some people thought "queer" originated that pose, but Allison reports, from that 1975 feminist writing institute, that big Bertha admonished them: *"Dare to be monstrous, she told us in that tone of irony that warned of puns and witticisms to follow"* (207). The tradition of antiassimilation, then, could be perceived as emanating from a 1970s working-class butch feminism, rather than a late 1980s New York queer coalition. Embedded in camp irony and wit (a discourse some writers of lesbian history deny to lesbians), these shared moments of Dorothy Allison and Bertha Harris at the feminist writer's institute could promote the kind of move that would embrace the insult of queer, in order to retrieve a contestatory site for political intervention.

Moreover, "queer" might reposition lesbian—moving the term out of its subcategorical position within feminism to one of (hopefully) equal status within discourses and practices of homosexuality. In order to safeguard the status of lesbian within feminist practices, and in association with gay men, Teresa de Lauretis organized a conference in Santa Cruz in 1990, proposing "queer" as a tactic that would so move the lesbian into a queer coalition that would, however, continue to trouble the conjunction between "lesbian AND gay." As de Lauretis explained it, in her introduction to the special issue of *differences* that was culled from the conference, "queer" was set at the site of difference, to call for an articulation of historical/material specificity in regard to sexual and gender practices where "and" had simply conjoined them (iv–vii). In other words, (some of them penned by Mary McIntosh), there is a separate development of lesbian and gay male history inscribed in their shared strategies.[2] Terms such as constructionism and queer, rather than inhabiting a gender-free or beyond-gender theoretical position, would be examined to reveal the uneven development of lesbian/gay politics along the social, historical axis of gender difference, while also forging a common front.

Persuaded by de Lauretis's call through queer to critically explore the homosexual divide, I wrote "Tracking the Vampire" for her conference and to be published in the ensuing collection of articles. For me, queer mobilized a vampiric (in)visibility within systems of representation that would feed along an axis of both gay and lesbian texts which had nourished me prior to feminism. Again, ever in dialogue with feminist constructions, I tried to retrieve "lesbian" from an ill-got *jouissance* that cast her in *Whatever Happened to Baby Jane.* Smarting (hopefully) at the feminist "recreational use of the lesbian" that assigned her to the wings in order to stage mother/daughter conjunctions, I hoped to provide an entrance for lesbian from upstage center by aligning her with homosexuality—the queer. Within that critical context, situating lesbian representational strategies in proximity to those of the gay, or homosexual, man, was intended as a correction to the way in which feminist discourses had subsumed or "topped" the lesbian. The social movement ever in mind, it also seemed high time to end the historical labor relations between the lesbian and the feminist activist movement which had domesticated lesbian labor. After all, the lesbian feminist had provided activist labor in many causes, not necessarily her own, such as abortion rights, and for which the straight feminist did not return the favor by, say, marching in PFLAG units in Pride marches. Where were those legions of feminists marching in support?

When I delivered the paper, "Tracking the Vampire," I was critiqued by the local community in Santa Cruz for performing "whiteness" and privileging complex, abstract theorizing, unavailable to working-class people. I revised my paper by founding the theorizing in my historically-geographically specific experiential situation that had produced the theory and by working anti-Semitic codes of blood along with vampiric images. This process of self-criticism and answerability to the local community seemed a familiar practice within lesbian feminist cultural production. However, the editors at the Pembroke Center for Teaching and Research on Women, who would publish the article in *differences*, had (to me) a surprising reaction to what I considered to be a standard materialist feminist correction. They sought to edit out the initial experiential foundation of the piece as an example of 1970s feminist essentialism. First they suggested that I italicize the personal base of the argument, so that it would read like a biographical sketch of the author, separated out from the theorizing. Then they sought to cut it entirely. I'm relating this publishing gossip, not to elevate the stature of my work, nor to seek some balm for wounds to my ego, nor to *j'accuse* those editors, but to compose a parable, bound in the business of publishing, that illustrates the shift in the reception of the construction of "lesbian" in representation, and situates that shift specifically within the rise of the term *queer*. The deconstructive break with the personal as political sought to reaffirm the author as floating signifier. Slippage, once perceived as privileged mobility, became the preferred mode of intellectual travel. The queer call was to return to that unmarked patriarchal, Eurocentric language of, well, the French and German philosophical traditions. "Philosophy to the fore!" cheered queer. Queer thus functioned as the sign of sexual politics cut loose from earlier, grassroots lesbian feminism.

BURIAL RITES OF THE FEMINIST BUTCH

From the developing perspective of queer, lesbian became conflated with what was once more specifically identified as radical feminist politics. The preponderance of socialist/materialist feminist practices in the 1970s was buried in such revisionism, along with the critique devised by working-class, manual-laboring butch feminists. Soon, in queer quarters, it seemed that all lesbian feminists had been wearing Birkenstocks and ripping off their shirts at the Michigan Womyn's Music Festival. Some of us chortled at the revisionist image of bar/butch/feminist dykes listening to acoustic guitars. We remembered, for example, the girl group called the Contractions, who whacked their electric instruments at top volume and flirted impossibly with the audience of dykes (sigh). The culture, always variegated by its wildly divergent feminisms was, through the charge of essentialism and the newly organized perspective of queer, being represented by one small subset. Slapping each other on the back, we joked, "was lesbian s/m invented by Gayle Rubin and Pat Califia in an argument with antiporn advocates?" Leafing through our old phone books and photos of friends flamed out in one affair after another, we snorted at the queer dykes' belief that they were originating the practice of multiple sexual partners, s/m scenarios, the use of sex toys, and the habit of hanging around bars. Beebo Brinker, Ann Bannon's 1950s seducer and abandoner, who found someone else's flannel pajamas in the faithful Laura's apartment, took it as a familiar sign of lesbian social practices, and her progeny peopled at least two succeeding decades. What a surprise, then, to learn that queer dykes associated such sexual promiscuity as more narrowly particular to a gay male culture that they would then need to assimilate and imitate. Butch feminists, it seemed, had been having monogamous, vanilla, Saturday-morning slight sex since the 1970s. We snickered. Then it wasn't funny anymore.

Such revisionist history thus promoted a queer ascension, through a valorization of gay male practices, arising from lesbian feminist ashes. The new queer dyke is out to glue on that gay male mustache and leave those dowdy, gynocentric habits behind. The *lesbian* body, perforated by discursive intrusions as early as Monique Wittig's, disciplined by materialist production as early as the manifestos of Ti-Grace Atkinson and the Combahee River Collective, and radiated out through the hard work of coalition-building, was spanked by the queers for its so-called ontological status and antisexual proclivities. Although, by now, we are surely bored with the spectacle of the debate over the essentialist charge, the charge continues to brand "queer" onto the disciplined, up-ended bottoms of what were once fleshly figures of lesbian desire. Further, queer's consort, "performativity," links "lesbian" to the tarnished sweating, laboring, performing body that must be semiotically scrubbed until the "live" lesbian gives way to the slippery, polished surface of the market manipulation of its sign. Better to circulate the queer dyke body through 'zines and fashion rags than to travel its orifices and tissues in Wittig's speculum-script. Body-less transcendence is produced through the process of semiosis. Isn't that the same desire for transcendence that was identified earlier by lesbian feminists as a masculine, Eurocentric trope? That gay male mustache, garnishing the lip of the queer dyke, then, also garnishes her critical strategies. Even if, as Peggy Shaw contends, testosterone is better in the hands of women, appropriating the masculine is not, obviously, beyond gender.

Right after those queer dykes slammed the door on the way out of lesbian feminism, the dowdy old women-centered places began to close down: most feminist and lesbian theaters, bookstores, and bars have disappeared. One of the underground movies making the circuit

last year is called *Last Call at Maud's*—about the last night at the oldest
lesbian bar in San Francisco and the end of many such lesbian bars. I
walk the streets of West Hollywood and the Village in New York to
jealously observe packed bar after bar of gay men. I stand in the book
chain A Different Light on a Saturday night in West Hollywood—one
of four or five lesbians among, say, fifty gay men. I'm flipping through
the 'zines. I'm checking out the special photo shots of daddy-boy-
dykes in *Quim*. Back on the streets. Everyone is looking good. I stand
outside the gym on Santa Monica, in front of the huge picture windows, reminiscent of shop windows, where I can watch everybody
working out. The women are looking strong. Slim. Young. I look down
at my aging, overweight, academic body. They've cleared us out, I
think. It's true—the Birkenstocks are gone, but so are what we used to
call "women of size" and well, uh, older women. Two of my gay male
friends call me up—they're freaking out because they're now in their
30s—how will they retain their sexual currency—do they have to
become tops—do they have to go over to the leather scene, where
older men still find them desirable? So now we all have *their* problems,
I think.

Never mind, I'll go to the theater. I like *Angels in America*—it has a
big cast and a big theme—a critique of nationalism and, well, I'm pretty
sure the angel is a lesbian. That's what we used to say about the Holy
Ghost—you know, the Father, the Son and. . . . Anyway, there are some
great one-person dyke shows making the circuit and lots of new lesbian
stand-up comics. Forget Broadway—we have "intimate" sites such as
P.S. 122, or I can always go to the movies with my other professor friends
and "read," as we say, something like *Single White Female* as signifying,
as we also say, lesbian. The privileging of gay male culture by queer
dykes, along with the disdain and mis-remembering of lesbian feminism, has produced the dwindling away of lesbian cultural resources—
socially and economically and theoretically. Oh well, I comfort myself
with the option of those lesbian luxury cruises sponsored by Olivia—if
only I could afford one. Then I'm caught up short with this thought—
those old dowdy lesbian feminist hangouts—almost all of them were
organized as collectives: theater collectives, bookstore collectives, food
collectives, collective living quarters. Lesbian dowdy politics had been
intrinsically tied to collective ownership and collective labor. They
locked the mode of material production to cultural production and to
the production of sexual, personal relationships . . . and then there was
interactive commodity dildoism. Does it matter that A Different Light is
not a collective and is, in fact, a chain? Is someone getting rich? Is
someone not? Does it matter?

UP (YOUR) MARKET

What was once a lesbian or gay community is now becoming a market sector. The *Journal of Consumer Marketing* ran an article that summarized the finding of several studies to discover just how lesbians and gays consume market goods. Several studies (some produced by gay public relations agencies) concur that gays and lesbians make more money per household than the U.S. average, buy more airline tickets, own more cars, are better educated, and spend more money on consumer goods. Clearly this market sector has disposable income. They are becoming a target market, but how are they accessible to the market? This study suggests that it is primarily through their publications. The article lists the *Advocate, Deneuve, Genre, On Our Backs, Out* and *10 Percent* as likely venues for effective ads. The new, glossy formats with upscale-looking models and ads encourage corporations to consider buying their pages.

Sarah Schulman has taken such studies to evidence a rising "management class," warning that there is a "class war emerging within the gay and lesbian world" ("Now for a Word from Our Sponsor" 6). She details how some gay organizations are even organizing to profit from HIV-positive buyers. Particularly poignant, notes Schulman, is the growth of viatical companies that purchase the life insurance policies of persons with terminal illnesses. After all, people with AIDS, who have no children or other heirs, may be eager to spend and thus sell their insurance money, at any percentage, to a viatical company. Schulman details how this new management class creates the image of a gay/lesbian market sector that conceals the class differences within it. She quotes from the literature published by the gay-owned Mulryan/Nash advertising firm—the one that marketed *Angels in America* to gay tourists and worked for the government of Holland to develop advertising that would attract gay tourists. Mulryan/Nash contends that 61 percent of gay people have college degrees, household incomes of $62,000, and CD players, work out in gyms, and drink sparkling water. Schulman contrasts these figures with some published in the *New York Times* asserting that homosexual men earn 12 percent less than heterosexual ones and lesbians 5 percent less than heterosexual women, who earn 45 percent less than heterosexual men. Schulman's conclusion, then, is that a privileged gay class is entering the market economy and creating a fiction that erases the "others" in what was once called a community. The aim is to produce sexual identities as powerful consumers with discretionary incomes and good taste.

The once-activist Queer Nation has formed the Queer Shopping Network of New York. "Queer" may be found on coffee mugs, T-shirts, and postcards sold at Gay Pride parades and in new marketing chains across the country. One can buy queer and wear it. In some circles, "queer" seems to be primarily constituted by body piercings, leather, and spike haircuts. One might applaud such signs of commodification as signs of success. Good. We are not necessarily poor, nor downwardly mobile. Lipstick lesbians are cute. Sex can be fun. We are visible, strong, making more money, dressing better, eating out, and enjoying sex.

Many "queer" academics write this affluent, commodity fetishism. Some are concerned with Rock Hudson's body, some with k. d. lang's and Cindy Crawford's photo display in *Vanity Fair,* others with the radical purchasing of dildoes—"subversive shopping," as Danae Clark refers to it in her article "Commodity Lesbianism." They invent queer discourse out of an addiction to the allure of the mass market. Fandom queered. *Melrose Place* reruns as Castro Street. Class privilege and the celebration of capitalism are compounded with the queer sex industry. Likewise, certain theoretical strategies have been embodied in new, surprising ways. The much-touted practice and theory of masquerade, once written as subversive cross-dressing, has literally turned into a uniform. Recent Gay Pride parades sport a uniformed color guard of Marines and the like, accompanying the flag. The people on the sidewalk cheer as the presumably "queer" or "gay" U.S. flag and military march by. If only we could make the military-industrial complex gay-friendly. From queer planet to queer Pentagon. Antiassimilationist in its move away from pleading civil rights, the queer movement insinuates sexual citizenship through affluence in the market and the willing participation in national agendas. Wouldn't it be victory for the movement if Colonel Margarethe Cammermeyer, mother of four sons, Vietnam vet, could be reinstated into the army?

MOMMIE DEAREST

The Reagan 1980s, ushered in by Joan Crawford's attack on any of those hideous wire hangers still found in the closet, produced a routing out of any associations with the iron curtain that continued to inform the political movements concerning alternative sexualities. Contesting capitalism, along with providing alternative economic practices such as collective ownership and labor, in discourses of so-called sexual dissidence was out. Following its successful purge, the privileged compound "queer performativity" ushered in the 1990s, having detonated the ground of lesbian feminism—shattering its socialist roots through the charge of essentialism. The trick was, as post–Berlin Wall discourse also performed, to invert the traditional meanings of political terminology, thereby confusing the actual development of power relationships. After the wall's fall, Euromediaspeak repositioned communism as signifying the Right and the reactionary and global capitalism as the leftist, outsider position. Such sleights of terminology masked material conditions: former property owners in the West appropriated the properties of the former East, while portraying themselves as the oppressed, shaking off the shackles of collective ownership. Similarly, the lesbian feminist position, imbricated with socialist/communist strategies, such as collective practices of ownership and labor, were represented as essentialist, reversing the nature of the critique in order to overcome its materialist practices with formal discursive ones. The rise of "queer performativity," then, accompanied the victory of global capitalism in the new Europe as well as the complete commodification of the sexual movement. The charge of essentialism rousted the iron curtain out of the closet.

The notion of the Bad Binary also functioned to resituate the queer movement within market strategies. Second terms were out. Hetero/homo made homo suspect. Likewise for capitalism/communism. After all, Baudrillard had already depicted the two as the twin trade towers in New York in his *Simulations*. Global capitalism could contain everything, all differences within its shifting economic zones, just as the new Individual could contain multiple subject positions. Down with the binary went oppositional economic and cultural alternatives. Queer emulated global capitalism in order to gain status within it. Certain revisions of history would have to be performed, of course, in order to cleanse any sense of oppositional affiliations from the sexual rights movement. Enter the case of Colonel Cammermeyer. Antiwar demonstrators? Not! Instead, the bid to reinstate the lesbian Vietnam hero into high ranks in the army revised the image and the agenda of the movement. Soldiers and marketeers of global expansion, avid and capable consumers, loyal fans, even (hopefully) good wives and husbands could gather under the banner of queer. Oppositional struggles fade before simple iterations that queer includes everyone who is antinormal and hypernormal all at once. Who could but envy us? At last we're competitive, as they say.

Nevertheless, those of us who were in a relationship, so to speak, with the old dowdy "I" of i-dentity politics, the "I" of dialogue or the dialectic, continue to interpret "presence" as politically showing up. As a base of operations, that "I" signals the old theatrical, the old dare I say communist, the old feminist collective dialogues of contradiction—"I know, let's do a show—I'll play," as Lois Weaver once said onstage to

Peggy Shaw, "Katharine Hepburn to your Spencer Tracy." Or, in the old communist sense, "I know, let's redistribute the land—let's collectivize the labor—what? It's not fair, given your college education, your student loan, your expertise? How can we work this out?" Or, in the old feminist sense, I can still hear the voice of the African American activist Bernice Johnson Reagon, speaking to a group of feminists struggling over issues of ethnicity and sexual practice. She described the experience of building coalitions:

> The first thing that happens is that the room don't feel like the room anymore. (The audience laughed) And it ain't home no more. It is not a womb no more. And you can't feel comfortable no more. . . . [Yet] the "our" must include everybody you have to include in order for you to survive. . . . That's why we have to live in coalitions. 'Cause I ain't gonna let you live unless you let me live. Now there's danger in that, but there's also the possibility that we both can live—if you can stand it. ("Coalition Politics," 359, 363)

The sound of dialogue, the collective, resounds in these threats and hurts of the clash of conflicting positions, or the joy of temporary agreement which, like Rome, is not made in a day, or by the fiat of a term like *queer* that sweeps down from the discourse to gather up oppositional positions by force of its own definition AS embracing AS multimulti, acting like the movies, or the old well-made plays that conclude all problems with a kiss, a marriage, or, in this case, a dildo.

And "presence"—showing up—at activist disruptions, at live performances, in collective venues, reclaims the "live"—the body—the visible—looking for lesbians in the political sense. It is "live" performance as politics, as theater, the play of positional masks, sweating flesh and clapping hands that finally animates what cyberpunks call the "meat." For presence as body, as visibility, in the collective, once abandoned, i-dentity once gone, promotes the new sense of performativity in which the body is a trope and performance part of the allure of reading and writing.

WORK NOT, WANT NOT

The year 1982 might be regarded as the Great Divide. Along with *Mommie Dearest*, the Barnard conference staged the outbreak of open conflict between the lesbian s/m community and the feminist antiporn adherents—a conflict that was never resolved. The debates were hot and the rifts were deep. What later became the "sex radicals" tired of feminism's het "missionary position," while the feminist critique stalled out in its persistent blindness to heterosexism. Moreover, the socialist critique remained obsessed with labor, ignoring issues around sexual practice and pleasure.

Meanwhile, the beginning of what would become the AIDS crisis was forging new alliances between lesbians and gay men. Patriarchal privilege aside, gay men were in life-or-death struggles around sexual practices. Sex was a given, open focus in their community, while the feminist community, where heterosexism forced a silencing of the debate they were afraid to continue, seemed to be formulating neo-puritanical prescriptions against erotic materials and the exploration of sexual pleasure. So lesbian feminists became queer dykes among gay men. The rise of the fundamentalist Right demanded a new, more aggressive political activism. The failure of government institutions to respond to the need for AIDS treatment became more and more reactionary. ACT UP, formed in the late 1980s in New York, produced "live" agitprop street performances within a coalition. For awhile. While some ACT UP organizations survived, others, such as the ones in San Francisco and Seattle, split into ACTS UPS, or whatever. Lesbians split from gay men over the focus of concern: is AIDS a gay male disease, or how do we also address the problems of the category "women," straight or lesbian, of color who bear a high incidence of AIDS? Latent feminist coalitions with other women, particularly women of color, still haunted the new dyke. It seems girls don't just wanta have fun, but they also don't wanta have none. In queer coalitions, proceeding out from New York's urban center, how could those queer dykes still remain in old feminist coalitions with women of color and third-world women?

If queer, as sex-positive and antiassimilationist, claims to cut across differences: bisexuals, transgendered people, s/m practitioners—and all the "antinormal" could be included in its embrace, and if it also claims multicultural representation at its base, then why do we read things like the following? Cherríe Moraga, the lesbian Chicana poet and dramatist writes:

> We discussed the limitations of "Queer Nation," whose leather-jacketed, shaved-headed white radicals and accompanying anglo-centricity were an alien-nation to most lesbians and gay men of color. (*The Last Generation* 147)

Even the queer enthusiast Michael Warner offers a chilling description of the "queer community" in his introduction to *Fear of a Queer Planet:*

> In the lesbian and gay movement, to a much greater degree than in any comparable movement, the institutions of culture-building have been market-mediated. . . . Nonmarket forms of association . . . churches, kinship, traditional residence—have been less available for

queers. This structural environment has meant that the institutions of queer culture have been dominated by those with capital: typically, middle-class white men. (xvii)

Terry Castle, in *The Apparitional Lesbian*, adds this dimension:

> As soon as the lesbian is lumped in—for better or for worse—with her male homosexual counterpart, the singularity of her experience (sexual and otherwise) tends to become obscured . . . to the extent that "queer theory" still seems . . . to denote primarily the study of male homosexuality, I find myself at odds with both its language and its universalizing aspirations. (12–13)

Charles Fernández, in "Undocumented Aliens in the Queer Nation," identifies *queer* as a "melting pot" term of "bankrupt universalism."

I think an important clue to the element in the notion and practice of queer that led to its embrace of commodification and its emulation of dominant class and gender practices may be found in Alexander Chee's historical account of the origins of Queer Nation:

> The name stuck simply for the sake of marketing. The original idea was this: choose a name around each action, keep responsibility with each individual and not with an institution. . . . People are tired of groups with egos, processes, personality cults, and politicking. So far Queer Nation is individuals confronting individuals. ("A Queer Nationalism" 15)

Chee underscores that any practice of continuity was a marketing choice. The queer retention of individualism, changing tactics, venue, and organizations, was designed to invigorate those who are "tired" of group processes. The interest, then, is not in collective agency—in fact, collectives are perceived as infected with "politicking"—but in the individual's action of intervention into the marketing process. In fact, if Chee is correct, Queer Nation arose as a direct contradiction to collective, group-process-oriented politics. At the same time, it does seem to unfurl that same old banner of the individual that liberal democracy keeps hanging out to dry. Sarah Schulman, writing from a slightly different perspective in *My American History*, indicates that the AIDS crisis catalyzed the correction of traditional forms of coalition-building. She offers "processing" as the problem, through which coalition-building became therapizing, continually postponing activism—a delay the new, fatal progress of AIDS could ill afford (6). Yet, when the process is aborted and the coalition simply iterated, the skills that had been learned in antiracist, antisexist training groups become lost and those dominant structures remain intact within the coalition.

Queer coalitions, then, in a hurry to get onto the streets, began to interrogate the "normal," as if outside of the normalizing operations of patriarchy, capital, and nation. For, without arduous attention to dominant contexts, single-issue politics operate within them. The term *queer,* then, circulating out from Queer Nation, asserts itself as an umbrella term without the hard rain of coalition-building. Thus it reinstates the dominant social structures, lending its power to those who are already vested in the system, with the exception of their sexual identification. Not surprisingly, then, white middle-class men will form the constituency. Their culture, sub or not, will continue to be representative.

YOU HAVE NOTHING TO WEAR BUT YOUR CHAINS

Now thoroughly depressed, I wonder if this writing is only nostalgic. The good old days of butch feminism. Not only. I mean, the child whines because she wants something she can't have—in the present. It isn't all fort/da, as the Freudians would have us believe—I mean, it isn't all because mommie left the room. If this writing did begin by wriggling through those spread thighs of the colossal Bertha Harris I erected to guard the portals between butch feminist and queer, it isn't satisfied to remain there, curled up in the fetal position, stammering fort/da to some Freudian who likes to watch. Toward a butch-feminist retro-future seeks an agenda that might animate both a modernist project of doing something historical about the future and the ironic, postmodern sense of retro that, by the conjunction, still performs a critique of the categories of historical past and future.

Employing *retro* in this way is in contradiction to the way the term and the practice are typically theorized. Critics such as Celeste Olalquiaga in *Megalopolis* contend that any retro future is always already

> attracted by an image of progress only possible to an apocalyptical fin de siecle as a melancholic appropriation—one that refuses to accept death, fetishistically clinging to memories, corpses, and ruins. (23)

Farting the old fetishistic gas, as usual. Crucial to my argument, however, is the way in which Olalquiaga discovers retro as a specifically gay male practice. She contends that the "two most conspicuous subcultures involved in retro fashion are children of the baby-boomer era: yuppies and young gay men" (32). Never to be left out, I want to imply queer dyke subculture in such practices. Here's how Olalquiaga sees it:

> While yuppies use money as a means of neutralizing difference, many young gay men use their bodies as a celebratory means of camouflage

and the absorption of difference. Rather than the explicit transvestism of drag . . . these men are prone to . . . the body as the territory on which infinite characters and personas can be explored on a daily basis. . . . Money and body alike, then, serve as conduits for the circulation of signs, enabling a swift exchange void of the weight of referentiality. It is not history or a peculiar culture that is being referred to in this way of quoting, it is rather an iconographic richness that is being happily cannibalized. (32)

Something in the style of retro quoting, then, makes it unspecific—the general play of signs that, finally, celebrates a significatory emptiness. The past is dead. This sense of retro depends upon a rather wide bandwidth of signs—that is, unlike drag, not signs of a specific historical or collective past. Retro butch feminism is more specific in its referent, butch feminism, than queer has been in its operations that would dismantle the generalized, revisionist lesbian feminism. So first the retro I have in mind requires a knowledge of the specific historical and discursive strategies of butch feminism to cite. Retro, in this sense, is a kind of discipline. On the one hand, retro confounds the melancholic nostalgia of a dead retro with an agenda for the future; on the other, it corrects the tendentious quality of utopian agendas with a camp citation of history. What does this mean? Partially, it mandates a reconsideration, back through queer, of a class-specific, self-consciously gendered political program that situates the practitioner within coalitional politics while playing out traditionally lesbian seduction scenarios within the political practice. Economic structures once again codetermine sexual politics and the inscription of the different histories of gay men and lesbians reconfigure what now seem to be common, agendered forms, which encourage the belief that there is another, nongendered discursive space within which such politics may emerge. The composition seeks a certain playful sobriety, oxymoronic compounds that actually do suggest, once again, agency and responsibility in a time which puts on a good show in order to distract the audience from the irreparable damage it inflicts on those who continue to play by its rules.

N O T E S

I am indebted to the organizers of the conference entitled "Queering the Pitch" in Manchester and to Karen Quimby and the other organizers of the "Queer Frontiers" conference at the University of Southern California for inviting me to deliver the keynote addresses that led to this chapter.

1. Both this chapter and its title overwrite the femme with feminist. Partially, this new conjunction means to place the butch and feminism in a similar desiring coupling, as the earlier butch/femme had suggested. Polemically, the conjunction also means to reforge a lost, troubled connection. However, "dropping" the femme is definitely part of the theoretical process here—an unhappy one. I can only hope that she will make me regret every minute of it—will force herself back into the theorizing. Thanks to Laura Harris for pointing out this problem in my article. I eagerly await her forthcoming femme flirtation with the discourse.

2. See McIntosh's notion of the triad of "queer," "feminist," and "lesbian" strategies at the conclusion of her article "Queer Theory and the War of the Sexes."

WORKS CITED

Allison, Dorothy. *Skin.* Ithaca: Firebrand, 1994.
Baudrillard, Jean. *Simulations.* Trans. Paul Foss et al. New York: Semiotext(e), 1983, 135–36.
Castle, Terry. *The Apparitional Lesbian.* New York: Columbia University Press, 1993.
Chee, Alexander. "A Queer Nationalism." *Out/Look* 12 (1991): 15–20.
"Daddy Boy Dykes." *Quim.* Winter 1991. 32–35.
de Lauretis, Teresa. "Queer Theory: Lesbian and Gay Sexualities: An Introduction." *differences* 3.2 (1991): iii–xviii.
Fernández, Charles. "Undocumented Aliens in the Queer Nation." *Out/Look* 12 (1991): 20–23.
Fugate, Douglas. "Evaluating the US Male Homosexual and Lesbian Population as a Viable Target Market Segment." *Journal of Consumer Marketing* 10.4 (1993): 46–57.
McIntosh, Mary. "Queer Theory and the War of the Sexes." In *Activating Theory: Lesbian, Gay, Bisexual Politics.* Ed. Joseph Bristow and Angelia R. Wilson. London: Lawrence and Wishart, 1993, 30–52.
Moraga, Cherríe. *The Last Generation.* Boston: South End Press, 1993.
Olalquiaga, Celeste. *Megalopolis: Contemporary Cultural Sensibilities.* Minneapolis: University of Minnesota Press, 1992.
Reagon, Bernice Johnson. "Coalition Politics: Turning the Century." In *Home Girls: A Black Feminist Anthology.* Ed. Barbara Smith. Brooklyn: Kitchen Table, Women of Color Press, 1983.
Schulman, Sarah. *My American History: Lesbian and Gay Life during the Reagan/ Bush Years.* New York: Routledge, 1994.
———. "Now for a Word from Our Sponsor." Paper delivered at the University of California at San Diego, January 1995.
Warner, Michael. Introduction. *Fear of a Queer Planet.* Minneapolis: University of Minnesota Press, 1993, vii–xxxi.

Afterword

LILLIAN FADERMAN

Is the lesbian-feminist of the older generation feeling like the mother—who had been "very advanced" in her youth—whose daughter, having just come of age, rudely rejects all mama's ideas as dated and dowdy though she only half understands them? Does the mother feel a sting of injustice in her daughter's lack of desire to listen to what mama had really been about in her shining youth? Does mama, with menopause looming on the horizon, feel betrayed and abandoned and worried sick by the favorite daughter who should now be paying her the tribute of wanting to follow closely in her footsteps instead of running off with strange young men?

What is it with this daughter? Is mother melodramatic and hysterical when she fears matricide? Is daughter bent on killing mother off to allay the anxieties of influence? Or is it that the irresponsible daughter wants to do away with her mother in order to squander without restraint the riches of an inheritance that she already enjoys? To what extent are lesbian-feminists justified in being perturbed that their successors are headed in all the wrong directions or in feeling outraged that those who have followed have undervalued and misunderstood them?

Many of us who came to lesbian life in the 1950s greeted the public rebirth of a feminist movement in the sixties with exuberance and relief because it articulated our deepest feelings. What feminists were saying—about sexism, for example, about male chauvinism and double standards and inequality—touched precisely on those dissatisfactions that had made us want to become lesbians in the first place. Feminism appeared to strike at the root of what had alienated us from the heterosexual world and to proffer solutions such as we had long invented in our most secret thoughts and felt forbidden to utter. Feminism encouraged us to articulate those repressed thoughts. It encouraged us to contribute the wisdoms we had learned as lesbians to the formulation of theory and the formation of practice.

Feminism also provided a space for lesbians to dream of an Amazon nation and a place to invent a women's culture. It swelled our ranks with women who came to understand through radical feminism that only a lesbian-feminist lifestyle was entirely consistent with their political ideals. It gave us pride by encouraging us to see that far from being "neurotic," as the 1950s considered lesbians, we had been pioneers and heroic role models in independent living and in loving free of the dangers and drawbacks of heterosexuality. And for lesbian academics, feminism provided, as Dana Heller suggests in the introduction to this volume, the tools and insights necessary for revolutionary reading and writing. So, it is no wonder that for many of us lesbians, feminism seemed to be our natural and only home, and other feminists seemed to be our natural and only allies.

The euphoria of the lesbian alliance with feminism was short-lived, since serious problems were manifested early, such as mainstream feminism's tendency to insult lesbians by tokenism or the homophobia of conservative feminists. But despite those problems, the gifts—the insights, the theoretical tools, the direct or indirect affirmations—that lesbians received from feminism were rich. The gifts were so valuable that those of us who remember them—and remember the earlier days when we lived without them—were shocked and even furious when we saw emerging a new generation that seemed to take for granted what feminism made possible and, with no little hostility to feminism, sought after what seemed like strange gods—queer alliances.

Those alliances were a shock because queer style and queer language appeared to be so different from lesbian-feminist style and language. But are queer ideas entirely different from lesbian-feminist ideas? On closer examination, aren't many of the perceived differences between lesbian-feminist theory and queer theory less substantive than stylistic and aesthetic? As a number of the contributors to this volume suggest, despite the annoying refusal of queers to credit lesbian-feminism, much of queer theory seems to be old wine in new bottles.

Lesbian-feminist ideology as it was established in the 1970s was, of course, diverse and complex and often a subject of internal debate, as was apparent from the constant battles within the movement. But perhaps to facilitate the conscious or unconscious intention of killing off the mothers, queers sometimes seem to want to present lesbian-feminism as monolithic, as Bonnie Zimmerman points out in her chapter,

"'Confessions' of a Lesbian Feminist." Lesbian-feminists are now being essentialized as puritan, ethnocentric, essentialist—everything that queers are not. However, ideas that are central to queerdom were also central to the thinking of many lesbian-feminists, including the formulation of theories and practices to counter racism as well as the direct challenge to puritanism through a valorization of nonmonogamy. Lesbian-feminists were in the forefront in articulating the debates with regard to sexuality and gender as social constructs; they were vitally concerned with the need for a more inclusive conception of woman; they were the ones who first formulated theories regarding sex as politics; they argued eloquently for the right to freer expression of sexual desire. Linda Garber has shown elsewhere that seminal lesbian-feminist poets such as Judy Grahn and Pat Parker promulgated in their 1970s works many of the ideas that are central to the concept of "queer" today.[1] It is no exaggeration to say that much of what queer daughters are and think would not have been possible without lesbian-feminist mothers.

"Postmodernist" thought that supposedly began the calling into question of the category of "woman" was, in fact, basic to lesbian-feminist theorizing. From the very beginnings of the movement in the late sixties and early seventies lesbian-feminist theoreticians in periodicals such as *The Furies* were insisting that lesbian-feminists must pay attention to differences of class and race, must not assume universals among women, must not carelessly insist on the category "woman" while describing only white, middle-class women. These issues of difference which were raised from the start became perhaps the primary area of focus and discussion among lesbian-feminists throughout the 1970s and into the eighties, leading much more directly than is currently being acknowledged to the "postmodernist" realization that "woman" is an unstable concept.

Far from being essentialist, the very basis of lesbian-feminism may be seen as social constructionist. What was absolutely integral to the lesbian-feminist movement was the concept that lesbianism was not a state that a few women were born into; rather, any woman could, should, and would become a lesbian once she understood sexual politics. Lesbian-feminism insisted that though a woman had spent her entire adult life as a heterosexual and had never before acknowledged an attraction to other women, she could elect to become a lesbian for political reasons and that sexual desire would follow that election. Lesbian-feminism was a clear demonstration of social constructionism because it maintained that sexuality, rather than being innate and fixed, had primary reference to what was happening in society.

What was also basic to lesbian-feminism, long before it was articulated by Judith Butler, Gayle Rubin, and other queer theorists, was the concept that gender was nothing but performance and had no essential connection to sex or sexuality. Lesbian-feminist dress, comportment, and occupations proclaimed that women could "usurp" all the territories that men once considered the exclusive domains of masculinity. It was basic to lesbian-feminist thought to believe that women could perform what had been considered "the masculine" just as well as, or better than, men could; and such (improved) performance included especially what had been considered most sacred to male prerogative—satisfying women sexually. In those ways lesbian-feminism problematized the essentialism of the notions of both sexuality and gender.

Because lesbian-feminists questioned gender essentialism, Michèle Barale rightly suggests in her chapter, "When *Lambs* and *Aliens* Meet," queer theory's interrogation of maleness should resonate particularly with them. As Barale points out, from the very beginning of their movement lesbian-feminists wanted to upset notions of normative masculinity, and that is exactly what male queers are bent on doing. One implement of the queer challenge to "maleness" has been drag, a ludic pursuit that did not charm lesbian-feminists of the seventies. But the nineties are very different from twenty years ago (thanks in part to the social changes lesbian-feminism wrought). Lesbian-feminist resentment of drag queens in the seventies had nothing to do with the fact that men were not acting like men or with any notion that gender presentation should be chromosomally appropriate. Rather lesbian-feminists were disturbed that drag queenery reified every stereotype about women that lesbian-feminism was trying to dispute. To dispute those stereotypes was revolutionary in the context of the times, and to confirm them by male performance of "the woman" was counterrevolutionary. Drag is less threatening now precisely because feminism has succeeded in making the point that there are all kinds of women and most of them transcend the stereotype. It is tautological that lesbian-feminists of the nineties would need to rethink views regarding males performing "woman" that are more than two decades old and that were developed in a patently different social milieu.

But in no way was it gender-fuck to which lesbian-feminists were opposed in the seventies. Lesbian-feminists had their own style of gender-fuck, which was androgyny. And they insisted that *anyone* could perform androgyny. It is ironic that queers make a great distinction between themselves and lesbian-feminists by disassociating from what they characterize as the timidity and seriousness of the earlier movement with regard to gender. Queers see lesbian-feminist style as a contrast to their own outlaw style. But, in fact, many lesbian-feminists were performing what was for their times an outrageous version of the game of gender and in doing so were outlaws in an era that was far less safe for outlawry than these fin-de-siècle times. By refusing to act like "women" were supposed to act and love like "women" were supposed to love, lesbian-feminists were saying there are many ways to be female that the category "women" (as opposed to "womyn") does not acknowledge. Lesbian-feminists were among the first to problematize the simplistic mappings of chromosomal sex to gender to sexual desire. In pioneering the gender outlawry of androgyny, lesbian-feminists made the Western world quite a bit safer for contemporary gender outlaws.

To insist on this point further, the very essence of the ludic style of queer can be traced back to what Sue-Ellen Case characterizes in her chapter, "Toward a Butch-Feminist Retro-Future," as "working-class butch feminism." Case traces early "queer" to the style and theorizing of Bertha Harris and her advice to "dare to be monstrous." As Linda Garber has shown, Harris was not the only lesbian-feminist mother of today's queer daughters.[2]

So if lesbian-feminists and queers agree on so many issues, what's the problem?

One of the many problems has to do with the basic feeling of lesbian-feminists which I characterized at the beginning of this chapter—of being slighted by their successors who sometimes seem to be reinventing the theoretical wheel, painting it in mauve and fuchsia, then passing it off as entirely original. At the least, lesbian-feminists would like some acknowledgment of the ways in which they have contributed to queer thought, perhaps even some admission that so many of the ideas of the mothers were as seminal to contemporary queer thought as the work of the poststructuralist fathers, who are invariably cited in queer scholarship, to the all-but-total neglect of the mothers.

Another very basic problem that lesbian-feminists have with queer scholars concerns audience. The language queer scholars deploy sometimes seems transparently aimed at what lesbian-feminists once called the "big boys" at the academy. Lesbian-feminist writing, in contrast, had as primary values clarity and accessibility, since its purpose was to speak directly to the community and in so doing to effect change. Queer theory may desire to effect change outside the academy, too, but its hermetic, sleep-inducing jargon and sentence structure place its production beyond the reach and patience of almost anyone other than queer theorists and perhaps its primary addressees—those who have power to proffer academic advancement. Whether it is the intention of queer theorists or not, queer theory appears resolutely elitist. (It is interesting, however, to entertain the possibility that queer theorists are less elitist in their use of language than a product or victim of their times: perhaps lesbian-feminists wrote so clearly in the 1970s because they composed either in longhand or on a typewriter, which did not encourage endless monkeying around with phrase and sentence. Does composing on a word processor, which affords such easy revision, result in super-Jamesianism—a building of one qualifying phrase on top of another on top of another, a torturing of language in a thwarted attempt to arrive at more clarity—which ends inevitably in no clarity?)

But perhaps the most substantive parting of the ways between lesbian-feminism and queer is queer theory's rejection, in the guise of challenging the binary gender system, of almost any focus on the politics of female sex and sexuality. *Female* is generally elided altogether in queer theory. This elision might be somewhat less objectionable if, as Carolyn Dever and Teresa de Lauretis suggest in their chapters in this volume, lesbians were more centrally implicated in the dominant queer discourses, which seem almost invariably to be concerned with masculinity—whether in relation to the male body and AIDS or the postmodern lesbian becoming male. De Lauretis's sad story of her coining the term *queer theory* in the desire to create an alternative to the phrase *gay-and-lesbian* (which had come to be used as one word) pinpoints the problem—she found that she had created a worse monster, since "lesbian" was soon altogether sidelined in "queer." De Lauretis now regrets with good reason "queer's" neutralization of differences among lesbians, gay men, transvestites, transgendereds, and others— differences that it is perilous to neutralize.

The first lesbian-feminists broke away from feminism and established their own space because they recognized that "feminism" in itself did not necessarily (though it might potentially) include lesbians, that lesbians needed a "lesbian-feminism" (which would be open to any woman who dared understand the possibilities she was offered). It is mystifying that female queers have not seen an analogous need to claim their own space but rather have let themselves be disappeared in what is essentially male queer space. Lesbian-feminists long ago understood that "mankind," which was supposed to mean "men and women," really meant "men," so they were careful to avoid such "inclusive" words and to mark a clear locus for themselves in language. They understood that language and conceptual space were inextricably intertwined. Queer females now seem to have given up entirely a conceptual space for themselves as lesbians in adopting the term and the concept "queer."

Has that move done away with the binary gender system, or has it created a discourse about one and only one gender? What have we gained to compensate for all that we have lost? The losses that Sue-Ellen Case delineates—the dwindling away of lesbian social, economic, and theoretical resources, which has been brought about by the privileging of gay male culture by queer dykes and the disdain and misremembering of lesbian-feminism—could be endlessly expanded.

The fact is, female queers cannot make a happy home with the male of the queer species any more than radical feminists could with heterosexual men. Despite the best good will on the part of male queers, despite decades of feminist gains, males, queer and straight, ultimately overshadow and overpower females, queer and straight. All space becomes male space unless females maintain a concerted effort to mark a space for themselves.

Why should this necessarily be so? Would that it were not. However, it remains indisputable that the world privileges *male* and places *female* in an auxiliary space. That this is so in the world is clear just by flipping TV channels or staying tuned to CNN. That it is equally so in queer theory is clear by perusing most of the classic queer texts, such as Diana Fuss's *Inside/Out* or queer journals such as *GLQ*. Even when females are "in charge" or individual males have no wish to be privileged, whenever there is no self-conscious move to foreground "female" it is disappeared and "male" becomes the universal or the only gender of importance.

Hence, despite the best good will on the part of some males, queer females are an auxiliary to the *real* queers, just as homosexual women were an auxiliary to the *real* homosexuals in the homophile movement of the 1950s, before lesbians consciously created their own political spaces. In the feminist movement, despite the occasional homophobia of some feminists, lesbians were never merely auxiliary, not only because of the crucial roles they played within the movement but—most especially—because lesbian-feminism made clear that *any* female could choose lesbianism—and, indeed, many females who entered the feminist movement as heterosexuals did. Lesbian-feminism created a powerful concept of slippage: any feminist could at any time become a lesbian-feminist.

If we examine the history of feminism and even its present state, it is hard to disagree with Karin Quimby ("Notes for a Musical History of Lesbian Consciousness") that feminism, both practical and theoretical, needs lesbians—to produce scholarship, fight legal battles, run its clinics, and march in its parades. But as Annamarie Jagose points out in her chapter, we now acknowledge that the notion of "shared womanhood" is problematic. Do lesbians still need feminism?

A true essentialist feminism is understood to be naive once we recognize that "shared womanhood" is a myth. But to apply what has been called "strategic essentialism" to feminism is a useful tactic. Strategic essentialism demands a recognition that though "woman" changes from era to era, from race to race and class to class, for as long as can be remembered females have ultimately had the *lesser* power in all nations, races, classes, etc., vis-à-vis their male counterparts. The abstract category "woman" to which all females have been taught they belong is still belittled and stigmatized in almost all cultures, and that stigmatization has awful effects on females, whether or not those females agree that "woman" really exists. Strategic essentialism as applied to feminism begins by acknowledging difference between females, but also acknowledges the need to band together under the banner "woman" wherever such banding can be mutually helpful to females.

Feminists made much of the concept "woman" because they saw "woman" as a category that needed defense. If things have gotten somewhat better for females in some parts of the world, it is because feminists helped make them better. But it is short-sighted to the degree of silliness to think that most of the battles have been won or that things will stay better unless there is an awareness of how easily what has improved can get bad again—and a fight against such regression.

What feminism has come to realize in the last years is that we can band together not as a monolithic whole but simply for the practical reason of helping to counter the problems—as different as they are from place to place and class to class—that are visited on females because they are female. Jagose quotes Judith Butler: "The deconstruction of identity is not the deconstruction of politics; rather it establishes as political the very terms through which identity is articulated." That seems like good sense as a theory. But somewhere down the line theory needs to move into practice or nothing gets improved. It may be true that queer theorists understand the uses of politics, but they have yet to devise a workable political plan. Perhaps postmodern female theorists have deconstructed identity for themselves, perhaps they can convince some few other females to step outside the category "woman," but the preponderance of the world is unfortunately not postmodern and will not be in the foreseeable future. That preponderance refuses to acknowledge such "stepping outside" and still adamantly defines and privileges people with reference to their genitalia. Lesbians as females—whether queer or not—suffer along with the rest of the socially constructed category of "womankind." To bring about changes in the ubiquitous "sexist" (to use a dated feminist term) systems that produce the suffering requires large numbers of people banding together and making demands. Numbers are vital, and lesbians alone do not have sufficient numbers, so coalitions are necessary.

Annamarie Jagose goes on to argue that the reification of the category "woman" does not secure a safe space from which to consolidate a feminist initiative. However, to get lost in the category "queer" makes any female initiative altogether impossible. Queer men have their own battles to fight, which are no less immense than ours, but they are different. And certainly at this point in their history they cannot be expected to fight on the female front. The tragedy of AIDS, which has required all their energy (and much of ours, as willingly as many of us have given it) is only the most immediately pressing instance of troubles that huge numbers of queer men have which are different from the troubles of most lesbians.

Cornel West points out in his influential book, *Race Matters*, that "blackness has no meaning outside of a system of race-conscious people and practices." *Black* has been constructed to mean primarily "to be subject to white supremacist abuse."[3] But having made that observation, West goes on to speak of the importance of black "coalition strategy." "Woman," too, is a created category that subjects females to sexist abuse. But since all females are, at the least, potentially subjected to that abuse in one form or another, whether or not they agree to being classified as "woman," some coalition with other females, however loose, is necessary if they wish to combat that abuse. The lesbian-feminist mothers understood that wisdom a quarter of a century ago. That understanding should serve as the most valuable inheritance of all to queer daughters.

NOTES

1. Linda Garber, "Lesbian Identity Politics: Judy Grahn, Pat Parker, and the Rise of Queer Theory," Ph.D. diss., Stanford University, 1995.
2. Ibid.
3. Cornel West, *Race Matters* (New York: Random House, 1994), pp. 39–43.

CONTRIBUTORS

Michèle Aina Barale is Associate Professor at Amherst College, where she teaches in the departments of English and Women's and Gender Studies. She is one of the editors of *The Lesbian and Gay Studies Reader* and is currently finishing *Below the Belt: Essays in Queer Reading.*

Jane Caputi teaches in the American Studies Department at the University of New Mexico at Albuquerque. She is the author of *The Age of Sex Crime* and *Gossips, Gorgons, and Crones: The Fates of the Earth.*

Sue-Ellen Case is Professor of English at the University of California, Riverside. She is the editor of *Performing Feminisms: Feminist Critical Theory and Theater* and co-editor of *Cruising the Performative.*

Kathleen Chapman is adjunct faculty at the University of Colorado, Denver, and University of Colorado, Boulder. She is working on an investigation of lesbian counterpublic spheres in Berlin of the 1920s.

Teresa de Lauretis is Professor of the History of Consciousness at the University of California, Santa Cruz. Her most recent book in English is *The Practice of Love: Lesbian Sexuality and Perverse Desire.*

Carolyn Dever is Assistant Professor of English at New York University. Her chapter is part of a larger project on the rhetorical function of the lesbian in feminist theory.

Michael du Plessis is Assistant Professor of Comparative Literature/ Humanities and English at the University of Colorado, Boulder. He has contributed to the anthology *Re-Presenting Bisexuality* and is completing a book-length study of bisexual, lesbian, transgender, and gay film and video.

Lillian Faderman is Professor of English at California State University, Fresno. She is the author of *Surpassing the Love of Men, Scotch Verdict,* and *Odd Girls and Twilight Lovers* and the editor of *Chloe Plus Olivia: An Anthology of Lesbian Literature from the 17th Century to the Present.*

Dana Heller is Associate Professor of English at Old Dominion University, where she teaches American literature, literary theory, and gender studies. She is the author of *The Feminization of Quest-Romance: Radical Departures* and *Family Plots: The De-Oedipalization of Popular Culture.*

Katie Hogan is finishing her dissertation, "'The Angel in the House': Women, AIDS, and the Politics of Sentimental Representation," at Rutgers University, for which she won the 1996 Pergamon–National Women's Studies Association Award for Graduate Scholarship in Women's Studies. In addition to publishing essays on gender and AIDS, she is currently co-editing *Gendered Epidemic,* to be published by Routledge. She lives in New York City.

Annamarie Jagose is Senior Lecturer in the Department of English at the University of Melbourne and author of *Lesbian Utopics.*

Karman Kregloe is a Ph.D. candidate in the American Studies Department at the University of New Mexico at Albuquerque. She is writing her dissertation on shifts in lesbian representations and politics in the United States.

Colleen Lamos is Associate Professor of English at Rice University. She is the author of essays published in *Joyce in Context, Lesbian Erotics,* and *The Lesbian Postmodern.* Her articles and reviews have appeared in *Signs, James Joyce Quarterly, Contemporary Literature, Pretext, NWSA Journal, Lesbian and Gay Studies Newsletter,* and *The Lesbian Review of Books.* She has just completed a book manuscript, *Going Astray: Gender and Sexual Errancy in T. S. Eliot, James Joyce, and Marcel Proust.*

Tania Modleski teaches in the English Department at the University of Southern California. She is the author of *Loving with a Vengeance: Mass-Produced Fantasies for Women, The Women Who Knew Too Much: Hitchcock and Feminist Theory,* and *Feminism without Women: Culture and Criticism in a "Postfeminist" Age.*

Karin Quimby is a doctoral student at the University of Southern California, where she is completing her dissertation, "Reading for the Lesbian Plot: Feminist Designs/Lesbian Intentions." She has published essays in *Lesbian Erotics* and *Cross Addressing: Discourse on the Border.*

Ruth Salvaggio is Professor of American Studies at the University of New Mexico, where she teaches critical theory and cultural studies. Among her books are *Enlightened Absence: Neoclassical Configurations of the Feminine* and the recent anthology *Women Critics: 1660–1820,* co-edited with the Folger Collective on Early Women Critics.

Bonnie Zimmerman is Professor of Women's Studies at San Diego State University, where she teaches a variety of courses on literature, lesbianism, culture, and theory. She is the author of *The Safe Sea of Women: Lesbian Fiction 1969–89* and co-editor of *Professions of Desire: Lesbian and Gay Studies in Literature* and *Lesbian Studies Continuing: Toward the 21st Century.* She has been a lesbian feminist activist for twenty-five years and hopes to remain one for at least twenty-five more.

INDEX